D0684581

THE
FEDERAL
CONDITION
IN CANADA

SERIES LIST

McGraw-Hill Ryerson Series in Canadian Politics
General Editor - Paul W. Fox

POLITICS: Canada, Fifth Edition, Paul W. Fox
CANADIAN FOREIGN POLICY, D. C. Thomson and R. F. Swanson
THE CONSTITUTIONAL PROCESS IN CANADA, Second Edition,
R. I. Cheffins and R. N. Tucker
POLITICAL PARTIES AND IDEOLOGIES IN CANADA, Second Edition,
W. Christian and C. Campbell
PRESSURE GROUP BEHAVIOUR IN CANADIAN POLITICS,
A. Paul Pross
POLITICAL PARTIES IN CANADA,
C. Winn and J. C. McMenemy
GOVERNMENT IN CANADA, T. A. Hockin
LOCAL GOVERNMENT IN CANADA, Second Edition
C. R. Tindal and S. Nobes Tindal
PUBLIC POLICY AND PROVINCIAL POLITICS,
M. Chandler and W. Chandler
POLITICAL CHOICE IN CANADA (Abridged Edition),
Harold D. Clarke, Jane Jenson, Lawrence LeDuc, Jon H. Pammett
CANADIAN FOREIGN POLICY: Contempory Issues and Themes,
Michael Tucker
POLITICS AND THE MEDIA IN CANADA,
Arthur Siegel
CANADA IN QUESTION: Federalism in the Eighties, Third Edition,
D. V. Smiley
THE L-SHAPED PARTY: The Liberty Party of Canada 1958-1980,
Joseph Wearing
WOMEN AND POLITICS IN CANADA,
Janine Brodie
THE REVISED CANADIAN CONSTITUTION: Politics as Law,
R. Cheffins and P. Johnson
THE FEDERAL CONDITION IN CANADA,
D. V. Smiley

Forthcoming

GOVERNMENT IN CANADA, Second Edition,
T. A. Hockin
CANADA'S JUDICAL SYSTEM,
Peter H. Russell
CANADIAN PARLIAMENTARY SYSTEM,
Paul G. Thomas
CANADIAN FOREIGN POLICY, Second Edition,
Michael J. Tucker

THE FEDERAL CONDITION IN CANADA

DONALD V. SMILEY
Professor of Political Science
York University

McGRAW-HILL RYERSON LIMITED

Toronto Montreal New York Auckland Bogotá Cairo Hamburg
Lisbon London Madrid Mexico Milan New Delhi Panama Paris San Juan
São Paulo Singapore Sydney Tokyo

THE FEDERAL CONDITION IN CANADA

Copyright © McGraw-Hill Ryerson Limited, 1987. All rights reserved. No part of this publication may be reproduced, stored in a retrieval system, or transmitted, in any form or by any means, electronic, mechanical, photocopying, recording, or otherwise, without prior written permission of McGraw-Hill Ryerson Limited.

ISBN 0-07-549072-2

1 2 3 4 5 6 7 8 9 0   G   6 5 4 3 2 1 0 9 8 7

Printed and bound in Canada

Care has been taken to trace ownership of copyright material contained in this text. The publishers will gladly take any information that will enable them to rectify any reference or credit in subsequent editions.

Canadian Cataloguing in Publication Data

Smiley, Donald V., date-
  The federal condition in Canada

(McGraw-Hill Ryerson series in Canadian politics)
Includes index.
ISBN 0-07-549072-2

1. Federal government - Canada.   2. Canada -
Politics and government - 1963-.*   I. Title.
II. Series.

JL65 1987 S55 1987   320.971   C86-094903-6

TABLE OF CONTENTS

This book is dedicated with respect and affection
to the memory of Walter Young

FOREWORD

Professor Donald Smiley has done it again. Having written a number of authoritative books and a great many learned articles on Canadian federalism, he has put pen to paper once more and produced another scholarly, reflective, provocative assessment of our system of government.

It is typical of Professor Smiley that he preferred to write a new book rather than revise his popular, previous treatise on Canadian federalism, *Canada in Question*, which has gone through three editions. Professor Smiley has an inquisitive and creative mind which is not only open to new ideas but actually welcomes them. Although this sort of intellectual curiosity is supposed to be the hallmark of an academic, it is unfortunately not always as evident as it is in Smiley's case.

This time Professor Smiley's inquiring mind has led him to reassess the forces at work in contemporary Canadian federalism, to reflect on recent developments and the literature in the field, and to arrive at conclusions which are considerably different from those he expressed in the several editions of *Canada in Question*.

The basic difference is that Smiley is now more optimistic about the future of federalism and the survival of Canada. As he notes in his Introduction, he now believes that our system of government is relatively stable and no longer in danger of imminent disintegration.

Coming from as keen and knowledgeable a critic as Donald Smiley, this judgement is welcome news. But his book is more than a message of good cheer. It is a learned and thoughtful appraisal of current Canadian federalism and all its attendant problems. Since our system has plenty of problems, there is much to reflect upon.

Having given an admirable brief review of the history of our Constitution, the author notes some of the difficulties which the new *Constitution Act* of 1982 has created. Since we now have a written Constitution which the judiciary has the last word in interpreting, the power of the courts, in particular the Supreme Court, has been increased enormously. Because the increase has been at the expense of the legislature, Parliament no longer can be said to be sovereign. The declaration of our rights and freedoms in a Charter which is to be interpreted by the courts also creates a vista of new issues.

Meanwhile, what Smiley calls "the continuing constitutional agenda" remains. This includes Quebec's place in the new Constitution, aboriginal rights, the status of the Northwest Territories and the Yukon, and the provinces' role in international matters such as the negotiation of free trade with the United States. Negotiations on matters like these will inevitably increase the importance of executive federalism, that is, the dealings between provincial and federal ministers and bureaucrats. But it will also enhance the role of political parties, which Smiley analyses carefully at some length.

He also examines the impact of French-English duality on federalism and the alienation of the peripheral areas of Canada from the centre. As a westerner by birth and upbringing, Professor Smiley has a particularly keen perception of the continuing grievances of western Canada. He reviews Prime Ministers Trudeau's and Mulroney's contrasting approaches to national issues and concludes by assessing the role of the provinces in the future development of Canadian federalism. His prediction is that the provinces may be less significant in the future than they have been in the past. The regional and cultural considerations which have supported the provinces may be displaced by cleavages of a different kind, reflecting local, personal, and group interests such as class, gender, and occupation.

It is a stimulating argument which is indicative of the quality of Smiley's book. No one has read more widely on the subject of Canadian federalism or thought more deeply about it than Professor Smiley — and no one has presented his trenchant opinions more succinctly. *The Federal Condition in Canada* will undoubtedly become as popular as *Canada in Question*.

University of Toronto   Paul W. Fox
September 22, 1986   General Editor

Introduction

Those who are familiar with my past writings are here reminded that this book is not, to my mind at least, a Fourth Edition of *Canada in Question*. The *Federal Condition* aims to be less "busy" and less concerned with detail, and here and there attempts to show the relevance to Canada of federal experience elsewhere. Further, I have backed away from anything which is a political economy of Canadian federalism. Despite my attraction to the political economy approach and the burgeoning secondary literature, I do not know enough to write in any adequate way about matters as complex and diverse as policies related to energy, consumer protection, water management, the control of the natural environment, the regulation of financial institutions, and so on. In particular, I have nothing to say about the crucial matter of fiscal federalism — a subject which I once tried to comprehend but which, I am now convinced, is so complicated that one should either cultivate it as a full-time specialty or leave it alone entirely.

The title of this book has been chosen with some care. What is being discussed is a relatively stable system of government. This assumption of stability most clearly distinguishes this analysis from my writings on Canadian federalism in the past two decades. In retrospect it appears that I, and most other observers of Canadian affairs, very much over-estimated the strength of Quebec nationalism and provincialist influences elsewhere in the country and very much under-estimated the capacity of the system to respond effectively to such divisive pressures. Thus, barring the ultimate nuclear disaster or a breakdown in the international economic order even more severe than that of the Great Depression, it seems reasonable to believe that in the forseeable future Canadians will be governed under some recognizable variant of federalism.

Despite the present context of the collapse of Quebec separatism, the less strident way in which provincial demands are expressed elsewhere in the country and the relative harmony of federal-provincial relations, it would be imprudent to believe that provincialist challenges to Confederation are behind us once and for all. Any sensitive reading of Canadian history would suggest otherwise. However, in Chapter IX, I argue that it seems likely that Canadian politics will come increasingly to revolve around cleavages other than those demarcated by provincial boundaries.

Chapter I is somewhat abstract and analytical. Although I believe it essential to what follows, some readers may prefer to skip it and proceed directly to the more specifically Canadian material which begins in Chapter II.

Honest scholars are required to acknowledge intellectual debts they cannot repay. The York Department of Political Science has been a stimulating environment for my work for just a decade now, and I have been helped in my studies of Canadian affairs by a varied and congenial group of departmental colleagues — particularly Janine Brodie, Fred Fletcher, Ian Greene, Ken McRoberts, David Shugarman, Douglas Verney and Reg Whitaker. York graduate students constantly stimulate my thinking and have been, with one or two exceptions, politely tolerant of my bemusement with new currents of thought related to such matters as neo-Marxism, feminism and dependency theory. Osgoode Hall Law School contains a number of imaginative constitutional lawyers and from members such as Marc Gold, Peter Hogg and Patrick Monahan I have been helped in my amateurish attempts to understand the Canadian Constitution. I must mention also four friends and former colleagues who each in his own way has made distinguished contributions to the literature of the federal system — Ed Black, Alan Cairns, Stefan Dupré and Peter Russell. Finally, the general editor of this series, Paul Fox, has, as in the past, drawn on his seemingly unlimited resources of good humour, patience and expert scholarly judgement in making this book something much better than it otherwise might have been.

Dorothy Fisk deserves great credit for transforming my longhand into a clean manuscript.

Donald Smiley
Toronto
May, 1986.

THE
FEDERAL
CONDITION
IN CANADA

I

Canadian Federalism: Some Analytical Perspectives

This chapter will provide a working definition of federalism, a discussion of the relation between federal governments and federal societies and an analysis of the implications of federalism for certain important political values and for the policy outputs of governmental systems.

What is Federalism?

A federal country will be designated here as one in which the most salient aspects of human organization, identification and conflict are linked to specific territories within that country. Conversely, in a non-federal country such organization, identification and conflict are not spatially demarcated. Territorial pluralism — federalism — is only one of the ways in which human beings are and can be organized. In a book published in 1963, Philippe Garigue argued that the dependency of the French-Canadian nation was perpetuated by federalism because French Canadians outside Quebec were a permanent minority, and he proposed a new regime in which francophones and anglophones would be politically organized as such wherever in Canada they lived.[1] In the Australian and Canadian lefts, there have been persistent strains cool or hostile to federalism on the general grounds that this form of government exaggerates cleavages based on territory and thus frustrates those founded on social and economic class. The corporatist option provides that the major actors in the making of public policy are not representatives of territorially demarcated communities but of national governments and national groupings of business and labour. More fancifully, if within a particular country gender should become the major point of identification and conflict, then federalism would be irrelevant — except in the unlikely and unhappy event that most of the males lived in particular parts of the country and most of the females in others.

1

Although the term federation is sometimes used to designate associations of private groups — the Canadian Federation of Agriculture or the Federation of British Industry, for example — it is more common to designate governmental systems alone as being federal. Among students of the subject, K. C. Wheare's definition is widely accepted: "By the federal principle I mean the method of dividing (governmental) powers so that the general and regional governments are each within a sphere co-ordinate and independent."[2] Wheare's formulation is in close agreement with that of A. V. Dicey in his *Introduction to the Study of the Law of the Constitution,* first published in 1885, where the "three leading characteristics of a completely developed federalism" were defined as: "the supremacy of the constitution — the distribution among bodies with limited and co-ordinate authority of the different powers of government — the authority of the Courts to act as interpreters of the constitution."[3] Implied in the Wheare-Dicey definition is another distinction characteristic of federalism: the powers of the central government are exercised directly over individual citizens and private groups rather than, as in a confederacy, through the states or provinces alone.

In a recent book, Preston King has challenged the view that federations are distinctive forms of political organization by virtue of the co-ordinate powers of central and regional governments, and he advances this alternative definition: "we propose that any federation be regarded as an institutional arrangement, taking the form of a sovereign state, and distinguished from other such states solely by the fact that its central government incorporates regional units in its decision procedures on some constitutionally entrenched basis."[4] Although King rejects the Wheare-Dicey formulation by way of a complex argument which I do not find persuasive, his definition is useful in directing our attention to the circumstance that in polities usually regarded as federations there is the constitutional entrenchment of the powers of the governments and/or the residents of the states, provinces or cantons in the structures and operations of the central government.

My working definition is this: a federation is a sovereign state in which:
1. There is a constitution which distributes the powers of government between central and regional governments and which provides some protection for the people and/or the governments of these regional units in the structure and operation of the central government.
2. The elements of the constitution related to the respective powers of the centre and the regions are not subject to change by the action of the central or regional governments alone.
3. Individual citizens and private groups are subject to the laws and other authoritative exercises of power by both the central and regional governments.

This definition is broad enough to comprehend those nations which serious observers usually designate as federations, and does not contain characteristics which are sometimes advanced as defining charateristics but do not in all cases prevail; for example, that the federal principle requires that there be equal representation of the regime in the upper chamber of the national legislature or that the residual powers (i.e., those which the constitution does not confer explicitly on either the central or regional authorities) be held by the regions.

It should be emphasized here that the definition given above is stipulative rather than normative; federalism is used neither as a "boo word" nor a "hurrah word." It is not very helpful and may be misleading to evaluate any particular set of governmental arrangements by the test of whether it conforms to a particular definition of federalism or otherwise. This kind of error was made by Marcel Faribault and Robert Fowler in their book on the Canadian Constitution published in 1965, "There is no place in a truly federal system for different classes of regional governments or a special status for any one of them. They must all have the same constitutional powers and jurisdiction."[5] Faribault and Fowler were arguing against a special status for Quebec in Confederation but did not advance any argument as to why such federal systems as India, which provide for different classes of regional government with different powers, were less "truly federal" than the United States where all the states have the same jurisdiction. To repeat, my purpose in defining federalism is solely to introduce a measure of clarity into the following discourse and not to provide a normative test by which governmental systems in Canada or elsewhere are to be evaluated.

Federal Governments and Federal Societies

Although federalism is about territorialism, federal arrangements in government do not protect spatially bounded differences indiscriminately. More specifically, the territorial interests, governmental and non-governmental, which are protected are those delineated by the boundaries of states, provinces or cantons. An amendment to the British North America Act of 1871 clarified the power of the Parliament of Canada to establish new provinces out of any Canadian territory not included in an existing province with the crucial proviso that the consent of a province was required for any alteration of its boundaries. There are similar constitutional guarantees for the territorial integrity of the constituent units in the American, Australian and Yugoslav federations. For any changes in the boundaries of its länder (provinces), the constitution of the Federal Republic of Germany, as amended in 1969, provides for the association of the central government with the wishes of the people in affected areas as expressed through referendums. However, the Indian constitution of 1949 permits the national parliament alone to alter state boundaries, and under these powers there was effected in 1956 a radical reorganization making such boundaries conform more closely to linguistic divisions.

To repeat, federalism does not protect all territorial particularisms but only those demarcated by the constitutionally guaranteed boundaries of state, provincial or cantonal governments. In this connection it is useful to consider Canada not as it appears on a map, but rather as it is experienced as we travel over it by airplane, automobile or train — to perceive the country in terms of what the geographer Cole Harris calls the "islands of settlement" separated from one another by vast expanses of water, bush, prairie, rock and tundra.[6] From Confederation to today it is these spatial concentrations of human habitation which have been protected by Canadian federalism. Harris puts it well:

It is of singular importance that among all these different scales of Canadian settlement (rural settlements, French and English linguistic communities, regional cities and thus hinterlands, regime) the provinces have become increasingly dominant. In effect, they are now the repositories of the country's fragmented form. At Confederation the local settlement was still the predominant scale of Canadian life, but settlements that once provided definition and defence for traditional ways have been overridden by modern transportation and communications. Their isolation and stability have largely gone, they survive in some urban shadow of an urbanized and industrialized society. In such a society horizons are broadened and the local defence of custom is superseded. The state assumes a growing symbolic and practical importance. In this situation, the Canadian province, with its constitutionally defined power, its growing political history, and a location which bears some relationship to the fragmented structure of the country, replaces both the local settlements that no longer support Canadian life, and the broader but amorphous regions that have no clear political definition. The provinces are crystal clear. Their territorial boundaries are precise. For all the arguments, their powers are explicit. Their scale is supportable within modern technology. As political territories that reflect something of the country's island structure, they enormously simplify Canadian reality and it is this simplified and thereby politically more powerful regionalism that now confronts the concept and sentiment of Canada.[7]

It must be emphasized that in Canada, as in other federations, the national and provincial boundaries demarcate the activities not only of governments but also of a very large number of institutions. Thus, Canadians organize themselves as such not only for the purposes of government but as Presbyterians, manufacturers, university teachers, playwrights and so on. Similarly, there is not only an Alberta political jurisdiction with its territorial boundaries and legislative powers protected by the Constitution but also an Alberta Red Cross, an Alberta Teachers Association, an Alberta Conference of the United Church of Canada, an Alberta Chamber of Commerce and an Alberta Federation of Labour.

We know a good deal less than we should about how federalism in government shapes and is shaped by other aspects of human organization.[8] Those groups whose exclusive or primary activities are in the influencing of governments in respect to matters about which both central and regional jurisdictions are active (for example, in Canada those concerned with the protection of the natural environment and with agricultural policies) will have strong incentives to constitute themselves along federal lines.[9] As the scope of governmental activity expands, however, and as groups like the Christian churches try more and more to influence governmental policies, associations whose major purposes are other than this will experience similar incentives — again in the Canadian case, cultural organizations, associations involved with ''amateur'' athletics and with the physically handicapped. Further, more than in most liberal democracies, certainly more than in the United States, a large number of ''private'' groups (for example, those of the native peoples, women, consumers, scholars, creative artists and so on) draw financial support from governments and must perforce organize themselves within the territorial boundaries of their respective donors. In these latter circumstances, it is not uncommon for governments to attempt to influence such associations for governmental purposes, sometimes to oppose governments at the other level.[10]

We might say then that in Canada, as in other federations, federal organization is a major circumstance not only of the governmental system, but also of other aspects of association. Within the social realm, structures and patterns of influence roughly parallel those of the governmental system; for example, one of the crucial factors contributing to the fragmentation and relative weakness of the trade union movement in Canada is the fact that, under the constitutional distribution of powers, most workers who bargain collectively do so under provincial rather than federal legislation and that many other matters of direct and immediate concern to workers are similarly within provincial jurisdiction. As I have suggested, there are powerful incentives for groupings of persons pursuing various kinds of social objectives to associate themselves on federal lines. And in a negative sense there appear to be relatively few influential private associations representing the interests of Canadians on a trans-provincial basis, for example, as residents of the prairie region; or on a sub-provincial basis, as residents of Labrador, Northern Ontario or the interior of British Columbia.

Both Canadian government and Canadian society are federalized in the sense that conflicts and identifications are demarcated by national and provincial boundaries. But what shapes what? Does Society decisively determine Government, or is it the other way round? In a formal sense, is Society the independent variable and Government the dependent variable? Or, to put it yet another way, do the causal arrows run from Society to Government or in the other direction?

In the 1950s an American political scientist, William S. Livingston, argued that, "Federalism is a function not of governments but of societies."[11]

> Thus: The [governmental] institutions themselves do not provide an accurate index of the federal nature of the society which subtends them; they are only the surface manifestations of the deeper federal quality which lies beneath the surface. The essence of federalism lies not in the constitutional or institutional structure but in the society itself. Federal government is a device by which the federal qualities of the society are articulated and protected.[12]

Livingston's society-control view of federalism and of the governmental process more generally was characteristic of the major trends of analysis in North American sociology and political science in the 1950s and 1960s. The prevailing paradigms have recently been described by Theda Skocpol in these terms:

> "government" was viewed primarily as an arena within which economic interest groups or normative social movements contended or allied with one another to shape the making of public policy decisions. Those decisions were understood to be *allocations* of benefits among elementary groups. Research centered on the societal "inputs" to government and on the distribution of governmental "outputs." Government itself was not taken very seriously as an independent actor, and in comparative research, variations

in governmental organizations were deemed less significant than the general "functions" shared by the political systems of all societies.[13]

During the 1960s and on into the next decade when French-English relations were putting severe strains on Confederation the society-centred view was very attractive to Canadian students of federalism, and in an article published in 1968 Michael Stein wrote:

> It seems to me that the concept of 'federal society' can be most usefully applied if it is confined to a society which is conterminously both 'polyethnic' and multilingual in make up . . . . Where a society is constituted of territorially based communities which are clearly differentiated by language and ethnicity, then one can expect to find a federal society. . . . A 'federal political system' then . . . is that form of political system (of a nation-state) in which the institutions, values, attitudes, and patterns of political action operate to give autonomous expression to both the national political system and political culture and to regional political subsystems and subcultures (defined primarily by ethnic-linguistic factors).[14]

In his 1977 Presidential Address to the Canadian Political Science Association, Alan C. Cairns strongly challenged the Livingston position. The task Cairns set for himself was to explain the continuing aggressiveness and vitality of the provincial governments of Canada. He said:

> The sociological perspective pays inadequate attention to the possibility that the support for powerful, independent provincial governments is a product of the political system itself, that it is fostered and created by provincial government elites employing the policy-making apparatus of their jurisdictions, and that such support need not take the form of a distinct culture, society, or nation as these are conventionally understood. More specifically, the search for an underlying sociological base, whatever its nature and source, as the necessary sustenance for viable provincial political systems, deflects us from considering the prior question of how much support is necessary. Passivity, indifference, or the absence of strong opposition from their environment may be all that provincial governments need in order to thrive and grow. The significant question, after all, is the survival of provincial governments, not of provincial societies, and it is not self-evident that the existence and support of the latter is necessary to the functioning and aggrandisement of the former. Their sources of survival, renewal, and vitality may well lie within themselves and in their capacity to mould their environment in accordance with their own governmental purposes.[15]

Although Cairns' analysis was devoted primarily to explaining the continuing power of the provinces, his attack on the society-centred view of Canadian federalism could similarly be applied to the central government by an argument to the general effect that Ottawa's strength arises from the national apparatus of government itself rather than the cultural, economic or non-governmental underpinnings of the Canada-wide community or the emotional commitments of citizens to that community.

The years since Cairns' address have witnessed an enormously complex and important debate among scholars about the role of the state.[16] Despite the many differences, there appears to be a new consensus emerging that states have a greater or lesser degree of autonomy in shaping economies and societies in contrast to the previous views which saw states largely as processors of societal elements. These new currents have a direct and obvious relevance for students of federalism.

Among Western neo-Marxist scholars in the last decade or so, the nature and function of the capitalist state has been a major focus of concern. In his influential *The State in Capitalist Society* first published in 1969, Ralph Miliband wrote: "Marx, himself, it may be recalled, never attempted a systematic study of the state," and despite the later contributions of Lenin and Gramsci, "Marxists have made little notable attempt to confront the question of the state in the light of the concrete socio-economic *and* political *and* cultural realities of actual capitalist societies."[17] In attempting to remedy the deficiency to which Miliband referred, neo-Marxists have differed in fundamental ways. Yet they agree that the capitalist state "is an expression, or condensation, of social class relations and these relations imply domination of one group by another."[18] To perform this role effectively and to maintain the capitalist mode of production and the relation of class domination it entails, the state needs a degree of "relative autonomy" from various "fractions" of the bourgeoisie who, in their pursuit of immediate self-interest, would otherwise act so as to destroy capitalism.

Non-Marxist scholars who, in terms of the title of a recent collection of essays, are "bringing the state back in" to social and political analysis are even more divergent in their perspectives than are the neo-Marxists.[19] What distinguishes the former group is its members' common conviction that, under certain circumstances, state actors have a degree of autonomy in capitalist states even from the most powerful of business interests.[20] Skocpol puts it this way: "Bringing the state back in to a central place in analyses of policy making and social change does require a break with some of the most encompassing social-determinist assumptions of pluralism, structural-functionalist developmentalism and the various neo-Marxisms."[21] She writes of the latter that "at the theoretical level, virtually all neo-Marxist writers in the state have retained deeply embedded society-centered assumptions, not allowing themselves to doubt that, at base, states are inherently shaped by classes or class struggles and function to preserve and expand modes of production."[22] Yet Skocpol warns us that it is unwise to "stand on their heads the society-centered assumptions." Studies of the state alone are not to be substituted for concerns with classes or groups; nor are purely state-determinist arguments to be fashioned in the place of society-centred assumptions. She also argues against seeking for "the grand system theories of the structural-functionalists or neo-Marxists"; more adequate explanations will be historically specific.[23]

This book is written from a vantage point similar to that of Skocpol. It diverges from neo-Marxism in two specific ways:

First, I believe it at least possible that the capitalist state (or more accurately, the most powerful of state actors) will develop goals and the capacity to pursue them effectively, incompatible in whole or in part with the interests of the dominant class. The circumstances under which this will be so need to be examined in particular circumstances. Second, the capitalist state responds to societal interests other than those of the dominant class. Neo-Marxists characteristically and, in my view, unconvincingly group such responses as exercises of the legitimation function. To put it another way, there are in capitalist states patterns of domination and subordination other than those of class in a Marxian sense, and much of democratic politics revolves around these non-class divisions. In particular, neo-Marxism ignores the impact of competitive party politics as an important determinant of state action. George Bernard Shaw shrewdly asserted that political parties gather money from the rich and votes from the poor with promises to protect each against the other. In his monumental study of the federal Liberal party between 1930 and 1958 Reginald Whitaker describes in rich detail how the party under King and St. Laurent successfully performed this complex balancing act.[24] King, in particular, shrewdly manipulated the business interests on whom the party depended for campaign funds and public opinion which was necessary to keep the party in power, by using the one to redress the balance when the other theatened to become dominant. Significantly, these manoeuvres enhanced the autonomy of the party and laid the groundwork for the ongoing assimilation between the party and the federal state. ''That the party never rejected the support of the vested capitalist interests, while at the same time never entirely losing its credibility with the voters as a party of democratic reform, left it precisely the flexibility and freedom of action to 'wheel and deal' in the centre of the political spectrum and to make the kind of practical accommodation necessary to maintain its hold on power.''[25]

Contemporary theories of the liberal-democratic state, both Marxist and non-Marxist, do not, in my view, give adequate clues to an operational definition defining the boundaries between the state apparatus and civil society. In Canadian terms, are the following (all very much dependent on public funds) to be regarded as parts of the state: the National Archives, public corporations acting in terms of commercial imperatives, mixed public-private commercial enterprises, children's aid societies, ''private'' groups like the Consumers' Association of Canada, the National Advisory Committee on the Status of Women, and associations of the native peoples? In another context Mary Eberts gives the example of ''national sports governing bodies that promote Canadian 'official' entries at international competitions, and are heavily funded by government, although 'private'.''[26] With the coming into effect of the Charter of Rights and Freedoms the delineation between state and non-state has become a crucial question for legal and judicial definition as well as political analysis.[27] Section 32(1) of the Charter enacts that its provisions apply to all matters coming within the jurisdiction of the ''Parliament and government of Canada'' and ''the legislatures and government of each province.'' Other sections refer to government institutions in a similarly imprecise way.

Much contemporary analysis, both Marxist and non-Marxist, tends to reify ''the'' state. It has been said that persons in the Anglo-Saxon political tradition have, in contrast to Europeans, a very weak concept of the state as distinguished from the operating institutions of government. Contemporary observers of both Western and Marxist persuasions have revived the European perspective, and

Alfred Stepan has encapsulated this view thus: "The state must be considered more than the 'government'. It is the continuous administrative, legal, bureaucratic and coercive systems that attempt to structure relations *between* civil society and public authority in a polity but also to structure many crucial relationships within civil society as well."[28] The general thrust of such a view causes the observer to exaggerate the unity of action of the state and to overlook the clashes among state actors which is the focus of attention of the "bureaucratic politics" school of political analysis. On the other hand, it is unwise to reduce the state to independent state actors as Eric Nordlinger has done in his *On the Autonomy of the Democratic State* in which he defines the state as "all those individuals who occupy offices that authorize them, and them alone, to make and apply decisions that are binding upon any and all segments of society."[29] Such reductionism neglects the relatively durable patterns of relations among state actors as provided for by the law and settled customs of the constitution.

The Federal Condition in Canada is written within the general perspective of Cairns' assertion that "contemporary Canadian federalism is about governments" and assumes that the federal and provincial governments have, under some circumstances at least, a real rather than "relative" autonomy in shaping economy and society.

Do the Formal Structures of State Power Matter?

Society-centred perspectives, both neo-Marxist and otherwise, are disposed to suggest that the way power is organized within governmental systems is not a significant determinant of the way these systems perform. In his 1972 book on American federalism, Michael D. Reagan wrote: "institutional patterns do not determine relationships of power but reflect them."[30] Although in his influential writings *The State and Capitalist Society* and *Marxism and Politics*[31] Miliband has made a lucid case for the "relative autonomy of the capitalist state," there is little in his writings to suggest that there are important consequences of such states being unitary or federal, parliamentary or congressional; of what kinds of electoral systems are in effect; of how members of the judiciary are chosen, and so on. Canadian neo-Marxists have shown some sensitivity to the federal dimension of Canadian political institutions, and Garth Stevenson particularly has related the continuing strength of federal and provincial governments to their support of different "fractions" of the Canadian bourgeoisie, and he has asserted, without any convincing evidence, that, "while the major accumulation functions have increasingly been assumed by the provincial states, the legitimation and coercion functions have continued to be performed to a much greater extent at the federal level."[32] However, neo-Marxists have been insensitive to other dimensions of the organization of state power in Canada. J. R. Mallory, in his *Social Credit and the Federal Power in Canada,* first published in 1954, attributed the provincialist interpretation of the British North America Act between the late 1890s and the beginning of the Second World War to the disposition of members of the judiciary to protect the system of private property against government regulation.[33] There appears to have been no follow-up of this kind of analysis of judicial review of the Constitution nor the application of class analysis to other dimensions of the Canadian constitutional order than federalism.[34]

The state-centred view is more disposed towards emphasizing the importance of the formal structures of governmental power, although in a logical sense one might assert the autonomy of the state and still maintain that the nature and extent of autonomy were not critically influenced by the way in which state power was internally organized.

In his *Constitutionalism and the Separation of Powers*, M. J. C. Vile criticizes the widespread behavioural view that formal structures are of relative unimportance. He writes: "The behaviourist's concern with 'social forces', and his emphasis upon the real stuff of politics, seem to lead him to the view that the behaviour which he sees as the sole content of politics is not in any significant way affected by the structure of constitutional rule, but is wholly determined by economic, racial, class and other factors."[35] In examining the writings of three observers within this general framework, Vile points to "the emphasis on 'human nature' to the exclusion of the mechanics of government, the underlying assumption that it is the relative power of 'groups' that provides the independent variables of the political system upon which all other factors depend, and the consequent belief that institutional structures can have little or no significant effect upon the outcome of political situations."[36] He argues: "The expression of the behavioural approach . . . errs . . . in underestimating the requirement of order in the political system, and in taking for granted the institutionalized order of constitutional states like Britain and the United States. Behaviourists concentrate on what happens within the ordered system founded by the constitution, ignoring the long-term stabilities which are the context of, and the prerequisites for, such behaviour."[37] Thus: "The study of politics must, therefore, very largely consist of the ways in which constitutional and political institutions, and the social forces and movements in a particular society, interact with each other; of the limits upon the extent to which stable constitutional modes of behaviour can be developed and maintained; and the effects they can have in moulding behaviour."[38] Vile's book is a persuasive analysis not only of institutional structures as explanatory variables, but also of the values which may be realized through particular structures of state power.

In a thoughtful article very much in the spirit of Vile's analysis, Richard Simeon in 1975 argued that political institutions in Canada do matter.[39] He referred to the various kinds of territorially-demarcated changes in Canadian society and asserted that political institutions are never neutral in determining the kinds of cleavages which develop in a political system, quoting E. E. Schattschneider to the effect that: "All forms of political organization have a bias in favor of the exploitation of some kinds of conflict and the suppression of others . . . Some issues are organized into politics while others are organized out." Simeon argued that the issues which are "organized into" politics were territorially bounded, while those which divided Canadians in other areas were "organized out." His general conclusion was that the "institutions are not simply the outgrowth or products of the environment and . . . they are not just dependent variables in the political system. They can also be seen as independent forces, which have some effects of their own; once established, they themselves come to shape and influence the environment.''[40]

The disposition of both behaviourists and Marxists to de-emphasize the consequences of the structure of state power is in large part a revolt against the formalism and aridity of the older forms of institutional analysis. For example, one can find little in the lucid, accurate and detailed account of the Canadian governmental system in Robert Macgregor Dawson's textbook, as revised in successive editions by Norman Ward, to indicate the consequences of these structures of power for the welfare of the Canadian people, the responses of governments to their needs and desires, political stability and so on. In the remaining sections of this chapter I shall attempt an analysis of how federal structures of government relate to certain liberal democratic values and the outputs of the political system.

Federalism and Liberal Democratic Values

Reginald Whitaker has pointed out that despite the vast amount of academic writing in both fields: ''there is . . . surprisingly little reference to federalism among democratic theorists, and perhaps even less consideration of democratic theory among students of federalism.''[41] Among influential contemporary theorists of democracy who have neglected federalism, although each has had his career in a federal country, Whitaker mentions C. B. Macpherson and J. Roland Pennock. So far as students of federal institutions and processes like Ivo D. Duchacek, G. F. Sawer, R. L. Watts and K. C. Wheare are concerned, there is single-minded focus on describing and analysing what must be about the most complex of institutional arrangements ever entered by humankind along with a corresponding neglect of normative democratic theory. Sawer's concluding paragraph in his *Modern Federalism* is typical of the stance of writers on federal institutions:

> If . . . an attempt is made to evaluate federalism in the range of institutional systems, I would say that it is a prudential system best suited to the relatively stable satisfied societies of squares such as abound in Canada, Australia, West Germany and Austria, and probably still constitute the majority in the U.S.A. It is not a swinging system. People are not likely to go to the stake, or the barricades, to defend federalism as such. They may undertake heroic actions for the sake of some value which federalism happens at the moment to favour, and may then even inscribe federalism on their banner — 'Liberty and Federalism' — 'Equality and Federalism' but never just 'Federalism'.''[42]

Interestingly, there is a persistent strain of federalist theory in France dating from Proudhoun and including in this century thinkers espousing a federal Europe, but neither in metropolitan France nor its former empire has there been any significant experience of federal institutions.

In an essay published in 1953, Franz Neumann posed two questions: ''Is there a value which inheres in federalism as such? Are there goals which can be attained only through federalism?''[43] His answer to both questions was ''No.'' Ranging widely through modern political experience, he demolished the arguments that federalism inherently and inevitably contains effective obstructions to the arbitrary exercise of governmental power, protects civil liberties and ensures responsive "grass roots" democracy.

Neumann's analyses were misleading. It is not, after all, relevant to evaluate whether federalism can in some absolute way guarantee certain key values. Obviously it cannot. Rather, the question is whether and to what degree liberal democratic values are better protected in particular circumstances by federalism than by some alternative kind of governmental arrangement.

Because it provides for two sets of co-ordinate political authorities and divides the citizenry into groupings for national and regional political purposes, federalism is difficult or impossible to reconcile with the interrelated ideas of popular sovereignty and nationalism which are at the foundations of the legitimacy structures of most modern states. Article 3 of the Declaration of the Rights of Man and of the Citizen thus articulated these ideas: "The basis of all sovereignty lies essentially in the Nation. No corporation nor individual may exercise any authority that is not derived therefrom." The preamble to the constitution of the Fifth French Republic adopted in 1958 affirms the "attachment" of the nation to the Declaration and enacts in Article 3 that, "National sovereignty belongs to the people, which shall exercise it through its representatives and by way of referendums." Article 20(2) of the constitution of the Federal Republic of Germany similarly provides that, "All state authority emanates from the people. It shall be exercised by the people by means of elections and voting and by specific legislative, executive and judicial organs." Other examples might be given.

It is necessary here to make a distinction between legal sovereignty and popular sovereignty. Legal sovereignty denotes the circumstance that within a particular territory there is a determinate legal superior to which all individuals and private groups and all the specific institutions of the state and exercises of state authority are subordinate. In the United Kingdoms constitutional system, Dicey defined parliamentary sovereignty in these terms: "Parliament (the Monarch, the House of Lords and the House of Commons acting together) has, under the English constitution, the right to make or unmake any law whatever; and further, . . . no person or body is recognized by the law of England as having a right to overrule or set aside the legislation of Parliament."[44]

Where, then, in a federal regime does legal sovereignty reside? Because all the agencies of the state, including (most crucially in a federation) the central and regional governments, derive their power from the constitution, it might be said that the constitution is sovereign, and Section 52(1) of the Constitution Act, 1982 states: "The Constitution of Canada is the supreme law of Canada, and any law that is inconsistent with the provisions of the Constitution is, to the state of the inconsistency, of no force or effect." But to claim that legal sovereignty, in the Canadian case or otherwise, resides in the constitution is indefensible because the constitution itself provides an authoritative procedure for its own amendment. This procedure will permit changes to be made in the amending procedure itself. Thus, in the most ultimate sense, sovereignty in a constitutional regime is in the authorities who have the power to determine the procedure by which subsequent amendments to the constitution can be made.[45]

However, the legitimating credentials of modern states are framed not in terms of legal sovereignty but of popular sovereignty, of the claim that the final powers of community action are vested in the people. Dicey, in a somewhat facile way, linked the legal sovereignty of Parliament to popular sovereignty by arguing that the objective of the conventions of the constitution was ''to secure that Parliament, or the Cabinet which is indirectly appointed by Parliament, shall in the long run give effect to the will of that power which in modern England is the true political sovereign of the State — the majority of the electors or (to use popular though not quite accurate language) the nation.''[46] This linkage was based on the somewhat benign view that the conventions of the constitution had evolved and would evolve to make the will of parliament responsive to the will of the majority of the electors. Further, Dicey appeared to ignore the circumstance that under parliamentary sovereignty Parliament itself had the unfettered discretion to determine how the popular will might lawfully be manifested — through elections, referendums, demonstrations, the various organs of expression and so on.

Lurking behind much of the acceptance of popular sovereignty as the ultimate credential of democracy is Rousseau's formulation in the *Social Contract* in which the community is united through an indivisible and inalienable general will. Such a concept is obviously incompatible with federalism.[47]

It was the Americans in the fateful summer of 1787 who invented federalism, and it was in the course of the struggle to have the constitution contrived in Philadelphia adopted that the confusion between legal and popular sovereignty which has since remained at the heart of American constitutional mythology originated.[48] The anti-Federalists who opposed the adoption of the proposed constitution were by the standards of the day democrats. They supported the proposition, almost unchallenged in Western political thought from the fifth-century Greeks onward, that republican government was possible only in small communities. Those supporting the constitutional settlement designed at the Philadelphia meeting were fearful of popular majorities, particularly those which would challenge property rights, and to frustrate the will of the people as embodied in such majorities, they sought to erect two safeguards. First, as brilliantly argued by Madison in the famous *Tenth Federalist Paper,* the size and the complexity of interests in the projected new nation would frustrate majorities being formed. Second, within the structure of government itself there was a complex of checks and balances which would, it was hoped, prevent any group of power-holders from abusing their authority in challenging individual rights or the general welfare. Despite these anti-democratic impulses, those who supported the adoption of the constitution found it politically necessary to press their case with the public of the several states on purportedly democratic premises. Thus it was decided that the constitution should be ratified not by the legislatures of the states but by state conventions elected to decide only that issue. Of even more significance, supporters of the constitution claimed that under it all the agencies of government derived their powers from the sovereign people. This ideological sleight-of-hand according to which the American people are sovereign but are effectually hobbled by their constitution from acting as such lies at the heart of the constitutional tradition of the United States. It is a tribute to the effectiveness of political socialization in the republic that successive generations of even the most sophisticated of its citizens have been able not only to live with this contradiction, but also to deny that it exists.

In general, then, federalism is difficult if not impossible to reconcile with sovereignty whether legal or popular. Whitaker is perceptive in writing, ". . . it is no exaggeration to suggest that the rise and persistence of federations has been a leading factor in the decline of the concept of sovereignty from the height of its prestige in the 16th to 18th centuries. Functioning federations seem a kind of standing reproach to the notion that a sovereign power, absolute, indivisible and inalienable, separate from and supreme over the society is a necessary element of any polity."[49]

In the mythology of popular sovereignty it is not just any group of people who can make a legitimate claim to be sovereign but only those who constitute a nation. The late Rupert Emerson wrote: "The nation is today the largest community which, when the chips are down, effectively commands men's loyalty, overriding the claims of both the lesser communities within it and those which cut across it or potentially enfold it within a still greater society reaching ultimately to mankind as a whole."[50] But what community in a federation is the nation in Emerson's sense: Quebec or Canada? Nigeria or Biafra? the Punjab or India? The Americans in the 1860s encountered and, by force of arms, resolved the conflicting claims of whether "We, the People of the United States" referred to in the preamble of the constitution meant that in the previous century an indissoluble union had been established or, alternatively, whether "We, the People" meant the people as constituted in their respective states retained the right to withdraw their states from the larger political community. Countries which are not federal may of course face the challenge of secessionist movements from one or more of their constituent areas. However, in a federation, movements for secession will usually start with the advantage that the sub-national communities which are partly or totally disaffected have already attained constitutional protection of their rights to self-government in relation to a number of important matters.

In a paper delivered in 1964, Pierre Trudeau made a perceptive analysis of the relation between federalism and nationalism.[51] He saw a paradox here in the sense that the cohesion and desire for autonomy of particular groups in federal states which made federalism necessary at the outset makes such regimes somewhat unstable. Because of the continuing strength of such spatially demarcated diversities, there is an ever-present impulse for those who wish to preserve the existing federation to counter such divisive forces by resorting to nationalistic appeals. This course of action is, however, fraught with danger, "Yet if nationalism is encouraged as a righful doctrine and noble passion, what is to prevent it from being used by some group, region or province within the nation? If 'nation algerienne' was a valid battle-cry against France, how can the Algerian Arabs object to the battle-cry 'nation kabyle' being used against them?"[52] Trudeau's enemy in this and other of his writings was the "national state," the sovereign state acting in the interests of a single ethnic/national group, and, as we shall see, he attempted to evolve an alternative source of political legitimation for federal political communities.

Much contemporary theory bases the credentials of democracy on the supremacy of the will of the majority rather than the sovereignty of peoples constituted as nations. But in a federation which majority should prevail, that of the whole political community or of its constituent states or provinces? Democratic theory appears not to have addressed this question. Willian H. Riker ends his 1964 book on federalism in eight nations with this somewhat surprising statement: "[I]f in the United States one approves of Southern white supremacy, then one should approve of American federalism. If, on the other hand, one disapproves of the values of the privileged minority, one should disapprove of federalism. Thus, if in the United States one disapproves of racism, one should disapprove of federalism."[53] Writing about the same time in his critique of the general disposition of the Canadian left towards centralization, Trudeau came to the opposite conclusion that, "other things being equal, radicalism can be more easily attained in a federal country than in a unitary one" because progressive measures can be implemented in the more progressive of the regional units when their people are ready for them.[54] However, neither Riker nor Trudeau makes a satisfactory general case for preferring national to regional majorities or the contrary. Riker's assertion is directed specifically to the United States in the 1960s and before, and he does not deal with the situations referred to by Trudeau in which regional majorities are more committed to liberal and democratic values than to regional ones. Neither does Trudeau take into account circumstances like those in Duplessis' Quebec where national majorities were more liberal than some regional majorities.

The analysis outlined above suggests that it is difficult or impossible to reconcile the operation of federal states with popular sovereignty, nationalism and majority rule or with a combination of these doctrines. Flaubert has one of his characters in *The Sentimental Education* expostulate against "an idiotic adoration of Authority" in these terms: "But why should the sovereignty of the people be more sacred than the divine right of kings? They are both fictitious! Away with metaphysics; we've had enough of ghosts! You don't need dogmas to keep the streets swept!" Trudeau did not go this far but suggested that the legitimacy of the modern state (especially the federal state) should be based not on passion but on reason, on a cool-headed consensus throughout the community that "no group within the nation feels that its vital interests and particular characteristics could be better preserved by withdrawing from the nation than by remaining within."[55] In his latter years as prime minister, Trudeau resorted to precisely the kinds of nationalistic appeals he had so deplored in his 1964 essay, and he asserted in the House of Commons on April 16, 1980: "We, who are here in Parliament, are the only group of men and women who can speak for every Canadian. We are the only group, the only assembly in this country, which can speak for the whole nation, which can express the national will and the national interest." Significantly, the prime minister's assertion that only Parliament or more accurately, the Liberal majority in the House of Commons, could legitimately articulate "the national will and the national interest" was, in the constitutional conflict of 1980–81, challenged by the governments of eight of the provinces and by a Supreme Court of Canada decision in September 1981 to the effect that convention would be breached if Parliament proceeded to bring about constitutional change in the face of such provincial opposition.

Contrary to both the pre-1965 Trudeau and to the assertion of Flaubert's character that "you don't need dogmas to keep the streets swept," some kind of legitimating myth would seem to be necessary to sustain federal states as well as other kinds of political communities in the exactions they make on their citizens. Rousseau put it well: "The strongest man is never strong enough to be master all the time, unless he transforms force into right and obedience into duty." The translation of "force into right and obedience into duty" is particularly difficult for federal states. As we have seen, federalism is almost a standing challenge to the major legitimating myths of democracy. Sawer is perceptive in pointing out that federalism is almost never defended for itself but only in association with more compelling values like liberty or equality.[56]

It seems possible to make three statements of general application to the effect that federalism contributes to the protection of liberal democratic values:

First, the constitutional distribution of functions and political resources between the central and regional orders of government is an obstruction to either set of officeholders abusing its powers. Experience suggests that pluralism among state agencies is a necessary, though perhaps not sufficient, condition for the avoidance of tyranny. Such pluralism can of course be established and sustained in unitary states through a constitutionally prescribed system of checks and balances among the various elements of government. However, federalism would seem to be a peculiarly effective device against the concentration and abuse of state power.

Second, the ongoing competition between the national and regional authorities in federal systems helps sustain civil freedoms and the rule of law. Whitaker states that ". . . it is impossible to imagine a functioning federalism in an illiberal polity."[57] At a minimun, the elites of the central and regional governments will demand the freedom to compete openly with one another and to appeal to the public for support of their respective positions. While it is possible to postulate a regime in which freedom of expression was restricted to such intergovernmental conflict, it is highly unlikely that state agencies would in fact impose such limitations. Thus the thrust of federalism is to sustain open debate about public affairs. In his book *The Welfare State and Canadian Federalism,* Keith Banting points out that whereas in the United Kingdom disputes among various central agencies concerned with income security take place in private, similar kinds of conflict in Canada are openly debated between federal and provincial governments.[58] Further, federalism tends to sustain the rule of law, and Dicey writes, "That a federal system can flourish only among communities imbued with a legal spirit and trained to reverence the law is as certain as can be any conclusion of political speculation. Federalism substitutes litigation for legislation, and none but a law-fearing people will be inclined to regard the decision of a court as equivalent to the enactment of a law."[59] Federalism then, provides both incentives and institutional procedures by which the actions of government can be subjected to challenge as to their legal validity both by other governments and by private citizens and groups.

Third, where (as is usual) popular preferences in respect to public policy are unevenly distributed throughout the territory of a country, then preferences will be more fully realized under federalism than under a unitary regime of uniform policies for the whole nation. A simple mathematical illustration can be given. Let us imagine a nation of five geographical units of 100 000 persons in which there are conflicting preferences about, say, the opening of grocery stores on Sunday. The preferences about these options are distributed as follows:

Unit	For	Against
A	60 000	40 000
B	30 000	70 000
C	80 000	20 000
D	65 000	35 000
E	10 000	90 000

In a federal situation, there would be open Sundays in A, C and D and closed Sundays in B and E with the preferences of 135 000 persons overridden. In a unitary circumstance, there would be Sunday closure against the wishes of 245 000 people.

The general proposition that public preferences are better realized under decentralization than centralization is a somewhat formal one which rests on assumptions that often do not prevail in the real world:

1. That there are no significant externalities in the policies of the constituent units. Thus these policies do not affect the interests of persons in other units. In an interdependent nation this condition is seldom realized, and an important justification for conferring powers on central governments is the desirability of dealing with such externalities.

2. That particular functions might be performed by either order of government and at approximately the same per capita costs. Again this is not always so. Sometimes it will not be possible, or possible only at prohibitively high per capita costs, for at least the smaller provincial or state units to provide particular services, for example, a highly developed system of graduate education. Thus there may be very considerable economies of scale in having the central government perform certain functions. In terms of less tangible advantages, one of the chief impulses for establishing and sustaining federations is that the residents of constituent units will have more influence in dealing with foreign nations than they would have as citizens of several smaller sovereign states.

3. That the only alternatives available in respect to particular functions of government are different choices by the constituent units and uniform nation-wide policies by the central government. There may be other options. If there are significant advantages in national uniformity, this may in some situations be attained through voluntary agreement among the state/provincial authorities rather than centralization as has come about in respect to many aspects of apprenticeship matters under the jurisdiction of the Canadian provinces. On the other side, central governments may put in place provisions which take into account the various circumstances of sub-national areas as is the case with Canadian federal policies of incentives directed towards industrial development.

4. That the state/provincial authorities are at least as responsive to popular preferences as is the central government. Such responsiveness is difficult to measure even in broad terms. However, as was the case in Huey Long's Louisiana and Dupplessis' Quebec, the constituent units of federations may in some cases sustain quasi-dictatorships less sensitive to the popular will than is the central government.

In summary, federalism can make significant contributions to sustaining democratic values. Some federal states, certainly Canada, have problems in evolving a compelling political legitimation because of the competing claims of national and state/provincial political jurisdictions, and the credentials of the political community as such are problematic. On the other hand, federalism erects some barrier against the mystification of the national-popular sovereignty justifications of political authority. The existence of two competing orders of government is valuable as a safeguard against the tyranny of any one set of office-holders and such competition sustains a regime in which crucial policy issues are openly debated. Federalism is pre-eminently a regime of law, and it sustains the rule of law. Under certain conditions, public preferences are more responsively translated into public policy in a federation than in a unitary state. These are in total very considerable advantages.

There are, however, two general circumstances of federalism which would appear to frustrate liberal democratic values: first, federalism is a very complex form of government. These complexities favour the relatively privileged and the sustaining of such privilege. The late John Porter wrote of Canadian federalism:

> Because the distribution of powers that now exists between the two levels of government taxes the capacity of the political scientist and the constitutional lawyer to understand it, and because it provides for a series of courses in the political science departments of universities, it is difficult to see what provincial autonomy means for most segments of the electorate. Consequently, it may be speculated that federalism as such has meaning only for politicians and civil servants who work the complex machinery they have set up, as well as for the scholars who provide a continuing commentary on it, but has very little meaning for the bulk of the population.[60]

While Porter's judgement was an exaggeration, he made a useful point. The complexities of federalism benefit not only professors and public officials but also privileged private groups which have the resources to understand and manipulate those intricacies.

Second, and this point is related to the previous one, the federal division of powers is an obstruction to making the governors effectively accountable to the governed and responsive to their preferences and interests. All contemporary federations have moved away from a situation in which each order of government carried out its constitutionally assigned responsibilities in relative isolation from the other to a situation of complex patterns of elite accommodation among federal and state/provincial governments. Albert Breton says of this: "The heart of co-operative federalism is secret deals, not the stuff on which a lively democracy thrives.''[61] In an era of big government, it is extraordinarily difficult to make holders of public office accountable for what they do, and federalism introduces a range of complications to this which is less present in unitary states.

Federalism and Public Policy

In this last section something will be said about the relation between federalism and public policy. More specifically, I will consider Dicey's proposition that "federal government means weak government."[62] Is the general impulse of federalism towards the non-interventionist state, towards sustaining the values which we now designate as neo-conservative?

Dicey gave plausible reasons for associating federalism with weak government:

> The distribution of all the powers of the state among co-ordinate authorities necessarily leads to the result that no one authority can wield the same amount of power as under a unitarian constitution is possessed by the sovereign. A scheme . . . of checks and balances in which the strength of the common government is . . . pitted against that of the state governments leads . . . to a certain waste of energy. A federation therefore will always be at a disadvantage in a contest with unitarian states of equal resources . . . Federalism, as it defines, and therefore limits, the powers of each department of the administration, is unfavourable to the interference or to the activity of governments. Hence a federal government can hardly render services to the nation by undertaking for the national benefit functions which may be performed by individuals . . . . A system meant to maintain the status quo in politics is incompatible with schemes for wide social innovation.[63]

He went on to state that "federalism tends to produce conservatism" because constitutional arrangements are hard to change, and this rigidity in itself was a barrier to the interventionist state.

In an influential article, "The Obsolescence of Federalism," published in 1939, Harold Laski supported the correctness of Dicey's association of federalism with weak government.[64] He argued that the "contracting capitalism" of the period in which he wrote "cannot afford the luxury of federalism":

> It [federalism] is insufficiently positive in character; it does not provide for sufficient rapidity of action; it inhibits the emergence of necessary standards of uniformity; it relies upon compacts and compromises which take insufficient account of the urgent category of time; it leaves the backward areas a restraint, at once parasitic and poisonous, on those which seek to move forward; not least, its psychological results, especially in an age of crisis, are depressing to a democracy that needs the drama of positive achievement to retain its faith.[65]

In general terms, Laski argued than in an age of "giant capitalism" federalism denied governments the necessary powers to deal with the problems confronting them.

There is a good deal of plausibility in the Dicey-Laski formulation. Certainly in Australia, Canada and the United States those on the left of the political spectrum have in general favoured centralization; in fact, the Australian Labor Party was officially committed to the abolition of federalism until 1975, while the right has for the most part supported state/provincial powers. J. R. Mallory in his analysis of the support of the Judicial Committee and of Canadian courts for provincial autonomy from the 1890s onward, attributes this disposition of the judges, most of whom were no doubt familiar with Dicey's association of federalism with weak government, to their support of the rights of private property.[66]

Nonetheless, federalism may, under certain circumstances, manifest impulses counterbalancing state interventionism. As we have seen, Pierre Trudeau argued that in federal states reform was more possible than otherwise because change was initiated by the more progressive sub-national jurisdictions. On this basis, it might plausibly be argued that because Saskatchewan had already put such programs in place, Canada established national schemes of medical and hospital insurance sooner than would have been the case if it had been a unitary state. It also seems reasonable to suggest that in the period of relatively buoyant public revenues between 1960 and 1980, both federal and provincial governments competed for the allegiance of Canadians through implementing measures of state intervention. In the present period of fiscal restraint, each order of government imposes obstacles to cut-backs the other wishes to make; for example, Ottawa has a stake in the provinces' maintaining existing levels of expenditures on health and post-secondary education; the provinces lobby for generous federal expenditures on unemployment insurance to forestall persons who have exhausted such benefits making claims for general welfare assistance.

In a study published in 1982, Keith Banting analysed how the structural characteristics of the governmental system had affected the development of the Canadian welfare state.[67] These are some of his major conclusions:

1. The existence of a comprehensive system for providing income security for Canadians cannot be attributed to the particular characteristics of our governmental arrangements. On the contrary, "the origins of the Canadian welfare state are to be found in the social strains and pressures generated by the transition from an agrarian to an industrial economy, and industrial nations with widely differing types of government — democratic and totalitarian, centralized and decentralized — have all made some form of collective adjustment for the income security needs of their populations . . . . the ubiquity of income security throughout the industrial world suggests that the existence of such programs does not depend primarily on the details of our form of government."[68]

2. [O]ther things being equal, countries with decentralized governments devote a smaller proportion of their resources to welfare than do countries with centralized governments. In comparative terms, federalism is clearly a conservative force in welfare politics, and the analysis of Canadian experience . . . supports this proposition."[69]

3. In the past two decades, the conservative impulses of divided jurisdiction have been in part offset by the competition between governments. A development in the same direction has been the willingness of the provinces to surrender

jurisdiction with respect to income security but not with respect to other matters through assenting to constitutional amendments in 1940, 1951 and 1964 which permitted Ottawa's involvement in unemployment insurance, contributory retirement pensions and survivors' pensions, respectively.

4. "On balance, federalism [in Canada] probably still does constrain the growth of income security spending, but only modestly. Certainly there is no compelling evidence to suggest that centralizing all responsibility for income security in Ottawa would substantially increase Canada's general commitments in this field, especially in the present period of large deficits at the federal level."[70]

Banting's focus was on Canadian income security measures since the end of the Second World War. His general conclusion that federalism had had a relatively modest impact on the development of the welfare state might have been modified had he analysed an earlier period. James Struthers' book on public policies related to unemployment policy in Canada between 1914 and 1941 showed how both federal and provincial governments used the intergovernmental distribution of powers to avoid responsibility for unemployed persons prior to the 1940 constitutional amendment which vested exclusive legislative jurisdiction over unemployment insurance in Parliament.[71] Throughout this period both Ottawa and the provinces asserted the traditional view that the municipalities had the primary responsibility for assistance to indigents. The federal government buttressed its avoidance of responsibility by referring to the constitutional distribution of powers which, it was claimed, denied the central authority juridiction in these matters. In some cases, the provinces rationalized their own failure to act in terms, not only of the historic role of the municipalities, but also of the overriding powers of Ottawa in respect to immigration which, it was claimed, had been exercised so as to increase the number of unemployed.

We should need detailed comparative studies in such fields as, for example, the control of environmental pollution, policies to reduce regional economic disparities, the support of higher education and the control of crime to make any definitive judgment about the association between federalism and weak government.[72]

Although much more investigation is needed to make any definitive judgements about the relation between federalism and the scope of government intervention, it is plausible to suggest that federalism results in unco-ordinated public policies. By co-ordination I mean the circumstance in which (1) the goals of public policy are explicitly formulated, (2) the goals of policy are ranked, and the less preferred are subsumed to more preferred objectives, and (3) scarce public resources are allocated to alternative uses in a context where the results of actual and proposed policies are measured as accurately as the existing state of such measurements permits. During the late 1960s and early 1970s there was a vast amount of effort expended in Ottawa and the provinces in pursuit of the rationalization and co-ordination of governmental operations on a jurisdiction-wide basis. It can be plausibly argued that such efforts resulted in intergovernmental conflicts becoming more widespread and less amenable to authoritative resolution than under the previous circumstances where many relations involved narrowly-defined measures outside the context of more comprehensive objectives.[73]

To the extent that effective government requires the rationalization of public policy, federalism stands squarely in the way of this goal. Some partial reconciliation of federalism and policy effectiveness might be made in a regime where the overlapping of jurisdictions was minimized and where, so far as was at all practical, the interdependence of central and state/provincial authorities was eliminated. However, in a remarkable article, "Can Federalism Make a Difference?" published in 1973, Vincent Ostrom argued that the fragmentation and overlapping responsibilities in the American federal system led to more effective public policies in respect to such matters as the quality of the natural environment and the control of crime and urban affairs than would exist under a regime in which public power was hierarchically organized.[74] Ostrom's basic case rests on the limits of rationality in large bureaucratic organizations, the advantages of having organizations of differing sizes involved in meeting different kinds of public needs and the possibilities of integration through "quasi-market" relations among public authorities. Further, "conflicts among public jurisdictions in a highly federalized political system will elucidate larger amounts of information about alternative solutions to public problems."[75]

As we shall see in Chapter IV, the Report of the (Macdonald) Royal Commission on the Economic Union and Development Prospects for Canada, published in 1985, took a sanguine view akin to that of Ostrom in respect to the possibilities of the fragmentation of state power inherent in federalism for facilitating adjustments in public policy in a volatile and unpredictable environment.[76] I am generally sympathetic to this kind of assessment. In general, federalism in its Canadian variant contributes both to the preservation of certain key democratic values *and* to effective public policy.

Appendix: The Use of "Region" in Canadian Political Discourse

The term "region" is widely and imprecisely used in Canadian political debate and analysis. (We almost never use "sectionalism" which is common in American discourse).[77] Sometimes Canada is divided into four regions: the Atlantic, Quebec, Ontario and the West; and sometimes into five, with British Columbia accorded the status of a region. Sometimes there is reference to Newfoundland as being separate from the Maritime region. Less commonly, the North (variously delineated) is given the status of a region. Regionalism is not only a term of discourse. Various kinds of statistics also are gathered and reported on a regional basis which has the inevitable disposition towards exaggerating differences among regions and ignoring differences within regions.

Scholars delineate regions within larger territories to demarcate areas which in one or more definable ways differ from those of contiguous areas. The way in which this is done depends entirely on the scholar's purpose:

The geographer Louis-Edmond Hamelin in his book, *Canadian Nordicity*, evolves a complex index of nordicity based on ten factors.[78] Some of these relate to physical divisions (latitude, temperature, precipitation, vegetation and so on), while others relate to human factors (accessibility by land, air services, density of population, economic activity, and so on).

In his *The Creation of Regional Dependency* the sociologist Ralph Matthews writes:

> It is easy to equate province with region, for provincial political social structures are by law and definition different from those of nearby areas, but any delineation of regional social structure must go beyond geo-political boundaries to determine the fundamental differences in family life, economic behaviour, religion, recreation, and other organizations and behaviours which comprise social life. Indeed, unless fundamental differences in social organization can be demonstrated to exist, there is little basis for declaring any territorial area to be a region distinct from adjoining territories.[79]

Matthews goes on to argue that social differences from contiguous areas are a necessary but not sufficient condition of a region, and "another necessary condition is some recognition by the people of a region that they, collectively, are different from other people by virtue of the distinctive social, cultural, and psychological characteristics of their place of residence."[80]

Peter McCormick, Ernest C. Manning and Gordon Gibson in their study of regional representation in the institutions and processes of the government of Canada equate region and province:

> A great deal of time and effort is being spent to avoid the logic that seems so straightforward to other federations: each province/state constitutes a regional unit and is entitled to special representation (in the central government) for that reason. In contrast to other regional divisions, province-regions have concrete historical and political existence; they correspond to one set of institutions that have real existence and meaning in the lives of most citizens. Their boundaries are unambiguous and their inhabitants easily recognizable.[81]

In political discourse we would do well in Canada to banish the term region from our vocabulary and speak instead of province. Not only do provinces have a concrete and unambiguous existence as political jurisdictions, but also as we have seen, provincial boundaries delineate those of a very large number of social and economic groupings. Regions, whether transprovincial or sub-provincial, have no such institutional underpinnings.

Notes

1. Philippe Garique, *L'option politique du Canada français* (Montréal: Les éditions Leorier, 1963).
2. K. C. Wheare, *Federal Government*, 3rd ed. (London: Oxford University Press, 1953), p. 11.
3. A. V. Dicey, *Introduction to the Study of the Law of the Constitution*, 7th ed. (London: Macmillan, 1908), p. 140.
4. Preston King, *Federalism and Federation* (Baltimore: Johns Hopkins University Press, 1982), p. 77.

5. Marcel Faribault and Robert M. Fowler, *Ten to One: The Confederation Wages* (Toronto/Montreal: McClelland and Stewart, 1965), p. 13.
6. Cole Harris, "The Emotional Structure of Canadian Regionalism," in The Walter L. Gordon Lecture Series, Volume 5, 1980–81 (Toronto: Canada Studies Foundations, 1981), pp. 9ff.
7. Ibid., pp. 19–20. Reprinted by permission.
8. A recent article should discourage easy generalizations about the relation between federal and unitary systems of government and the structure of non-governmental associations. See William D. Coleman and Wyn P. Grant "Regional Differentiation of Business Interest Associations: A Comparison of Canada and the United Kingdom," *Canadian Journal of Political Science* 18, no.1 March 1985): pp. 3–30.
9. Helen Jones Dawson, "National Pressure Groups and the Federal Government", in A. Paul Pross, ed. *Pressure Group Behaviour in Canadian Politics* (Toronto: McGraw-Hill Ryerson, 1975), pp. 27–58.
10. An example of the latter, with some adverse implications for federal-provincial harmony, has been Ottawa's action in providing financial support for native groups pressing legal claims against the provinces. For a study detailing the complex interactions between interest groups and intergovernmental relations related to the trucking industry, see Richard J. Schultz, *Federalism, Bureaucracy and Public Policy: The Politics of Highway Traffic Regulation* (Montreal and Kingston: McGill-Queen's University Press, 1980).
11. William S. Livingston, *Federalism and Constitutional Change* (Oxford: Clarendon Press, 1956), p. 4.
12. Ibid., p. 2.
13. Theda Skocpol, "Bringing the State Back In: Strategies of Analysis in Current Research," in Peter R. Evans, Dietrich Rueschemeyer and Theda Skocpol, eds., *Bringing the State Back In* (New York: Cambridge University Press, 1985), p. 4. Italics in original.
14. Michael Stein, "Federal States and Federal Societies," in J. Peter Meekison, ed., *Canadian Federalism: Myth or Reality* (Toronto: Methuen, 1968), pp. 40–41.
15. Alan C. Cairns, "The Governments and Societies of Canadian Federalism," *Canadian Journal of Political Science* 10, (December 1977): p. 699.
16. Evans et al., *Bringing the State Back In*, is valuable for views of non-Marxist writers. For an analysis of contemporary class-based approaches to the state see Martin Carnoy, *The State and Political Theory*, Princeton, N.J. Princeton University Press, 1984.
17. Ralph Miliband, *The State in Capitalist Society* (London: Quartet, 1973 printing), p. 8. Italics in original.
18. *Carnoy, The State and Political Theory*, p. 250.
19. See Evans et al., *Bringing the State Back In*.
20. Skocpol "Bringing the State Back In," pp. 9–14.
21. Ibid., p. 6.
22. Ibid., p. 5.
23. Ibid., pp. 28–29.
24. Reginald Whitaker, *The Government Party: Organizing and Financing the Liberal Party of Canada. 1930–1958* (Toronto: University of Toronto Press, 1977).
25. Ibid., p. 402.
26. Mary Eberts, "The Equality Provisions of the Canadian Charter of Rights and Freedoms and Government Institutions," in Claire F. Beckton and Wayne Mackay, research coordinators, *The Courts and the Charter*, vol. 58 of the research studies prepared for the Royal Commission on the Economic Union and Development Prospects for Canada (Toronto: University of Toronto Press, 1985), p. 146.
27. Eberts, "The Equality Provisions of the Charter," pp. 133–221, is a valuable and detailed treatment of the legal issues here.
28. Quoted in Skocpol, "Bringing the State Back In," p. 7.
29. Eric A. Nordlinger, *On the Autonomy of the Democratic State* (Cambridge, Mass.: Harvard University Press, 1981), p. 11.
30. Michael D. Reagan, *The New Federalism* (New York: Oxford University Press, 1972), p. 159.
31. Miliband, *The State and Capitalist Society* and also Ralph Miliband, *Marxism and Politics* (Oxford: Oxford University Press, 1977).

32. Garth Stevenson, "Federalism and the Political Economy of the Canadian State," in Leo Panitch, ed., *The Canadian State: Political Economy and Political Power* (Toronto: University of Toronto Press, 1977), p. 86.
33. J. R. Mallory, *Social Credit and the Federal Power in Canada* reprint (Toronto: University of Toronto Press, 1976) Chapter 10.
34. However, Rianne Mahon in a very perceptive essay written from a neo-Marxist perspective has analysed the workings of the unequal representation of social and economic interests within the Canadian federal state. "Canadian Public Policy: The Unequal Structure of Representation," in Panitch, *The Canadian State*, pp. 165–198.
35. M. J. C. Vile, *Constitutionalism and the Separation of Powers* (Oxford: Clarendon Press, 1969), p. 295.
36. Ibid., p. 297.
37. Ibid., p. 302. Italics in original.
38. Ibid., p. 314.
39. Richard Simeon, "Regionalism and Canadian Political Institutions," in J. Peter Meekison, ed., *Canadian Federalism: Myth or Reality,* 3rd ed. (Toronto: Methuen, 1977), pp. 292–304.
40. Ibid., p. 297.
41. Reginald Whitaker, *Federalism and Democratic Theory* (Kingston, Ontario: Queen's University, Institute of Intergovernmental Relations, Discussion Paper, 1983), p. 1.
42. G. F. Sawer, *Modern Federalism* (London: C. A. Watts, 1969), pp. 186–187.
43. Franz Neumann, *The Democratic and the Authoritarian State* (New York: Free Press, 1957), chapter, "On the Theory of the Federal State," pp. 216–232.
44. Dicey, *Law of the Constitution,* p. 38.
45. Edmond Cahn has argued that the provisions in the United States Constitution for its amendment was a distinctive contribution to constitutional experience. Prior to that, written constitutions and other basic legal codes were deemed to be "fundamental law" because of inspired, preternatural or divine authorship "and thus not properly subject to subsequent change." Edmond Cahn, ed., *Supreme Court and Supreme Law* (New York: Simon and Schuster, 1971), chapter "An American Contribution," pp. 1–25.
46. Ibid., p. 424.
47. Whitaker, *Federalism and Democratic Theory,* pp. 10–11.
48. There is a vast literature on the contriving of the American constitution, but the best single treatment I know is that of Gordon Wood in his monumental *The Creation of the American Republic 1776–1787* (New York: W. W. Norton, 1969).
49. Whitaker, *Federalism and Democratic Theory,* p. 5.
50. Rupert Emerson, *From Empire to Nation: The Rise to Self-Assertion of Asian and African Peoples* (Boston: Beacon Press, 1960), pp. 95–96.
51. Pierre Elliott Trudeau, *Federalism and the French Canadians* (Toronto: Macmillan of Canada, 1968), chapter "Federalism, Nationalism, and Reason," pp. 182–203.
52. Ibid., p. 192.
53. William H. Riker, *Federalism: Origin, Operation, Significance* (Boston: Little, Brown, 1964), p. 155.
54. Pierre Elliott Trudeau, "The Practice and Theory of Federalism," in Michael Oliver, ed., *Social Purpose for Canada* (Toronto: University of Toronto Press, 1961), p. 372ff.
55. Trudeau, *Federalism and French Canadians,* p. 189.
56. Sawer, *Modern Federalism,* pp. 186–187.
57. Whitaker, *Federalism and Democratic Theory,* p. 34.
58. Keith G. Banting, *The Welfare State and Canadian Federalism* (Montreal and Kingston: McGill-Queen's University Press, 1982), p. 80.
59. Dicey, *Law of the Constitution,* p. 175.
60. John Porter, *The Vertical Mosaic* (Toronto: University of Toronto Press, 1965), p. 384.
61. Albert Breton, Supplementary Statement, *Report of the Royal Commission on the Economic Union And Development Prospects for Canada,* 3 volumes; vol. 3 (Ottawa: Minister of Supply and Services Canada, 1985), p. 493 (The Macdonald Report).
62. Dicey, *Law of the Constitution,* p. 167.
63. Ibid., pp. 167–168.

64. Harold Laski, "The Obsolescence of Federalism," in A. N. Christensen and E. M. Kirkpatrick, ed., (New York: Holt, 1941), pp. 53–76.

65. Ibid., p. 57.

66. Dicey, *Law of the Constitution,* Note 33.

67. Banting, *Welfare State,* particularly Chapter 10, "State Structures and Policy Patterns."

68. Ibid., pp. 171–172.

69. Ibid., p. 172.

70. Ibid., p. 175.

71. James Struthers, *No Fault of Their Own: Unemployment and the Canadian Welfare State, 1914–1941* (Toronto: University of Toronto Press, 1983).

72. On taxation, see D. G. Davies, *International Comparisons of Tax Structures in Federal and Unitary Countries,* Research Monograph No. 16 (Canberra: The Australian National University, Centre for Research on Federal Financial Relations, 1976).

73. Donald V. Smiley, *Canada in Question: Federalism in the Eighties,* 3rd ed., (Toronto: McGraw-Hill Ryerson), chapter 4, "Executive Federalism."

74. Vincent Ostrom, "Can Federalism Make A Difference?," *Publius: The Journal of Federalism* 3, no. 2 (Fall 1973), pp. 197–238.

75. Ibid., p. 230.

76. Breton, Supplementary Statement, pp. 146–148.

77. An exception is Alan Cairns' classic 1968 article on the relation between the electoral system and the party system, "The Electoral System and the Party System in Canada 1921–1965," *Canadian Journal of Political Science* 1, no. 1 March 1968), pp. 55–80.

78. Louis-Edmond Hamelin, *Canadian Nordicity* (Montreal: Harvest House, 1979).

79. Ralph Matthews, *The Creation of Regional Dependency* (Toronto: University of Toronto Press, 1983), p. 15.

80. Ibid., p. 16.

81. Peter McCormick, Ernest C. Manning and Gordon Gibson, *Regional Representation: The Canadian Partnership* (Calgary: Canada West Foundation, 1981), p. 17.

II

The Canadian Constitutional Inheritance

Constitutional Dimensions of Canadian Federalism

It was suggested in the previous chapter that the public officials of Canada have a significant degree of autonomy from societal constraints and that the way power is structured within the governmental system has an important independent effect on the behaviour of those officials and the allocative outputs of the system. Thus any adequate analysis of Canadian federalism must pay some considerable attention to its constitutional dimensions, using this latter term, for the moment, in a comprehensive and somewhat imprecise fashion. It is true that processes which are usually regarded as other than constitutional are important, and I wrote in 1962: "The federal aspects of the Canadian constitution, using this term in its broadest sense, have come less to be what the courts say they are than what the federal cabinets and bureaucracies in a continuous series of formal and informal interactions determine them to be."[1] This statement was made during a period when, in comparison with both earlier and later times in the history of Confederation, judicial review was playing a somewhat restricted role in delineating the respective powers of the federal and provincial authorities. Yet even at the time this statement was made, it was somewhat misleading, and W. R. Lederman has pointed out:

> [T]he test of the constitution as authoritatively interpreted in the courts remains very important. It tells us who can act in any event. In other words, constitutionally it must always be possible in a federal country to ask and answer the question – What happens if the federal and provincial governments do not agree about a particular measure of cooperative action? Then what legislative body has the power to do what? And even though federal-provincial agreement on some matter may come at the end of difficult negotiations, the question and answer just referred to will have influenced

the result because the answer is a primary element in defining the bargaining power of the federal government on the one hand and the provincial governments on the other.[2]

Peter Russell has made the same point: "Students of federalism should not look upon 'executive federalism' and 'judicial federalism' as mutually exclusive processes," and he describes how, in the "virtual explosion" of constitutional litigation after 1975, both federal and provincial governments have attempted to strengthen their bargaining positions against one another by resorting to the courts.[3]

What Is the Canadian Constitution? and What Can We Reasonably Expect from It?

The term constitution as applied to a contemporary state can be used in either a broad or a narrow sense. The Pepin-Robarts Task Force on Canadian Unity gave this very broad definition:

> A constitution is a set of fundamental laws, customs and conventions which provide a framework within which government is exercised in a state. A constitution contains essentially (1) the basic principles, objectives and rules which command the political life of a society; (2) the definition of the principal organs of government in all four branches – the legislative, the executive, the judicial and the administrative — their composition, functions, powers and limitations; (3) the distribution and coordination of powers between the two orders of government if the form of government is a federal one; (4) the definition of relationships between the governors and the governed, particularly the rights of the latter.[4]

A more restricted definition of the constitution of a state is that collection of legal rules which both authorize the exercise of governmental power and specify the procedures by which such power is wielded. This is the law of the constitution, the legal rules which control and, in cases of conflict override, other expressions of the power of the state and the rules to which the courts of law will give meaning and effect. As we shall see, the law of the Canadian Constitution is only a part of our Constitution; the other part is constitutional convention.

Schedule 1 of the Constitution Act, 1982, lists some 25 previous measures which, with the 1982 enactment itself, are designated as the Constitution Acts, 1867 to 1982. This designation of the law of the Canadian Constitution includes the formerly-designated British North America Act of 1867 and subsequent amendments to that Act, measures for bringing provinces and territories into Confederation since 1867 and the Statute of Westminster enacted by the Parliament of the United Kingdom in 1931 to give legal recognition to the sovereignty of Canada and the other dominions. Section 52(1) of the Constitution Act, 1982 states: "The Constitution of Canada is the supreme law of Canada, and any law which is inconsistent with the provisions of the Constitution is, to the extent of the inconsistency, of no force or effect."

If we revert to using the term constitution in a broader rather than a narrower sense, we can say that the Canadian Constitution includes not only the elements specified in the 1982 Act, the law of the Constitution, but also constitutional conventions. A. V. Dicey in his classic *The Law of the Constitution* defined constitutional conventions as "customs, practices, maxims or precepts which are not recognized or enforced by the Courts [and which] make up a body not of laws but of constitutional or political ethics."[5] He wrote that the conventions of the United Kingdom's constitution had one common characteristic in that "they are all, or at any rate most of them, rules for determining the mode in which the discretionary powers of the Crown (or of the ministers as servants of the Crown) ought to be exercised."[6] In more recent times, Dicey's specification of constitutional convention was broadened to apply to certain elements of the relations between British authorities and those of the former colonies in the Empire/ Commonwealth, and, in the context of Canadian constitutional debate in the early 1980s, to the conduct of federal-provincial relations. Sir Ivor Jennings crisply summarized how a constitutional convention could be distinguished from other traditions, precepts or practices: "We have to ask ourselves three questions: first, what are the precedents; secondly, did the actors in the precedents believe they were bound by a rule; and thirdly, is there a reason for the rule?"[7]

In its decision delivered on September 28, 1981 the majority of the Supreme Court of Canada made a formulation of the relation between law and convention and of the relation between the two which will undoubtedly be influential, if not totally authoritative, in subsequent discussion about the Canadian Constitution.[8] One of the major issues involved in this decision was whether by convention the Parliament of Canada required the agreement of the provinces before requesting the Parliament of the United Kingdom to make amendments to the Canadian constitution involving the powers of the provinces. The majority made a very clear distinction between the law and conventions of the constitution and denied that through well-established practice conventions might "crystallise" into law. Thus:

> Those parts of the Constitution of Canada which are composed of statutory rules and common law rules are generally referred to as the law of the Constitution. In cases of doubt or dispute, it is the function of the courts to declare what the law is and since law is sometimes breached, it is generally the function of the courts to ascertain whether it has in fact been breached in specific instances and, if so, to apply such sanctions as are contemplated by the law, whether they be punitive sanctions or civil sanctions such as a declaration of nullity. Thus, when a federal or provincial statute is found by the courts to be in excess of the legislature which has enacted it, it is declared null and void and the courts refuse to give effect to it. In this sense it can be said that the law of the Constitution is administered or enforced by the courts.[9]

On the other hand:

> The conventional rules of the Constitution present one striking peculiarity. In contradistinction to the laws of the Constitution, they are not enforced by the courts. One reason for this situation is that, unlike common law rules, conventions are not judge-made rules. They are not based on judicial

precedents but on precedents established by the institutions of government themselves. Nor are they in the nature of statutory commands which it is the function and duty of the courts to obey and enforce. Furthermore, to enforce them would mean to administer some formal sanction when they are breached. But the legal system from which they are distinct does not contemplate formal sanctions for their breach.[10]

The majority gave as an example of a possible breach of convention the refusal of the Queen, the Governor General or a lieutenant-governor to assent to a bill passed by Parliament or a provincial legislature. This would be a gross breach of convention and would undoubtedly lead to a serious political crisis. Yet the courts would refuse to recognize the invalidity of the vetoed bill.

In his critique of the 1981 decision, Peter Russell has made a persuasive argument that the majority of the Supreme Court drew too strict a line between law and convention.[11] One of Russell's basic points is that there are several instances in both English and Canadian law in which courts have, in fact, given legal effect to the conventions of the constitution. His conclusion follows Dicey's to the effect that, while it is necessary to distinguish law and convention, these two elements together are the "constitutional law" of the realm.

So far as federalism is concerned, all but a small part of the law of the Canadian Constitution (as law was defined in the 1981 decision of the Supreme Court) consists of the distribution of legislative powers between Parliament and the provinces. Thus, the procedures governing the interactions between the federal and provincial executive authorities are in the realm of custom, practice and convention rather than of law. (The question put before the Supreme Court in 1981 as to whether convention required provincial agreement for Resolutions of the Parliament of Canada requesting Westminster to amend the constitution has been resolved once and for all by the Constitution Act, 1982 which provides for a wholly domestic amending procedure and thus removes this matter from the realm of convention.) However, the processes of executive federalism have evolved rapidly over the past generation, and informed and disinterested observers might well differ as to what customary practices had attained the status of constitutional conventions. For example, since the Second World War lengthy intergovernmental consultations have taken place in respect to the five-year fiscal arrangements between Ottawa and the provinces. Would convention be breached if a future federal government by-passed such consultation and affected changes unilaterally as it would have the undeniable legal power to do? Has the federal power to disallow provincial legislation been in abeyance so long – the last disallowance was in 1943 — and is this power so contrary to contemporary norms of Canadian federalism that its exercise would be a challenge to convention? What if an incoming provincial government released some or all of the hitherto confidential information about the dealings between Ottawa and its predecessor? In general, there is little law or established convention regulating federal-provincial relations and a considerable amount of doubt and dispute about the norms governing those relations.

The law and conventions of the Constitution are external restraints on the conduct of office-holders. So long as the constitutional order is sustained, breaches of the law of the constitution will result, sooner or later, in invalidation of such breaches by the courts; offences against convention will bring about other penalties.[12] Political experience suggests the crucial importance of such restraints for human freedom and dignity; despots are almost never benevolent. Yet even a meticulous regard for law and convention is not enough; these must be complemented by constitutional morality or what the Germans call "the spirit of constitutional comity." In a paper published in 1978, J. A. Corry made a cogent argument to this effect.[13] From his perspective, the conventions of the Canadian Constitution based on the tradition of British parliamentary government had a persuasive majoritarian disposition and this was necessary and appropriate to safeguard "the interests of the whole."[14] However, Canada is an "incorrigibly federal country," and "any constitution that gives parliament the powers necessary to safeguard the interests of the whole will be open to the overriding of the preferences of Quebec on particular points." Thus, "in the constitutional law of a federal state, particularly where the interests and sensitivities of minorities are involved, only in the rarest circumstances should nation-wide majorities insist on getting everything the constitution makes possible."[15] The solution is "a meticulous constitutional morality, a mutual comity which never overlooks advance notice and consultation, always strives for accommodation."[16]

But what then can Canadians reasonably expect from their Constitution? In the recent past, certain influential participants in the national debate have made patently unrealistic claims about what the Constitution can be and should be expected to do.

First, despite a good deal of heady rhetoric surrounding the Charter of Rights and Freedoms, the Constitution cannot "guarantee" human rights. What the Charter does do, and all that such an instrument can do, is to enunciate that nation's desire to honour certain claims — many of these specified in a very general way — and to transfer to the courts from legislatures and executive agencies a very wide discretion in defining and ranking these claims. Section 1 of the Charter enacts that "The Canadian Charter of Rights and Freedoms guarantees the rights and freedoms set out in it subject only to such reasonable limits prescribed by law as can be demonstrably justified in a free and democratic society." I have elsewhere suggested that no prudent consumer would buy a refrigerator with such an open-ended "guarantee."[17] Section 1 does no more and no less than to confer on the judiciary the authority to determine what limits in the specified rights can be "demonstrably justified in a free and democratic society." Further, under Section 33 either Parliament or a provincial legislature may override most of the rights specified in the Charter. In addition, apart from certain provisions relating to the French and English languages, the Charter is subject to amendment by the action of Parliament and of the legislatures of at least two-thirds of the provinces having in aggregate at least half the population of all the provinces. To repeat, the Constitution does not guarantee the rights of individual citizens or private groups in any absolute or certain way but rather enacts a procedure by which a group of specified rights are to be interpreted and ranked when they come into conflict with other private or public claims.

The rights which are more effectively and unequivocally guaranteed by the Constitution are those of the governmental authorities. Thus:

1. As we have seen, individual legislatures may override the Charter as it impinges on their own jurisdictions and may by acting together cause the Charter to be amended.
2. Under Section 43(a) of the Constitution Act, 1982, the boundaries of a province can be altered only with the consent of its legislature.
3. Section 38(3) permits individual provinces to dissent from amendments derogating from provincial powers and rights, and in such situations the amendment is of no effect in the dissenting province(s).

Secondly, the constitution cannot realistically be expected to serve as a compelling symbol of Canadian unity or a coherent statement of Canadian purpose. *The Constitution and the People of Canada,* a document introduced into the Federal-Provincial Conference on the Constitution in February 1969 said this:

> The first element in Canada's Constitution in the view of the Government of Canada should be a statement — a preamble — on the objectives of the federation. The basic role of the Constitution is, of course, to define the system of law and government which shall prevail in Canada. But before doing this, the Constitution must express the purpose of Canadians in having become and resolving to remain associated together in a single country, and it must express as far as this is possible in a constitution what kind of country Canadians want, what values they cherish, and what objectives they seek.[18]

The notion that a new Canadian Constitution should serve as a statement of national goals and commitments ran through the constitutional debates from the late 1960s onward, and in one instance, Peter Newman suggested that the new Constitution be written by poets rather than politicians and lawyers.

The Canadian Constitution as we have received it since 1982 demonstrably fails as a coherent and compelling expression of "what kind of country Canadians want, what values they cherish, and what objectives they seek." The preamble to the Charter goes no further than to state, "Whereas Canada is founded upon principles that recognize the supremacy of God and the rule of law." A constitution meant to serve as a national creed would scarcely contain anything like the following definition from the Sixth Schedule of the Constitution Act, 1982 relating to the redefinition of provincial ownership over natural resources:

> 51 1 (b) production from a forestry resource is a primary production therefrom if it consists of sawlogs, poles, lumber, wood chips, sawdust or any other primary wood product, or wood pulp, and is not a product manufactured from wood.

If Canadian schoolchildren in their patriotic exercises are required to learn and recite even less turgid parts of the nation's Constitution than the one just quoted, it is devoutly to be hoped that they would receive assistance against their oppressors by way of the protection of Section 12 of the Charter to the effect that "Everyone has the right not to be subjected to any cruel or unusual treatment or punishment."

To write a constitution in lucid and evocative language without the kinds of qualifications which abound in the Constitution Act, 1982 would be to turn over to the courts what many of us would regard as an undue amount of power to determine what the Constitution meant. Two examples from the experience of other nations can be given. The First Amendment to the constitution of the United States enacts, in part, that Congress shall make "no law . . . abridging the freedom of speech, or of the press." The American courts have not been willing to interpret this constitutional prohibition as literally as it is written, and there is a complex jurisprudence determining the permissible limits of the power of the Congress in restricting freedom of expression. In similar fashion Section 92 of the constitution of Australia provides that "trade, commerce, and intercourse" among the States shall be "absolutely free." From the beginning of the Commonwealth there has been a vast amount of judicial decision about what the apparently unequivocal term "absolutely free" means in particular circumstances. In general, the constitution is law, its primary audience is lawyers and judges rather than the wider public of citizens, and the requirements of good law and good rhetoric are quite different.

Another reason why it is unrealistic to expect a constitution to be a coherent national creed is that this document is a resultant of the conflicting values and interests of its framers.[19] Most of the durable and effective constitutions in force today (those of Australia, Canada and the United States, for example) were contrived by the most powerful and experienced politicians of the time, and federal constitutions almost by definition are reflections of conflicting pressures towards unity and state/provincial autonomy. As has been the case at other times and in other nations, the Constitution Act, 1982 reflects a series of complex compromises, and its lack of logical coherence and evocative symbolism is a resultant of such compromises.

What a constitution can do is to confer on the office-holders of government the legal authority to govern and to give the people a measure of protection against such powers being exercised in excessive and arbitrary ways. The constitution of the United States has been called a sword and a shield, a power-conferring and power-limiting instrument. Underlying all particular constitutions is the affirmation of constitutionalism expressed in Lord Acton's well-known aphorism about power corrupting and absolute power corrupting absolutely, expressed more colourfully by E. M. Forster, "As soon as people have power, they go crooked and sometimes dotty as well, because the possession of power lifts them into a region where normal honesty never prevails."[20] Corry puts it well; "[T]he main service of a good constitution is to put obstacles in the way of bad government,"[21] and, as we have seen, he argues that in the Canadian case even an adherence to the law and conventions of the Constitution by office-holders needs to be reinforced by a commitment on their part to constitutional morality. In an ultimate sense, though, the capacity of a constitution to thwart bad government depends on the governed rather than on their political masters:

> If the constitution safeguards an area of freedom that is generally congenial to the people and gives them means and processes for asserting their rights, an alert people eager to conserve their freedoms will use the constitution to thwart bad government. But a stream cannot rise higher than the source, and a people not capable of governing themselves well will not use the opportunities a good constitution affords.[22]

The Federal Constitution: The Legacy of 1787

In the summer of 1787 the "men of Philadelphia" invented federalism, one of the most important inventions ever made in the art of government. Subsequent federations may reasonably be regarded as prototypes of the American model adjusted to other traditions and circumstances. As we shall see, the Confederation settlement did have important federal elements but in other ways was a deliberate rejection of some of the most crucial elements of the American constitutional system. It has been affirmed that Canadian politics is both an American game played according to British rules and a British game played according to American rules, a dispute that could be resolved, if at all, only by some agreed-upon definition of what is meant by "rules." However that may be, one perspective for the understanding of the Canadian constitutional system is that of examining how British constitutional traditions have been adapted to our Canadian imperative of territorial and cultural diversity by way of the American device of federalism.

The basic elements of the 1787 constitutional settlement in the United States were these:

First, the powers of government were divided between the central government and the states by each deriving its powers from the constitution. When the American politicians came together in Philadelphia, they had two models for the organization of power before them, and their circumstances led them to reject both. The first was "national" — we would call it unitary — according to which whatever powers were possessed and exercised by the states were at the discretion of the central authorities. However, the revolution had been precipitated by the British authorities' assertion of their unfettered legal powers to regulate the affairs of the colonies. It was unthinkable to most of the delegates that the newly independent states would surrender such powers to another central government, even one under the control of the Americans themselves. The second model was "confederal" in which the central authority would be exclusively, or almost exclusively, dependent on the constituent states for carrying out its will; but this was the very kind of regime from which the delegates wished to escape. Although many persons believed at the time and even later that it was both practically and theoretically impossible to design a two-tier system of government without one set of political authorities existing at the discretion of the other (sovereignty in this view was inherently indivisible) this is precisely what the American constitution-makers did.

Second, individual citizens of the United States would be subject to the powers of both the central government and the governments of their respective states. This was the solution to a very practical problem. If, under the confederal form, the central authority attempted to force the compliance to its will of one or more of the states, the result would be civil war, and the challenge of the Confederate States to the national government did bring about such a war less than 75 years later. Yet under less crucial circumstances, the conferring of significant legislative powers, binding individual citizens, on the national authorities and the establishment of a national legislature, executive and judiciary meant that the will of the central government could be expressed through the peaceful processes of law making and law enforcement.

Third, the constitution included provisions by which it might subsequently be amended. Edward Cahn has pointed out that from the time of Oliver Cromwell's Instrument of Government of 1663 to the United States Constitution of 1787, written constitutions (and projected constitutions like the one for Carolina drawn up by John Locke) were regarded as being unsusceptible to future alteration, and "in the philosophic aspect of the matter, a written constitution was deemed to possess superior dignity and force because it mirrored the principles of natural law which everyone agreed were fixed, immutable and permanent."[23] Yet the United States Constitution, in Article 5, did provide a procedure for its own amendment, and some scholars have also argued that some or most of its framers foresaw constitutional adaptation through evolving processes of judicial review of the constitution.

Fourth, the supporters of the constitution (most crucially in the debates preceding its ratification by conventions in the states) defended the settlement in terms of popular sovereignty. The preamble to the constitution began "We the People, of the United States." It was decided that the constitution as drawn up by the Philadelphia Convention should be submitted for ratification to popularly-elected conventions in the several states rather than to the governmental authorities of those states. But in a deeper philosophical way, the constitution was propounded by its supporters as providing for a regime based on the sovereignty of the people. In one sense this was something of an ideological sleight-of-hand on the part of the supporters of the constitution. Opponents of the settlement which emerged from the Philadelphia Convention — the "anti-Federalists" — were on the whole the democrats of their day, and they staked out their opposition on the proposition, accepted by most political thought from the classical Greeks onward, that democracy was possible only in small republics. The supporters of the new arrangements countered this with the assertion that, under the projected constitution, all those on whom the powers of government were conferred derived their powers from the sovereign people. However, the complex way by which the constitution divided governmental authority made it virtually impossible for the people to act, and it was deliberately designed to do this. Thus the American constitution was, and is, an anti-majoritarian instrument whose rationale has been derived from a theory of popular sovereignty.

Fifth, the new constitution enacted a complex separation of powers between the executive and legislative branches of the national government. The 1787 document can be understood adequately only against the background of constitutional experimentation in the various states from 1776 onward as these newly-independent jurisdictions sought new bases for political authority. Much of this experimentation involved the nature of executive power and the relation between executive and legislature. In part, American adherence to the principle of the separation of legislative and executive powers combined with a complex system of checks and balances between the two branches was the reflection of a desire to return to the "balanced constitution" which George III and his ministers had allegedly destroyed by the corruption of Parliament and in part a manifestation of the framers' adherence to Montesqieu's more general constitutional theory stressing the division of state powers as a necessary prerequisite for the avoidance of tyranny.

Sixth, in one of its last acts before being displaced by the new national government established under the constitution, the Continental Congress in the Northwest Ordinance of July 1787 provided for the creation of new states in the territory north of the Ohio River. As in Canada eight decades later, only a small part of the area of the United States in 1787 fell within the boundaries of the federating states. The Northwest Ordinance provided that in the area in question there should be formed not fewer than three nor more than five states, and when any state had attained a population of 60 000 free inhabitants, it should have the rights and obligations of other states.

Seventh, the states as such were recognized in the operations and structures of the central government. The most important intrastate dimension here was the Senate with two representatives from each state chosen by the state legislature. The president and vice-president were to be chosen by electors chosen in the states. In both instances the states with smaller populations received a disproportionate voice.

These, then, were the major elements of the American constitutional system forged in the late eighteenth century: the constitutional distribution of powers between national and state authorities with the activities of each impinging directly on the individual citizen; the provisions for the subsequent amendment of the constitution; the ideological underpinnings of the constitution in popular sovereignty; the separation of legislative and executive powers; provisions by which new states might enter the union and the recognition of the state communities in the structures and functioning of the national government.

The Canadian Federal Constitution: The Legacy of 1864–67

The Confederation settlement of 1864–67 was a rejection of several of the fundamental constitutional principles upon which the American republic was founded. In part this rejection was deliberate and explicit; in some other dimensions it was a resultant of the particular circumstances facing the Fathers of Confederation.

The distribution of the powers of government between the central and the state/provincial authorities is perhaps the most crucial defining characteristic of federalism, and it was here that the British North American politicians of the 1860s most deliberately and decisively diverged from the American model. Section 8 of the American constitution specified the powers of the Congress, and the Tenth Amendment of 1791 enacted that ''The powers not delegated to the United States by the Constitution, nor prohibited by it to the States, are reserved to the States respectively, or to the people.'' John A. Macdonald in the Confederation Debates expressed the Fathers' rejection of the American model in these terms:

> We have strengthened the General Government. We have given the General Legislature all the great subjects of legislation. We have conferred on them, not only specifically and in detail, all the powers which are incident to sovereignty, but we have expressly declared that all subjects of general interest not distinctly conferred upon the local governments and local legis-

latures shall be conferred upon the General Government and Legislature.
— We have thus avoided that great source of weakness which has been
the source of the disruption of the United States.[24]

The device here was to specify in a Sections 92 and 93 of the British North
America Act the exclusive legislative powers of the provinces while under Sect-
tion 91 Parliament was given the power to legislate for ''the Peace, Order, and
good Government of Canada, in relation to all Matters not coming within the
Classes of Subjects by this Act assigned exclusively to the Legislatures of the
Provinces.'' However, Section 91 went on to enumerate ''for greater Certainty,
but not so as to restrict the Generality of the foregoing terms of this Section''
some 29 classes of subjects on which Parliament might legislate. The most plausible explanation for the decision to enumerate these powers is that the (then)
current understanding of ''Property and Civil Rights,'' a subject of exclusive
provincial jurisdiction under Section 92(13), included several matters which the
Fathers wished to be matters of Dominion authority.

Not only did the British North America Act confer what were then regarded
as the most important classes of power on the Dominion — Macdonald's ''all
the great subjects of legislation'' — but it also went on to provide that the national
authorities might by unilateral action involve themselves in the provinces' exercise of what otherwise were the latter's exclusive legislative powers under Sections
92 and 93. What might reasonably be designated as the quasi-unitary elements
of the Confederation settlement were the following:

1. Through the provisions for reservation and disallowance of bills enacted
   by provincial legislatures the provinces were put into the same constitutional relation with the Dominion as was the Dominion itself in respect to
   the authorities of the United Kingdom.
2. Under Section 92 10(c) Parliament might declare ''Works'' wholly situated
   within one province to be ''for the general advantage of Canada or for the
   advantage of Two or more of the Provinces.'' When such action was taken,
   the facilities so designated came under the jurisdiction of the Dominion.
3. The Dominion cabinet and Parliament were given the power to come to
   the aid of Roman Catholic and Protestant minorities in education if the
   rights of these groups under Section 93 were encroached upon by the
   provinces. Under such circumstances, there could be an appeal to the
   federal cabinet, but if the cabinet's efforts to right the situation were ineffective Parliament might enact ''Remedial laws.''
4. ''The Parliament and Government of Canada'' were given under Section
   132 the powers necessary to carry out international obligations binding the
   Dominion as part of the British Empire even though the matters involved
   were otherwise under provincial jurisdiction. Canada at that time of course
   had no independent power to commit the nation in international affairs.
5. Under Section 101 Parliament was given the power to establish a ''General
   Court of Appeal for Canada'' and ''any additional Courts for the better
   Administration of the Laws of Canada.'' Unlike the United States where
   there has been from the beginning national and state court systems, Canada
   has had a unified judicial system. However, under the provisions of Section

101 giving Parliament the power to establish whatever courts it chose, it was, and is, possible for the federal authorities to create a complex of courts dealing with the laws enacted by Parliament, with the courts under provincial administration being left to interpret and enforce provincial legislation alone.

It was not only in the judicial sense that the Fathers of Confederation rejected federalism, but also in the elimination from the new Dominion of several of the devices of Upper Canada — Lower Canada duality which had developed in the largest province of British North America as a response to the persistence of the two linguistic and cultural communities under the regime of the Act of Union. These dualistic procedures were a paradigm of what contemporary students of government call consociationalism: from 1842 onward ministries were headed by a leader from each of the two sections; there was some recognition of the double-majority procedure by which measures applicable to one or the other section were enacted only with the consent of a majority of the legislators from that section; apart from the heads of successive ministries, there was a considerable bifurcation in the executive council and the departments of government; prior to Queen Victoria's decision in 1857 to make Ottawa the permanent seat of government, the capital perambulated between the two sections. These devices reflected English-French duality and also contributed to the political deadlock whose resolution was a major purpose of the Confederation settlement. J. M. S. Careless has written of the period between 1841 and 1857:

[F]or all the quasi-federal structure in Canada, there was no effective separation of sectional from common concerns within the single legislature. The cumbersome expedient had frequently confused the two, and so made for angry friction. Certainly Upper or Lower Canadians tended to adopt the view that the province was one or two just as the occasion suited them. . . If quasi-federalism was a response to duality, it aggravated rather than resolved inherent Canadian differences.[25]

Other federations have been formed by units entering into a closer political union and this of course happened at Confederation in terms of the incorporation of the maritime colonies into the new Dominion. However, so far as the Canadas themselves were concerned, Confederation was a partial disentanglement, with the matters on which the two sections (under the Act of Union) were most at odds now conferred on the new provinces of Ontario and Quebec.

Sections 92 and 93 of the British North America Act gave the provinces a significant degree of exclusive legislaltive power, but this was not paralleled by the willingness of the first politicianss of the new Dominion government to permit the provincial jurisdictions to run their own affairs.[26] Although it had been Quebec pressures which had resulted in the Dominion emerging as a federal political community, albeit in a somewhat attenuated sense, the first premier of the province was the choice of Cartier, and in the next two decades there was frequent direct involvement of Ottawa in Quebec affairs. However, effective elements of provincial autonomy in Nova Scotia and Ontario developed some time earlier, and the groundwork for such autonomy received a foundation in legislation enacted by Parliament in 1873 which prohibited dual membership in the House of Commons and a provincial legislative assembly.

The Confederation settlement also diverged from the American tradition in respect to the conditions under which new provinces might enter the Dominion. As we have seen, the Northwest Ordinance of 1787 regulated the way in which states might be established with precisely the same rights and powers as the pre-existing ones, and by 1870 some 18 new states had come into the Union under such provisions. The Canadians on the other hand adopted the familiar colonial-imperial rules by which the circumstances under which territories within the country's borders could progress to self-government and new provinces be established would be determined by the Dominion authorities.[27]

There is nothing in the British North America Act, or the thinking of those who designed it, which showed any sympathy for the principle of popular sovereignty.[28] All the Fathers were anti-democrats; none believed in universal male suffrage without a property qualification. The preamble to the United States Constitution spoke of "We, the People"; the British North America Act of "the Provinces of Canada, Nova Scotia and New Brunswick." Unlike the American, the Canadian Constitution, as it emerged from the negotiations of 1864–67, was not submitted to ratification by popular conventions; the one intervening provincial election, that of New Brunswick in 1865, resulted in a decisive defeat for the Confederation forces. In short, the British North America Act of 1867 was an instrument of governments alone which embodied almost no hint of democracy or popular sovereignty.

The Confederation settlement was thus a decisive rejection of several of the most essential elements of American constitutionalism: the co-ordinate powers of national and regional authorities with residual powers conferred on the states; popular sovereignty; the separation of legislative and executive powers and the stipulation by pre-existing law of the procedures by which new states might be established. There was thus a marked reluctance to accept federalism in the form the Americans had invented. Most of the English-speaking Fathers would have preferred a unitary solution, or, in the language of the day, a "legislative union." Precisely how they visualized a legislative union is not clear, although it seems unlikely that many would have favoured the elimination of all intervening governments between the Dominion and the local authorities, and in the maritime colonies these latter jurisdictions existed in only a rudimentary form. The Fathers were no doubt familiar with the New Zealand system established in 1852 in which governmental powers were divided between a national authority and six provincial councils with the powers of the latter being subject to the discretion of the former.[29] So far as the rights of the French Canadians were concerned, some of the English-speaking Fathers might have seen as desirable an arrangement like that of the Act of Union of 1707 (uniting England and Scotland) by virtue of which the Scottish community received protection for its distinctive religious, legal and educational institutions without the principle of the sovereignty of the United Kingdom Parliament being breached. Peter Waite in his *Life and Times of Confederation* published in 1962, argued that, "most of the members of the Canadian coalition government thought of federation largely in terms of the composition of the central legislature . . . The basics of the federal principle lay in the central legislature and in the balance between the House of Commons on the one hand and the Senate on the other."[30] Even the French-Canadian Fathers saw the rights of this community receiving their primary protection through the workings of central institutions rather than through the distribution of legislative powers between the Dominion and Quebec authorities. "Cartier, like Sir Étienne Taché, was confident, perhaps too confident, that French-Canadian privileges would be defended better by French-Canadian ministers in a central government than by a local legislature."[31]

Not withstanding all of these breaches of the federal principle as the Americans had invented it, in both the thought of the Fathers and in the substantive terms of the Confederation settlement, the new Dominion emerged in important dimensions as a federal union with two sets of governmental authorities, each drawing its powers from a constitutional document which neither could at its own discretion amend. In his book-length analysis, *The French-Canadian Idea of Confederation 1864–1900* published in 1982, A. I. Silver makes a richly documented argument that, contrary to Waite, the French-Canadian Fathers saw the primary protection of the rights of that community in provincial powers and that only such a Quebec-centred approach would receive a significant degree of acceptance for Confederation in the province of Quebec.[32] To repeat, the pressure of the French Canadians did result in the Dominion emerging with features which were in a significant sense federal.

The most innovative dimension of the Confederation settlement was the combination of federalism, albeit federalism in a compromised form, with the Westminster model of parliamentary responsible government. This combination was repeated, in all cases with a greater or lesser degree of attention to the Canadian experience, in the founding of the Australian federation during the last years of the nineteenth century and of several of the nations of the new Commonwealth after the Second World War. Robin Winks has written that, "Canadian history is in many ways embedded in the history of every Commonwealth member nation. One cannot study the history of Africa — of Nigeria, for example–without knowing Canadian history."[33] The attainment of responsible government in the British North American colonies had taken place less than two decades before, and the Fathers had neither the incentive nor the desire to give up this newly-won principle for an American-type separation of legislative and executive powers. Jennifer Smith, in a recent article, has argued that in pre-Confederation British North America, the preference for parliamentary as against republican forms had not been definitively settled, although the winning of responsible government was an important victory for the former, and that Confederation itself constituted the decisive acceptance of parliamentarianism, what she designates as the "unity principle." Thus: "The Canadians prized parliamentary government for its strength, order and authority. They repudiated its republican rival for lacking authority, for yielding to the clamorous mob, for fragmenting power, in a word, for weakness."[34] According to Smith's analysis, the Fathers believed they could combine the parliamentary principle with federalism because a clear line could be drawn between Dominion and local matters. "For the founders politics at the national level was to be a politics concerned with the 'great questions', mostly economic, in which everyone had a stake. They conceived of a national political discourse liberated from local concerns, especially the dangerous kind having to do with nationality."[35]

In my view, Smith's analysis is at fault in ignoring the concerns of the founders for building protections for local, regional and cultural issues into the structures of the central government itself. The composition of the Senate was the most contentious single issue resolved by the Fathers and the issue on which the scheme of union nearly foundered. Just as crucially, the British North American politicians at the Westminster Conference of 1866 agreed on the representation of the provinces in the Cabinet of the new Dominion with Ontario allocated five places (including that of the prime minister), Quebec four and the Maritime provinces two each. Thus there was some expectation that local and provincial interests would have some outlet in the workings of the national authority. However, Smith is quite accurate in emphasizing the predilection of the Fathers for "strength, order and authority" in the affairs of the new Dominion, characteristics noticeably lacking in the United Province of Canada under the Act of Union regime. I shall argue in the last section of this chapter that the persisting legacy of Confederation has been executive dominance over the governmental process.

The phrase in the preamble to the British North America Act of 1867 that the provinces wished to be united into a Dominion "with a Constitution similar in Principle to that of the United Kingdom" expressed the desire of the Fathers of Confederation that the prevailing conventions of British parliamentary government under the Crown be perpetuated in Canada — at least at the Dominion level. Some of these conventions were included in the British North America Act itself; for example, the provisions of Section 20 that there be at least one session of Parliament each year and of Section 54 that a measure for the raising or expenditure of public funds might be introduced only in the House of Commons (rather than the Senate) and by a minister of the Crown. It is also reasonable to suppose that the Fathers included the independence of the judiciary in their concept of a "Constitution similar in Principle to that of the United Kingdom," and Section 99(1) provided that the judges of the superior courts of the provinces should "hold office during good behaviour" subject to removal "by the Governor General on address of the Senate and House of Commons." However, the most important convention of responsible government, that, to remain in office, a government must retain the support of the House of Commons, was not provided for in the explicit terms of the Act.

The Confederation settlement created the two provinces of Ontario and Quebec out of the former United Province of Canada established by the Act of Union of 1840, and thus the British North America Act contained the constitutions of Ontario and Quebec. Along with those of the other provinces, these were, under Section 92(1), to be amendable by the respective provincial legislatures "except as regards the Office of Lieutenant-Governor." Although there was some controversy about whether the legislature of Quebec should have one chamber or two, the provincial constitutions of Ontario and Quebec were not major concerns in the framing of Confederation. Some of the Upper-Canadian politicians, George Brown in particular, preferred that the province be organized along the lines of municipal government without legislative control of the executive. However, this ɪot to be, and from the beginning, the Canadian provinces adopted and ɹɪned the basic elements of the Westminster model.

Procedures for Amending the Canadian Constitution: 1841–1982

I suggested in Chapter I that legal sovereignty in a state resides in those persons and groups which have the authority to amend the constitution, especially the authority to amend the amending procedure itself and thus to determine how subsequent amendments can be effected. Formal amendment is only one of the procedures of constitutional change, but as William S. Livingston has pointed out, "It differs from the others in that it is superior to them and may be employed to transcend or repudiate any change that may be brought about by other means."[36] Since the 1920s the procedure by which the Canadian Constitution is amended has been a contentious issue, and some of the most fundamental debate about the nature of the Canadian political community has revolved around this issue.

Until the Constitution Act came into effect on April 17, 1982, the most important elements of the Canadian Constitution were subject to amendment by action of the Parliament of the United Kingdom. However, it had long been established that Westminster would so act only on the request of the Canadian authorities. The central part of the Constitution, the British North America Act of 1867, was a contrivance of the British North American politicians. The UK authorities influenced only two not very essential elements of the Act: in order not to offend the United States, the new political community was not to be called a "Kingdom" as the British North Americans wished, and there was to be a provision permitting the appointment of extra Senators to deal with deadlocks between that body and the House of Commons.[37] But the practice that the United Kingdom in amending the Canadian Constitution would act only on the request of the Canadian authorities antedated Confederation. The Act of Union of 1841 uniting the formerly separate colonies of Upper and Lower Canada was a British solution to Canadian problems as these had been brought to a climax in the Rebellions of 1837. However, on two subsequent occasions the act was amended by Westminster in response to requests of the Canadian authorities: in 1848 to give French a limited status as an official language and in 1856 to provide that, in the future, members of the Legislative Council be chosen by popular election.

In the period between Confederation and the late 1920s, the relatively few amendments to the Constitution made by Westminster were not very significant in the evolution of the Canadian political community, and the amending procedure itself was not the subject of much debate.[38] This latter subject was projected onto the public agenda by the declaration of the Imperial Conference of 1926 that, "They [Great Britain and the Dominions] are autonomous Communities within the British Empire, equal in status and in no way subordinate one to another in any aspect of their domestic or external affairs, though united by a common allegiance to the Crown, and freely associated as members of the British Commonwealth of Nations." In 1927 there was a Dominion-provincial conference convened for the purpose of attempting to evolve a procedure by which the Canadian Constitution could be amended without resort to the Parliament of the

United Kingdom. No agreement could be reached, and at the request of the Canadian authorities, the Statute of Westminster (enacted by the UK Parliament in 1931 to give legal effect to the declaration of the 1926 Conference) provided in Section 7(1) that, "Nothing in this Act shall be deemed to apply to the repeal, amendment or alteration of the British North America Acts, 1867 to 1930, or any order, rule or regulation made thereunder." Thus, because the federal and provincial governments had failed to agree on a domestic amending procedure, the UK Parliament remained as the amending authority for the Canadian Constitution.

In 1949 the Parliament of Canada, without the advice or consent of the provinces, requested and received from the UK Parliament certain powers to amend the "Constitution of Canada." However, Westminster was still to remain the amending authority in with respect to amendments relating to the legislative powers of the provinces, the rights of the French and English languages, the educational rights of denominational minorities and the constitutional provision that no House of Commons could continue more than five years. The precise scope of the power of the Parliament of Canada to amend the Constitution was never determined, although in a 1980 reference the Supreme Court of Canada decided that "it is not open to Parliament to make alterations which would affect the fundamental features, or essential characteristics given to the Senate as a means of ensuring regional and provincial representation in the federal legislative process."[39]

The story of the repeated failure of the federal and provincial governments to arrive at a domestic amending procedure from 1927 to 1981 is a tangled one which does not need to be repeated here. At federal-provincial conferences held in 1950, there could be no agreement as to whether or not amendments related to the legislative powers of the provinces required the agreement of all the provinces. In 1964, all eleven governments seemed for the moment to have arrived at agreement in the Fulton-Favreau formula, which provided that the most crucial parts of the Constitution were subject to amendment only with unanimous provincial consent — with such rigidity being somewhat tempered by procedures permitting some limited and voluntary inter-delegation of powers between Ottawa and the provinces — but the government of Quebec subsequently withdrew its support from this arrangement. The so-called Victoria Charter drawn up at the federal-provincial conference of June 1971 contained a domestic amending procedure as a part of a broader constitutional settlement, but again Quebec's consent was denied.

As the dramatic events leading up to the putting into place of the Constitution Act, 1982 made clear, there were two contentious and unresolved questions related to the procedure for amending the Canadian Constitution:

First, what degree of provincial consent was required before the Parliament of Canada might appropriately request an amendment from Britain? A document issued by the government of Canada in 1964 (apparently after having been circulated to the provinces without any having dissented from its text) enunciated as one of the "principles" which had evolved in relation to the amending procedure that "the Canadian Parliament will not request [of the UK Parliament] an amendment directly affecting federal-provincial relations without prior consultation and agreement with the provinces.'' This principle did not emerge as early as the others, but since 1907, and particularly since 1930, has gained increasing recognition and acceptance. The nature and degree of provincial participation in the amending process, however, have not lent themselves to easy definition.''[40] The last sentence emphasized the unresolved ambiguities. The Supreme Court of Canada addressed this issue in its decision of September 28, 1981 in deciding on the constitutionality of the federal Parliament's resolution requesting Westminster to amend the Canadian Constitution to provide for a wholly domestic procedure by which the Constitution might subsequently be amended and for a Charter of Rights and Freedoms. In a very complex decision, a majority of the members of the Court decided that, as a matter of strict law, Parliament had the right to pass such a Resolution. However, another majority of somewhat different composition decided that for Parliament to so proceed without a substantial measure of provincial consent would be a breach of constitutional convention and that because only two provinces, Ontario and New Brunswick, had agreed to the Resolution, this condition had not been met. This majority on the Court refrained from specifying in any more exact way what number or combination of provinces would need to assent to a proposed amendment to meet the substantial-consent convention. However, almost at the same time that new constitutional arrangements of 1982 came into effect, the Supreme Court of Canada upheld a previous judgement of the Quebec Court of Appeal that Quebec's consent was not required for the Resolution.[41]

Secondly, had the UK authorities any discretion in respect to requests made by the Parliament of Canada for the amendment of the Canadian Constitution? From the Statute of Westminster onward, Canadians interested in such matters were embarrassed that the failure to agree on a domestic amending procedure resulted in an otherwise sovereign state's being placed in the humiliating position that the most fundamental of its constitutional processes involved the parliament of another nation. However, as the dramatic events of 1980–81 demonstrated, the difficulty was more than symbolic. Thus, when Canadians disagreed about the validity of a particular request to Westminster from the Parliament of Canada, the United Kingdom authorities were forced into choosing between the Canadian disputants. In the context of the resolution introduced into the Parliament of Canada in October 1980, it was the opinion of the federal government, supported by Ontario and New Brunswick, that the equality of Canada and the United Kingdom as sovereign nations dictated that Westminster honour any request made by the Parliament of Canada. The contrary view of the dissenting provinces, supported by a report of the Foreign Affairs Committee of the British House of Commons, was that the UK Parliament had a continuing guardianship role to ensure that any Canadian resolution did not threaten the essential federal features of the Canadian constitutional system. By enacting the terms of an agreement between the federal government and all the provinces but Quebec concluded in Noverber 1981, the UK authorities made their final intervention in Canadian constitutional affairs.[42]

A Domestic Amending Procedure:
The Constitution Act, 1982

The proclamation of the Constitution Act, 1982 gave Canadians a domestic amending procedure and removed this crucial matter from the sphere of regulation mainly by convention to regulation by constitutional law.[43] The provisions related to amendment, along with other elements of the Canadian Constitution, remain as enactments of the UK Parliament, and that body, in the most strict of legal senses, could alter or repeal any or all of these provisions (A. V. Dicey in his classic *Law of the Constitution,* referred to the old aphorism that Parliament might do anything but make a man a woman or a woman a man; this statement antedates gender-change operations, and Parliament retains the plenary power to determine the legal gender of a person who has undergone such surgery). However, if for any perverse reasons Westminster should engage itself in the amendment of the Canadian Constitution, it is almost inevitable that such action would be repudiated by the Canadian government and Parliament and would not be regarded as legally valid by the Canadian courts.

These are the major elements of Part V of the Constitution Act, 1982, "Procedure for Amending Constitution of Canada":

First, following previous law and practice there are several procedures for amendment related to different aspects of the Constitution:

1. Section 42 provides that Parliament may amend the Constitution in matters related to "the executive government of Canada or the Senate and House of Commons." However, this power does not include the right to change the powers of the Senate, the method of selecting Senators, the residence qualification of Senators or the number of members by which provinces are entitled to be represented in the Senate.

2. Section 43 provides that amendments relating to one or more provinces but not all provinces can be made with the consent of the Parliament of Canada and the legislatures of these provinces. The section refers specifically to the alteration of provincial boundaries and the use of French and English languages within a province. In respect to the latter subject, amendments related to the status of the official languages in New Brunswick under Sections 16–20 could be made with the consent of the legislature of that province and Parliament; this would be true as well for changes in the constitutional status of the two languages in other individual provinces, but not with respect to the constitutional entrenchment of the educational rights or linguistic minorities.

3. Section 41 provides that certain amendments require the consent of all the provinces and of Parliament. These include the monarchical elements of the Constitution; amendments to the amending formula itself; subject to Section 43, the use of the English and French languages, and the composition of the Supreme Court of Canada.

4. Section 38(1) enacts that amendments to the Constitution not subject to other amending procedures can be made by action of the Parliament of Canada and the legislatures of two-thirds of the provinces having in aggregate at least half the Canadian population. This section of course regulates the crucial matter of the distribution of legislative powers between Parliament and the provinces.

The same procedure relates to the proportionate representation of the provinces in the House of Commons; the powers of the Senate and the method of choosing Senators; the number of members to which each province is entitled in the Senate; the extension of existing provinces into the Territories, and the establishment of new provinces.

There appears to be nothing on the public record to indicate the kind of bargaining that went on between the federal and provincial governments in assigning various elements of the Constitution to the differing amending procedures, particularly of those requiring unanimous provincial consent and those subject to the provisions of Section 38(1) requiring only the consent of two-thirds of the provinces having in aggregate half the population of all the provinces. The following five points, however, might be noted:

1. There seem to be unresolved ambiguities related to the Supreme Court of Canada. Under Section 101 of the British North America Act of 1867 (now the Constitution Act, 1867) the Parliament of Canada has enacted the circumstances related to the size, composition and jurisdiction of the Court. The Constitution Act, 1982 does not include the Supreme Court Act and other legislation relating to the Court in the specification of the Constitution of Canada. Yet Section 41(d) enacts that changes in the composition of the Supreme Court are subject to unanimous provincial consent and Section 42(d) that other changes relating to the Court require the consent of two-thirds of the provinces containing in aggregate half the Canadian population.

2. The amending formula itself can be amended only with unanimous provincial consent. However, Section 49 provides that within 15 years of the coming into effect of the Act a First Ministers Conference is to be convened to review the amending procedure. The unanimous consent provision will obviously make it extremely difficult to amend the amending formula, especially with respect to meeting Quebec's objection to that formula.

3. In consenting to the provisions of Section 42(1)(f) requiring the consent of two-thirds of the provinces for the creation of new provinces, the government and Parliament of Canada surrendered their former power (exercised in the bringing of all the provinces but the original four into Confederation) to establish new provinces under the terms that Ottawa decided so long as such action did not involve any changes in the boundaries of existing provinces.

4. Apart from constitutional provisions related to the use of the French and English languages in individual provinces, the Charter of Rights and Freedoms may be amended with the consent of Parliament and the legislatures of two-thirds of the provinces having in aggregate at least half the population of all the provinces. Considering the extravagant rhetoric of some supporters of the Charter as to its "guaranteeing" human rights, one might have expected this part of the Constitution to be subject to amendment only by unanimous provincial consent.

5. Sections 38(2) and (3) provide that a provincial legislature may "dissent" from an amendment which "derogates from the legislative powers, the proprietary rights or any other rights or privileges of the legislature or government of a province," and in such cases that amendment will have no effect in that province unless and until the legislature revokes its dissent. Section 40 goes on to enact that when an amendment is made which transfers provincial legislative powers

relating to "education or other cultural matters" from provincial legislatures to Parliament, Canada shall provide "reasonable compensation" to dissenting provinces.

Contrary to the wishes of the Trudeau government in 1980–81, the amending procedure contains no provision for involving the people in the amending process by way of popular referenda. Prime Minister Trudeau and his colleagues believed that Canadian public opinion was disposed to prefer national power to that of the provinces, and because of this (and perhaps also because of some general ideological support for popular sovereignty), the federal government included in its resolution of October 1980 a provision for a referendum in cases where Ottawa and the provinces differed about a proposed amendment. However, this clause was opposed by all the provinces — with the momentary exception of Quebec at one point in the First Ministers Conference of November 1981 — and the federal authorities gave way. Interestingly, there was, at the time, almost no public discussion of the constitutional settlement of 1981–82 being submitted to ratification by the Canadian people. Reginald Whitaker has pointed out the Canadian political tradition's hostility to direct democracy even when, as in 1980–82, fundamental constitution choices are involved.[45] From a different perspective Stephen A. Scott writes:

> Anglo-Canadian public law is deeply legitimist, placing a great weight on strict legal continuity. Law must be made according to law, and not otherwise: that is by the persons, and according to the processes, prescribed by law . . . This approach probably results from the notion that the law-making power — indeed the public authority generally — is to be derived from the law itself, rather than from the people. The Constitution Act, 1982 represents no departure from this legitimist tradition.[46]

To repeat, what Canadians mean by democracy is representative democracy unmixed with popular elements and according to which those whose credentials derive from popular elections have the unfettered power, as conferred and regulated by the Constitution, to make any and all choices for the political community.

Part V of the Constitution Act, 1982 specifies more clearly than did previous law and convention the procedures according to which the provinces can participate in the amending process. It had been established in 1875 that amendments to the Canadian Constitution might validly be made only in a joint address of both the Senate and the House of Commons. However, the provincial governments retained the right whether or not to submit proposed amendments to their respective legislatures, and with respect to several amendments, the provincial administrations gave consent on their own authority. Under the Constitution Act, 1982 amendments derogating from the powers of a province can be made only with the consent of a majority of the members of the Senate, the House of Commons and of the legislatures of that provinces, and the "dissent" of a province from an amendment — along with the subsequent revocation of such a dissent — can be made only with the agreement of a majority of the members of its legislature. Furthermore, an amendment may be initiated either by the Senate or the House of Commons or by a provincial legislature. In the latter case, Parliament — as well as the legislatures of the other provinces — would appear to be under a constitutional obligation to debate and vote upon the provincial proposal.

Under Section 47 the consent of Parliament to a constitutional amendment opposed by the Senate can be made by the House of Commons overriding the Senate's objections after 180 sitting days of Parliament. Under the Constitution as it existed up to that time the two chambers had the same powers with the sole exception that a resolution for the raising or expenditure of public moneys had to be introduced in the House.

In conclusion, something needs to be said about the constitutions of the provinces and the amendment of these constitutions. The British North America Act of 1867 contained the constitutions of Ontario and Quebec, a necessary element of the Confederation settlement because two new provinces were being created out of the former United Province of Canada. However, these provincial constitutions did not constitute a major focus of controversy at the time of Confederation, and, unlike Americans and Australians, Canadians have been little concerned with these constitutions of sub-national jurisdictions.[47] Section 92(1) of the British North America Act conferred on the provinces the exclusive power to legislate in respect to ''The Amendment from Time to Time, notwithstanding anything in this Act, of the Constitution of the Province, except as regards the office of the Lieutenant Governor.'' The courts have had little occasion to determine the scope of the provincial amending power.[48]

Judicial Review

Judicial review is the procedure by which courts of law consider laws and executive acts in the light of whether or not these conform with the terms of a constitution and then validate or invalidate such expressions of legislative or executive will accordingly. The British North America Act of 1867 did not provide explicitly for judicial review. The domestic constitutional system of the United Kingdom did not include such a procedure, since the Crown in Parliament was sovereign, and there could be no legal challenge to its will. From the early days of the British Empire, however, it had been customary to allow appeals to the Crown against enactments of colonial legislatures, and this procedure had been formalized in the recognition by imperial statute of the Judicial Committee of the Privy Council in 1833. The Judicial Committee was drawn from members of the House of Lords who had had previous experience at the bar or on the bench. As Peter Russell has pointed out, judicial review as a device for passing on the validity of Canadian legislation in the early years of Confederation ''might have been as much a corollary of imperialism as of federalism.''[49] The British North America Act was an imperial statute and according to the Colonial Laws Validity Act enacted by the UK Parliament in 1865, laws of colonial legislatures were invalid if they conflicted with imperial law. However, as it happened, judicial review of the British North America Act both by the Judicial Committee and the Canadian courts did not evolve as an instrument for imperial control of Canadian affairs but rather as a practical device for delineating the respective legislative powers of the Parliament of Canada and the provinces.

The *Constitution Act, 1982* gives judicial review a somewhat more explicit role in the Canadian constitutional system than it had before.[50] Section 52(1) states: "The Constitution of Canada is the supreme law of Canada, and any law that is inconsistent with the provisions of the Constitution is, to the extent of the inconsistency, of no force and effect." Within the context of the Canadian constitutional tradition, it may be supposed that the courts of law are charged with the authoritative determination of such consistencies or inconsistencies. Article 2(1) as part of the Charter of Rights and Freedoms enacts: "Anyone whose rights and freedoms, as guaranteed by this Charter, have been infringed or denied may apply to a court of competent jurisdiction to obtain such remedy as the court considers appropriate and just in the circumstances."

Until 1949 the Judicial Committee of the Privy Council was the final appellate body in Canadian constitutional cases, and in such matters the Supreme Court of Canada was very much a subordinate body. In 1951, the late Bora Laskin, then professor of law at the University of Toronto, wrote: "As Privy Council decisions multiplied, the Supreme Court became engrossed in merely expounding the pronouncements of its superior. The task of the Supreme Court was not to interpret the constitution but rather to interpret what the Privy Council said the constitution meant."[51] Such subordination was buttressed by the circumstance that many cases decided by the Judicial Committee came on appeal from provincial appellate courts, by-passing the Supreme Court entirely, and in 1938 such appeals had outnumbered those from the Court by 329 to 138.

There is a vast amount of analysis of the Judicial Committee's record in interpreting the Canadian Constitution.[52] From the late 1890s onward the Committee embarked on a course of giving the provincial powers over "property and civil rights" an expansive interpretation while narrowly limiting Parliament's general power related to "Peace, Order and Good Government" and the enumerated federal power over "trade and commerce". Most of the vigorous controversy about the Privy Council's role in interpreting the Canadian Constitution dates from the decade of the 1930s, during which time that body denied Parliament the powers deemed necessary by many informed Canadians to deal with the desperate circumstances of the Great Depression and further decided that Parliament did not have the jurisdiction to implement international obligations incurred by Canada if these involved matters within the scope of provincial legislative power — just when the nation had attained the legal status of a sovereign state.

Until perhaps two decades ago, it was conventional among English-speaking Canadians to be very critical of the Privy Council's record in interpreting the Constitution. One line of criticism affirmed that the Committee had strayed from the accepted rules of statutory interpretation in dealing with the British North America Act, and a very influential report commissioned by the Senate and published in 1939 suggested that this should be righted by a constitutional amendment which would, in effect, direct the judicial authorities to adhere to these canons.[53] A different approach suggested that the Privy Council had been uninformed about and insensitive to the exigencies of Canada and, in particular, to the need for strong federal powers to deal with the social and economic circumstances of modern life. In a sense these two lines of criticism were logically irreconcilable although some observers were able to support both at once.

Quite understandably, French-Canadian students of the Constitution were on the whole sympathetic to the record of the Judicial Committee in strengthening provincial powers. In a 1951 article, Louis Phillippe Pigeon, who became a member of the Supreme Court of Canada in 1967, wrote:

> A great volume of criticism has been heaped upon the Privy Council and the Supreme Court on the ground that their decisions rest on a narrow and technical construction of the B.N.A. Act. The decisions on the whole proceeded from a much higher view . . . . They recognize the implicit fluidity of any constitution by allowing for emergencies and by resting distinctions on matters of degree. At the same time they firmly uphold the fundamental principle of provincial autonomy, they staunchly refuse to let our federal constitution be changed gradually by one device or another to a legislative union. In doing so they are preserving the essential condition of the Canadian constitution.[54]

Pierre Elliott Trudeau gave his assent to this view in 1964: "It has long been a custom in English Canada to denounce the Privy Council for its provincial bias, but it should perhaps be considered that if the law had not moved in this direction, Quebec separatism would not be a threat today: it might be an accomplished fact."[55]

In recent years, some English-Canadian scholars have taken a more favourable view of the Judicial Committee's work. Using a highly technical approach, G. P. Browne in a 1967 book made a lengthy argument that that body did not stray from the accepted rules of statutory interpretation in its decisions on the British North America Act.[56] J. A. Corry, from a very different point of view, wrote in 1978:

> I am not concerned here whether *Citizens Insurance Co. v. Parsons* and the Local Prohibition Case were correct legal interpretations of Sections 91 and 92. The important point is that at the time they were handed down they were correct in the political sense. They left parliament with about as much power as it had public support and moral authority to exercise. Their decentralizing interpretations were in pretty close harmony with the balance of forces in this loose-jointed country.[57]

The Judicial Committee's work had a lasting effect on the division of legislative power between Parliament and the provinces. After an examination of the Supreme Court's record since 1949, Peter Hogg, in a 1978 article, concluded that the Court had generally adhered to the doctrines formulated by the Privy Council.[58] In more specific terms, the Court had given a somewhat more expansive interpretation of the trade and commerce power "but not very much," and in respect to Parliament's general power to legislate in respect to "Peace, Order, and Good Government" it had, in the recent anti-inflation reference, denied Ottawa's claim that such legislation could be justified under "p.o.g.g." although the measure was upheld as an exercise of federal emergency power.

What are courts really doing when they engage in the process of judicial review? This is an extremely complex and subtle subject, about which judges themselves and the scholarly analysts of their behaviour are in disagreement. At one pole it might be argued that judges are here involved in a process of purely legal reasoning in which decisions follow from a mechanical, though highly intricate, process of terminological clarification and analysis. The other pole is that judges have free rein to indulge their own non-legal preferences in interpreting the Constitution but rationalize what they do in a kind of legal discourse which obfuscates the real determinants of their decision.

No sophisticated person would accept either the positivist or the legal realist accounts of judicial review in the bold and unqualified way that they have been stated above. Judgements in constitutional cases cannot be derived solely from a process of legal reasoning; if they could, one would expect fewer disagreements in such cases among judges who are roughly equal in professional competence. Neither are judges completely unfettered by pre-existing law and judicial decisions. Apart from purely legal considerations, the judge of a Canadian appellate court might be influenced by the following considerations:

1. Whether in his or her view the nation or the province was the primary political community. Patrick J. Monahan writes of the *Anti-Inflation Reference:*

> The different approaches of Laskin, CJ and Beetz, J in that case are not explicable in terms of some narrow issue of 'legal' analysis. The differences between them are much more profound and pivotal. The chief justice is essentially operating from an ideal of pan-Canadian nationality. Implicit in the chief justice's view is the belief that the federal government must be given the necessary tools to regulate virtually any aspect of the economic life of the nation. The judgment of Beetz, J is premised on a contradictory conception of community. The foundation of his analysis is the primacy of provincial communities. For Beetz, J these communities must be preserved and defended, even if this means frustrating the designs of national economic planners. In short, this ostensibly narrow dispute about the meaning of the British North America Act implicates political concerns of the highest order.[59]

2. Whether the law or executive act which is being challenged comes within the ambit of the legitimate exercise of power by the state. In his admirable *Social Credit and the Federal Power in Canada* published in 1954, J. R. Mallory wrote of the 1930s:

> Increasingly, constitutional case law had become a reflection of conflict over the major issues of social and economic policy. If they are looked at in this way, one-half of the important leading cases in Canadian constitutional law involved an attempt by the state to interfere with the free disposal by individuals of their property . . . It is impossible to avoid the conclusion that the resulting spheres of authority of the Dominion and the provinces are the incidental outcome of a clash between individualism and collectivism. Then, only on the surface has this struggle been a conflict between two conceptions of federalism.[60]

Mallory's general point is that, within the context of Canada in the 1930s, the denial by the judicial authorities of federal powers to engage in certain social and economic activities meant that, in effect, these activities could not be undertaken by government at all, and he attributes such judicial conduct in large part to the desire of the courts to sustain the existing system of property relations. Similarly, it is reasonable to attribute a series of Supreme Court decisions from the 1950s onward invalidating certain provincial and municipal restrictions on civil liberties on the grounds that these encroached on federal power over the criminal law to the judges' abhorrence of such anti-libertarian measures.

3. How will the decision be received by the bar, the bench and the community of legal scholars? In a seminar some years ago, an American professor of constitutional law suggested, half-facetiously, that sovereignty in the United States resided in the *Harvard Law Review*. His argument was that the constitution was the supreme law of the land but that the constitution was what the Supreme Court determined it to be and that, in making such determinations' members of the Court were decisively influenced by those who wrote for the country's most respected legal journal. Judges of a nation's final appellate court are, after all, professionals, solicitous as are other professionals of the good opinion of their colleagues. Thus, although this can only be guessed, one can reasonably suppose that judges of the Supreme Court of Canada will want to avoid having their handiwork laced in print by such respected constitutionalists as Peter Hogg, W. R. Lederman and Peter Russell or having their individual opinions discussed as examples of shoddy judicial craftmanship in constitutional law classes at the Dalhousie Law School. The public to which such judges will respond will no doubt be wider than that of academic legal scholars and will include senior and respected members of the bar and the bench.

4. How will the decision impinge on the institutional legitimacy of the court? In particular, the Supreme Court of Canada has become a more important and visible actor in the Canadian system of government. We can suppose that legitimacy considerations will have some impact on judicial decision making, although the precise nature of the influence is indeterminate.

5. What will the consequences of the decision be in terms of public policy and the relative balance of power between federal and provincial governments? As a matter of principle, some Canadian judges, at least, would stoutly deny that they follow a "result-oriented jurisprudence" in judicial review of the Constitution. We might well treat such denials with some skepticism. In cases involving the division of legislative powers it is to be expected that judges will have some concern for the impact of their decisions on the relations between the federal and provincial governments and on the federal balance. It is commonly accepted that the September 1981 decision of the Supreme Court of Canada concerning the constitutionality of Parliament's resolution providing for a domestic amending procedure and a Charter of Rights was a crucial factor in influencing Ottawa and the provinces to engage in one more round of constitutional negotiations, and it is reasonable to suppose that members of the Court were aware of their important political role when they rendered their respective decisions. In examining the recent record of the Court in umpiring the federal system, Peter Russell detects an "uncanny" balancing of federal and provincial powers and

attributes this in part to pressures on the Court to "even things up" and thus to sustain the credibility of the Court as an impartial arbiter.[61]

From the mid-1970s onward two developments have enhanced the importance of the Supreme Court of Canada as umpire of the federal system:[62]

First, amendments were made by Parliament to the Supreme Court Act which strengthened the Court's role in constitutional matters. One important change eliminated the right of private litigants to appeal to the Court in civil cases where the amount at issue was over $10 000. In 1970–71 some 83 of 151 cases heard by the Court were appeals as of right compared with 16 of 117 cases in 1980–81. Up until the 1974 amendment most of the cases decided by the Court were in the field of private law, and many of those did not involve important matters of legal principle. Along with narrowing the right to appeal, the 1974 legislation extended the power of the Court to grant leave to appeal from other courts; in 1970–71 only 15 of 151 cases heard by the Court involved its own leave to appeal compared with 74 of 117 cases in 1980–81.

Second, in the mid-1970s there was what Russell has called a "veritable explosion of constitutional litigation," and several of the decisions rendered by the courts have been about matters in respect to which fundamental interests of the federal and provincial governments were at stake. From the first to the second half of the 1970s there was a fourfold increase in the number of constitutional cases coming before the Supreme Court of Canada, many of them at the initiative of governments themselves and, in other situations, with governments supporting private litigants. During this latter period, federal-provincial relations were characterized by deep conflicts, and G. Bruce Doern and V. Seymour Wilson pointed to the increased focus on regulatory issues as against fiscal matters in respect to which conflict could be more easily resolved through intergovernmental bargaining.[63] Many of the decisions rendered by the Court in recent years have involved matters of crucial interest to the federal and provincial governments: the control over the development of natural resources and the public revenues from such development, telecommunications, language policy, the respective roles of Ottawa and the provinces in constitutional change, and so on.

Has the Supreme Court in its recent decisions been biased againts the provinces? As we have seen, Russell has discovered "an uncanny balance in the net effects of the Supreme Court's decisions on the constitutional ressources of the two levels of government." Two other legal scholars, Gilbert L'Écuyer and Peter Hogg, have also denied that the Court has had a centralist bias.

Gilbert L'Écuyer, in a study commissioned by the Quebec Department of Intergovernmental Affairs and published in 1978, concluded that the Supreme Court had in fact been more favourable to the federal government than had been the Judicial Committee.[64] However, in interpreting the Constitution, the Court had been faithful to the letter and the spirit of the British North America Act which had been an expression of "une vision centralisatrice" — more faithful than the Privy Council. Thus, according to L'Écuyer, the centralizing nature of judicial decisions was a result of the nature of the Constitution itself rather than, as claimed by the Court's critics, a biased pattern of judicial interpretation.

Peter Hogg in his article "Is the Supreme Court Biased in Constitutional Cases?" published in 1979, answered "No."[65] The circumstance of judges being appointed by the federal authorities does not in itself lead to bias. Once a judge has been appointed, "he has nothing to hope for or fear from the federal government. Constitutional guarantees and powerful political traditions of judicial independence render the judge invulnerable to any kind of governmental action." Further, "The truth is, I suspect, that the federal government does not see the winning of constitutional law cases as a major policy objective, does not see the role of the Supreme Court in constitutional cases as being of major importance in determining balance of power between the centre and the provinces, and does see that any evidence of packing the court would provoke a storm of protest."[66] Although the "objective fact of judicial independence" would not in itself preclude judges from adopting a sycophantic stance towards those who appointed them, such a stance would bring contempt from the legal profession from whom they are drawn and whose respect they cherish. After examining the record of the Supreme court in judicial interpretation of the Constitution since 1949, Hogg concluded that "the Supreme Court of Canada has generally adhered to the doctrine laid down by the Privy Council precedents, and where the court has departed from these precedents, or has been without close precedents, the choices between enacting lines of reasoning have favoured the provincial interest at least as often as they have favoured the federal interest. There is no basis for the claim that the court has been biased in favour of the federal interest in constitutional litigation."[67]

Another important issue is whether judicial review is an appropriate procedure for umpiring the federal system. Paul Weiler has made a vigorous argument that it is not.[68] He posits two models of judicial decision making. The first "conceives of the judge as the adjudicator of specific, concrete disputes, who disposes of the problem within the latter by elaborating and applying a legal regime to facts, which he finds on the basis of evidence and argument presented to him in an adversary process." The competing model is that of the judge as policy maker who makes decisions "through essentially the same mode of reasoning as other actors in the governmental system." Weiler's argument is essentially that courts are highly sophisticated institutions for resolving "specific, concrete disputes" but are inadequate as umpires of the federal system:

> [F]ederalism questions are not amenable to stable legal principles. Our judges are working with a century-old document whose basic objectives are largely irrelevant to modern legislative problems. The courts are left to fill such empty verbal categories as 'peace, order and good government', property and civil rights, etc. . . . . All the courts can really do is to act on some intuitive sense that the immediate legislation (being challenged) just goes too far. Unfortunately, no one can propose any legal standards to tell how far is too far.[69]

Weiler recommends that federal-provincial bargaining be substituted for judicial review in delineating the respective jurisdictions of the two orders of government, and he argues that such bargaining in the relative absence of judicial decision has been highly effective in determining the respective roles of Ottawa and the provinces in the control of the economy through fiscal and monetary measures and in the evolution of the Canadian welfare state.[70] He would confine judicial review in division-of-powers matters to these very few situations in which there are "two statutes apparently relevant to one factual situation" and would make it impossible for private citizens or groups to mount legal challenges to federal or provincial laws or executive acts on division-of-power grounds.

Despite Weiler's strictures on judicial review, it is very unlikely that it will be entirely displaced by intergovernmental bargaining in the delineation of the respective jurisdictions of the federal and provincial authorities. Nor would this be in my view desirable. So long as the Constitution is the "supreme law of Canada" it is appropriate that this be subject to final and authoritative interpretation by the courts, even though in doing so judges obviously cannot be guided exclusively by stable and neutral legal principles.

The political nature of Canadian constitutional jurisprudence has been enormously enhanced by the extensive use of the reference.[71] Under the Supreme Court Act and corresponding legislation related to the senior appellate court in each province, the Governor in Council and the lieutenant-governor in council respectively may submit questions for the opinion of these courts, and according to the Supreme Court Act, the Supreme Court is required to hear appeals on reference decisions rendered by the provincial courts. The final appellate courts in both the United States and Australia have refused to deliver reference decisions on the general grounds that to pronounce on matters not involving particular litigants in concrete disputes would be an inappropriate assumption by the courts of a function which is essentially of an executive nature. In the Canadian context, decisions rendered on reference are in a narrowly technical sense advisory only. However, the distinction between reference decisions and those delivered in the ordinary course of litigation has become blurred, and it is broadly accurate to say that the constitutional validity of the two kinds of decisions is equal. About a third of the decisions rendered by the Judicial Committee were placed before that body on reference, and, in the past decade, some of the most important division-of-power decisions by the Supreme Court have come in reference cases, including the power of Parliament to alter the composition and powers of the Senate: Parliament's power to request constitutional amendments from Westminster; jurisdiction over natural resources off the coast of Newfoundland; federal power to enact legislation restraining inflation and so on.

Judicial review then, has become a much more important process in shaping the Canadian Constitution than it was 25 years ago, and, in particular, the Supreme Court of Canada has become a much more visible and contentious actor in the governmental system. These general developments were given an enormous impetus by the coming into effect of the Canadian Charter of Rights and Freedoms in 1982, and we are very close to a situation in which most of the work of the Supreme Court is in the realm of constitutional adjudication. There are three likely consequences of the emergent situation:

First, we can expect the provinces to demand a role in determining the jurisdiction and composition of the Supreme Court of Canada and/or the appointment of its members. Section 41(d) and Section 42(d) of the Constitution Act, 1982 appear to anticipate this. 41(d) provides that amendments to the Constitution affecting the composition of the Supreme Court can be made only with the consent of Parliament and all the provincial legislatures, while 42(d) specifies that other amendments related to the Court require the agreement of Parliament and at least two-thirds of the provinces having in aggregate at least half the population of all the provinces. There have been conflicting interpretations of these sections by legal scholars. My view is that the federal authorities retain their unlimited powers to determine the jurisdiction, composition and personnel of the Court but that when changes in these respects are by amendment incorporated into the Constitution, these changes will be subject to subsequent amendment according to the respective provisions of Sections 41(d) and 42(d). At any rate, we can expect strong influences from the provinces and elsewhere to federalize this increasingly crucial institution and to incorporate basic provisions related to it in the Constitution.

Second, we can expect more public interest than before as to who is appointed to the Court and the jurisprudential philosophy of appointees and prospective appointees. Under existing practices federal judicial appointments are made by the cabinet on the advice of the minister of justice except for chief justices who are recommended by the prime minister. From 1966 onward the federal authorities have submitted tentative choices to the National Committee on the Judiciary of the Canadian Bar Association which makes its own investigation and reports whether, in its judgement, the candidate is well qualified or not qualified.[72] So far as the Supreme Court is concerned, there has been relatively little interest in who was appointed except in the relatively restricted circles of the bar and the bench. Further, as Hogg has suggested, it appears that the federal authorities did not have as an important concern the jurisprudential philosophies of judges; otherwise, it would be difficult to explain the choices of Louis-Joseph Pigeon in 1967 and Jean Beetz in 1974, Quebecers with well-known records favouring the powers of the provinces.[73] Russell suggests that the principal effect of the Charter will be "its tendency to judicialize politics and politicize the judiciary."[74] In the case of the Supreme Court of Canada at least, it is unlikely that this will be politicization in the partisan sense; the last appointment of a person with a background in elective politics was that of Douglas Abbott in 1949. Of the incumbent members of the Court, only one of the justices has ever contested an election, and this election was only a brief interlude in an otherwise non-partisan career, and a person who had been prominently associated with the party in power in Ottawa might well be disqualified, regardless of his or her credentials, for a position on the highest appellate court. Rather, it is reasonable to expect that both the appointing authorities and an increasingly broader public of individuals and groups which feel that their values and interests are affected by the Court will more and more take into account the ideologies and jurisprudential philosophies of appointees and prospective appointees to the Court.

Third, as the Supreme Court becomes a more visible and consequential actor in the governmental system, we can reasonably expect that its legitimacy will be increasingly challenged. Because the jurisdiction, composition and personnel of the Court are under the exclusive control of the federal authorities, its legitimacy to act as an impartial umpire of federalism is somewhat compromised. On an even more fundamental level, the courts have been propelled into a vastly extended role in judicial review of the Constitution against a background in which Canadians have denied the reality of judicial power. According to common misunderstandings, the legislatures enact laws, executives execute laws, and courts interpret laws according to stable and neutral legal principles. According to the mythology, judges do not have power; they perform intricate functions analagous to those of, say, surgeons or airline pilots. Under the emergent circumstances, it is inevitable that this mythology will become increasingly unpersuasive despite the valiant efforts of the judges themselves to sustain it, and as the courts, not just the Supreme Court of Canada, but the courts in general, increasingly challenge the values and interests of important elements of Canadian society, some new reservoir of judicial legitimacy will have to be found.

The Federal Constitution and the Charter of Rights and Freedoms[75]

The coming into effect of the Charter of Rights and Freedoms on April 17, 1982 was, by a very wide margin, the most important change ever effected in the Canadian constitutional system. Up until this decisive break with our constitutional past, Canadian constitutional evolution had been on the whole incremental, and even the Confederation settlement preserved major elements of continuity. Interestingly, we have conferred on that element of our governmental system most attuned to incremental change, the judiciary, the task of adjusting us to the new constitutional order.

Prior to 1982 Canadians had lived under a regime of parliamentary sovereignty qualified by a division of legislative powers between Parliament and the provinces. There were few constraints on this sovereignty: Section 20 of the British North America Act of 1867 provided for annual sessions of Parliament; Section 50 enacted that no Parliament should sit for more than five years; Section 93 conferred certain protections for the educational rights of denominational minorities in the provinces, and Section 133 certain protections for the French and English languages in Dominion and Quebec affairs. Under such circumstances, judicial review of the Constitution was concerned almost exclusively with delineating the legislative powers of Parliament and the provinces. Canadian constitutional law, as designated in the subtitles of two widely-used texts on that subject, was defined in terms of this division.[76]

By the time the first version of the Charter as contained in the resolution was put before Parliament in October 1980, the preponderance of both expert and lay opinion in Canada had come to favour the constitutional entrenchment of human rights. However, the "notwithstanding" provisions of Section 33 of the Constitution Act, 1982 contain a very crucial compromise between entrenchment and the principle of parliamentary sovereignty, a compromise without which the support of some of the nine provinces (i.e., all those except Quebec) who assented to the constitutional settlement of November 1981 would have been denied. Section 33 enacts that Parliament or the legislature of a province may expressly declare an enactment of these legislatures to be operative despite its being contradictory to a provision of the Charter relating to fundamental freedoms (speech, conscience, religion, freedom of association, etc.), legal rights of people charged with or convicted of offences against the law, and equality rights related to non-discrimination on the basis of "race, national or ethnic origin, colour, religion, sex, age or mental or physical disability.'' It is provided that such a declaration shall cease to have effect five years after it comes into force, although Parliament or a provincial legislature may re-enact a declaration.

It is as yet too early to assess the implications of the notwithstanding clause for the regime of rights established by the Charter. The National Assembly of Quebec has taken maximum advantage of the provision to express its refusal to accept the legitimacy of the Constitution Act, 1982 and the way that change was effected. Neither Parliament nor the legislature of any of the other provinces has issued a declaration as made possible under Section 33. Some critics of the Charter have argued that it nullifies the ''guarantees'' of rights contained in that document. There have been more benevolent views. Some observers have suggested that the notwithstanding powers will be used very sparingly and that governments and legislatures will, in all but the most unusual circumstances, find it politically inexpedient to override either the Charter or the way it has been interpreted by the courts. It has also been conjectured that the courts will be bolder than otherwise in overturning federal and provincial measures because the judges are aware that they do not have the ultimate authority in respect to such matters.

Within the context of this work, the focus must be the consequences of the Charter for federalism and national unity. The successive federal Liberal governments in their approach to constitutional reform from the first federal-provincial conference on the Constitution to the coming into effect of the Constitution Act, 1982 believed such consequences were profound. A document *Federalism for the Future* introduced into the 1968 meeting by Prime Minister Pearson outlined Ottawa's general constitutional strategy from which successive federal governments did not diverge in any essential way in the next decade and a half.[77] *Federalism for the Future* declared that constitutional review and reform should be comprehensive rather than piecemeal and should proceed in three successive stages: (1) the constitutional entrenchment of human rights, including linguistic rights (2) reforms in the institutions of the government of Canada (Parliament, the Supreme Court of Canada, the federal public service and the National Capital Region) to make those institutions more representative of the country's diversity (3) the distribution of powers between the federal and provincial authorities. The general rationale for this strategy was contained in the prime minister's assertion that ''we have proclaimed our belief that the rights of people must precede the rights of government,''[78] and in the latter stages of the constitutional review process which culminated in the 1982 change, the federal officials designated the Charter, and asserted its primacy, as ''the people's package'' as against the ''government's package'' for which some of the provinces were pressing. In the context of Bill 60 introduced into Parliament in 1978 and which contained a comprehensive provision for the constitutional entrenchment of rights, Alan Cairns lucidly elaborated federal thinking about this matter:

A basic vehicle for attaining that transcendent loyalty (to Canada) was the proposed Charter of Rights and Freedoms. The proposal for an entrenched Charter binding on both levels of government, and as comprehensive as possible, was an attempt to move in an American direction and thereby

THE CANADIAN CONSTITUTIONAL INHERITANCE   **59**

confirm the pre-eminence of citizens over institutions . . . and ensure that rights and freedoms are inalienable. The Charter would establish "new rights for Canadian citizens to live and work wherever they wish in Canada."

So central was the Charter to the federal strategy that one of the two federal conditions for constitutional renewal was its inclusion in the Constitution, and its application to both levels of government. The resultant rights and freedoms were to be country-wide in scope, enforced by a national supreme court, and entrenched in a national Constitution beyond the reach of fleeting legislative majorities at either level of government. The consequence, and one very clear purpose, was to set limits to the diversities of treatment by provincial governments, and thus to strengthen Canadian as against provincial identities.[79]

In Canada as elsewhere there is an intricate relation between those claims and interests which are advanced by citizens as members of territorially delineated sub-national groupings (most importantly in the Canadian case as residents of particular provinces) and those that they make as members of nation-wide groupings. The thrust of the Charter in terms of both political sentiment and political mobilization will almost certainly be in a nationalizing direction although it is as yet too early to make any definitive judgement about how important this disposition will be. We have just come through a period in which the provincializing tendencies in the governmental system were stronger than at any previous period in Canadian history. We now appear, largely though by no means exclusively as a result of the Charter and the debate surrounding it, to be in a situation of profound rights-consciousness, and the rights so claimed are other than those of persons as members of provincial communities.

The Persisting Tradition: Executive Dominance over the Governmental Process

The most elemental and persisting tradition of the Canadian constitutional system is executive dominance over the governmental process both in Ottawa and the provinces. Thomas Hockin speaks of the tradition of a "collective central energizing executive as the key engine of the state" as being at the heart of the Canadian governmental experience. Mark Sproule-Jones in a recent essay, one of the very few analyses to attack the most fundamental of our political structures, begins, "This article argues that Canada was, and remains, a colonial political system. The colonial masters have gone, but have been replaced by a new, indigenous set. The major institutional arrangements of the original colonies were Crown and executive dominated. The major political arrangements of the modern political system are Crown and executive dominated."[80]

Jennifer Smith has argued that, "the issue of parliamentary versus republican government was not settled before Confederation. It was settled by Confederation . . . in the face of some sympathy for the republican alternative, a fact that undoubtedly contributed to the founders' preoccupation with the question."[81] She goes on: "The Canadians prized parliamentary government for its strength, order and authority. They repudiated its republican rival for lacking authority, for yielding to the 'clamorous mob', for fragmenting power, in a word, for weakness.''[82] With somewhat less explicit consideration, the provinces also structured themselves according to the parliamentary principle. In Chapter IV, I shall analyse some of the consequences of both these two competing orders of power and jurisdiction being organized in terms of "strength, order and authority." Campbell Sharman in one of the very few analyses of provincial constitutionalism ever made, has recently written that, "it is only a slight exaggeration to say that the present Constitution Act (of British Columbia) is an ennobling act for executive dominance of the governmental process."[83]

In its recent report, the (Macdonald) Royal Commission on the Economic Union and Development Prospects for Canada demonstrates the continuing allegiance of most Canadians to the tradition of executive dominance. The report states: "The bias in favour of executive dominance in our system has gone too far and needs redress."[84] However, the commissioners stoutly reject any effective measures towards that end. They recommend an elected Senate with only a six-months' veto over bills passed by the House of Commons on the grounds that, "An elected Senate which actually used the powers of the present Senate to mitigate, veto and amend legislation could indeed complicate responsible government. Moreover, a government with a majority in the Commons might seldom have a Senate majority."[85] Thus: "Our aim is to ensure regional sensitivity and to temper majority rule. It is not to override the vital principle of responsible government." The report is similarly conservative in its rejection of the proposal that party discipline in the House of Commons be weakened to permit MPs to function openly as representatives of their regions. "Party discipline is deeply entrenched in our parliamentary tradition. Moreover, it is a vital device for ensuring policy coherence and for achieving responsible government. We do not wish to tamper with such a fundamental element of the present system."[86]

The consequences of combining the Westminster model with Canadian federalism will be discussed in more detail in Chapter IV. The following general observations can be made here:

1. The centralizing and majoritarian structures of power within the national government frustrate the territorial pluralism which made federalism necessary at the beginning and sustain federalism.

2. The alleged virtues of the Westminster model in making power holders accountable are very much compromised by circumstances in which the actual locus of much important decision making is in a complex of intergovernmental interactions.

The most overt circumstance of executive dominance over the Canadian governmental process is the continuing existence of the War Measures Act as a federal statute. The act was passed by Parliament at the beginning of the First World War and was closely patterned on the United Kingdom's Defence of the Realm Act. Section 2 of the War Measures Act states that "The issue of a proclamation by Her Majesty, or under the authority of the Governor in Council, shall be conclusive evidence that war, invasion, or insurrection, real or apprehended, exists and has existed for any period of time therein stated, and of its continuance, until, by the issue of a further proclamation it is declared that the war, invasion or insurrection no longer exists." Section 3 provides that when the act is in force, all orders and regulations issued by the Governor in Council "shall have the force of law" and that "for greater certainty, but not so as to restrict the generality of the foregoing terms" the federal cabinet may take action in respect to:

(a) censorship and the control and suppression of publications, writings, maps, plans, photographs, communications and means of communication;

(b) arrest, detention, exclusion and deportation;

(c) control of the harbours, ports and territorial waters of Canada and the movement of vessels;

(d) transportation by land, air, or water and the transport of persons and things;

(e) trading, exportation, importation, production and manufacture;

(f) appropriation, control, forfeiture and disposition of property and of the use thereof.

Section 4 goes on to provide that the Governor in Council may prescribe the penalties for violations of orders and regulations made under the act provided that such penalties shall not exceed a fine of five thousand dollars or five years imprisonment or both.

The War Measures Act was in effect throughout both World Wars and for considerable periods after hostilities ended and during the Quebec crisis in the fall of 1970.

There are thus two Canadian Constitutions: the normal Constitution and the one which prevails when the War Measures Act is in effect. Under the first, Canadians live under a regime which is both parliamentary and federal. However when the executive invokes the War Measures Act, this is put in abeyance; the Governor in Council may take actions which would otherwise require the approval of Parliament and may encroach on matters otherwise within provincial legislative jurisdiction. The implication of the Charter of Rights and Freedoms for such emergency powers is unclear. While actions taken by the executive would clearly be reviewable by the courts to determine whether these violated the Charter, it seems unlikely under all but the most unusual circumstances that judges would attempt to second-guess the cabinet in respect to the fundamental requirements of national security.

During the 1970 crisis, members of the government suggested the desirability of legislation less sweeping than the *War Measures Act* to be proclaimed in conditions of domestic disturbance. However, nothing came of this, and the issue has almost disappeared from the agenda of constitutional debate. The circumstance that the War Measures Act remains on the statute book is a dramatic illustration of the Canadian tolerance for executive dominance.

Notes

1. Donald V. Smiley, "The Rowell-Sirois Report, Provincial Autonomy and Post-War Canadian Federalism," *Canadian Journal of Economics and Political Science* 28 (1962): p. 59.
2. W. L. Lederman, "Some Forms and Limitations of Cooperative Federalism," *Canadian Bar Review,* 45 (September 1967): p. 410.
3. Peter H. Russell, "Introduction," in Peter H. Russell, ed., *Leading Constitutional Decisions,* 3rd ed. (Ottawa: Carleton University Press, 1982), p. 21.
4. The Task Force on Canadian Unity, *Coming to Terms: The Words of the Debate* (Ottawa: Minister of Supply and Services Canada, 1979), p. 29. Reproduced with permission of the Minister of Supply and Services Canada.
5. A. V. Dicey, *Introduction to the Study of the Law of the Constitution,* 7th ed. (London: Macmillan, 1908), p. 413.
6. Ibid., p. 418.
7. Sir Ivor Jennings, *The Law of the Constitution,* 5th ed. (London: London University Press, 1959), p. 134.
8. Reference re Amendment of the Constitution of Canada (Nos. 1, 2 and 3), (1981) 125 D.L.R. (3rd).
9. *Re Resolution to Amend the Constitution* 1 S.C.R. 1981a p. 877.
10. Ibid, p. 880. Both quotes: Reprinted with permission of Canada Law Book, Inc., 240 Edward Street, Aurora, Ontario, L4G 3S9.
11. Peter Russell, "Bold Statement, Questionable Jurisprudence," in Keith Banting and Richard Simeon, eds., *And No One Cheered: Federalism, Democracy and the Constitution Act* (Toronto: Methuen, 1983), pp. 216–221.
12. Dicey argued that in the United Kingdom context, breaches of the fundamental conventions of the constitution — such as, for example, the failure of the Crown to call Parliament into session annually or the refusal of a ministry which had lost the confidence of the House of Commons to resign — would result in a breach of the *law* of the constitution. Chapter XV. However, this close association between an unconventional action and illegality would not always prevail under the more comprehensive usage of the term convention which has now become common.
13. J. A. Corry, "The Uses of a Constitution," in *The Constitution and the Future of Canada,* Special Lectures of the Law Society of Upper Canada (Toronto: Richard de Boo Limited, 1978), pp. 1–15.
14. Ibid., p. 2.
15. Ibid., p. 3.
16. Ibid., p. 9.
17. Donald V. Smiley, "A Dangerous Deed: The Constitution Act, 1982," in Banting and Simeon, *And No One Cheered,* p. 91.
18. The Right Honourable Pierre Elliott Trudeau, *The Constitution and the People of Canada,* (Ottawa: Privy Council of Canada, 1969), pp. 4–6. Reproduced with permission of the Minister of Supply and Services Canada.
19. There was a rash of proposals in the 1960s and 1970s for a new constitution to be written by a constituent assembly composed of persons other than the elected politicians of the day. As I have suggested, experience suggests this is a non-starter. The actual framing of a constitution after a political bargain has been consummated is simply a matter of legal draftsmanship. To expect persons other than politicians to conclude such bargains is, in the Canadian context, naive.
20. E. M. Forster, "What I Believe," in E. M. Forster, *Two Cheers for Democracy* (London: Penguin Books, 1965), p. 82.
21. Corry, "Uses of a Constitution," p. 4. M. J. C. Vile also puts it well, "The essential point about constitutions is not that they could restrain a society of bad men, but that they may channel political behaviour in certain directions rather than others, that the ordinary citizen will not be subject to the whims of good or bad men, but will have some certainty of essential continuities of action when the personnel of government changes. The aspirations towards a government of laws and not of men is inherently incapable of being realized, but a government of men subject

to the restraint of certain rules is not." M. J. C. Vile, *Constitutionalism and the Separation of Powers,* (Oxford: Clarendon Press, 1967), p. 298.

22. Corry, "Uses of a Constitution," p. 4. Reproduced from "The Uses of a Constitution," L.S.U.C. Special Lectures, 1978, *The Constitution And The Future of Canada*, with the permission of Richard De Boo Publishers and The Law Society of Upper Canada.

23. Edmond Cahn, "An American Contribution," in Edmond Cahn, ed., *Supreme Court and Supreme Law* (New York: Simon and Schuster, 1971), p. 8.

24. *The Confederation Debates,* February 6, 1865, quoted in Peter B. Waite, ed., *The Confederation Debates in the Province of Canada, 1865: A Selection* (Toronto: McClelland and Stewart, 1963), p. 44.

25. J. M. S. Careless, *The Union of the Canadas: The Growth of Canadian Institutions, 1841–1857* (Toronto: McClelland and Stewart, 1967), p. 210.

26. Essays by Bruce Hodgins and Robert C. Edwards, by Brian Young and by Kenneth Pryke detail the ways in which the Macdonald government controlled the affairs of Ontario, Quebec and Nova Scotia respectively in the first years of Confederation; see Bruce W. Hodgins, Don Wright and W. H. Heick, ed., *Federalism in Canada and Australia: The Early Years* (Waterloo: Wilfred Laurier Press), 1978.

27. For an analysis of the tradition in British North America and its comparison with that of the United States, see Lewis Herbert Thomas, *The Struggle for Responsible Government in the North-West Territories 1870–1897* 2d ed. (Toronto: University of Toronto Press, 1978), Chapter One. For a recent account of the political and constitutional evolution of the North, see Gurston Dacks, *A Choice of Futures: Politics in the Canadian North* (Toronto: Methuen, 1981), Chapter 3.

28. Bruce W. Hodgins, "The Canadian Political Elite's Attitude Toward the Nature of the Plan of Union," in Hodgins, Wright and Heick, *Federalism in Canada and Australia,* pp. 43–60. From a broader perspective, Reginald Whitaker argues that democracy has had little place in the Canadian constitutional tradition in the past and the present. See his "Democracy and the Canadian Constitution," in Banting and Simeon, *And No One Cheered,* pp. 240–260.

29. W. P. Morrell, *The Provincial System in New Zealand, 1852–1876* (Christchurch, New Zealand, 1964.

30. P. B. Waite, *The Life and Times of Confederation, 1864–1867* (Toronto: University of Toronto Press, 1962), pp.110–111.

31. Ibid., p. 110.

32. A. I. Silver, *The French-Canadian Idea of Confederation, 1864–1900* (Toronto: University of Toronto Press, 1982), particularly Chapter II, "Confederation and Quebec."

33. Robin Winks, "Cliché and the Canadian-American Relationship," in Richard A. Preston, ed., *Perspectives on Revolution and Evolution* (Durham, N. C.: Duke University Press, 1979), p. 18.

34. Jennifer Smith, "Intrastate Federalism and Confederation," in Stephen Brooks, ed., *Political Thought in Canada, Contemporary Perspectives* (Toronto: Irwin, 1984), p. 269.

35. Ibid., p. 272.

36. William S. Livingston, *Federalism and Constitutional Change* (Oxford: Clarendon Press, 1926), p. 13.

37. However, the British North Americans were successful in avoiding a procedure by which the Senate, if it came into conflict with the House of Commons, might be swamped by the appointment of the number of senators necessary to become the second chamber's opposition. Section 26 of the British North America Act of 1867, which provision was never put in effect, permitted the Queen on the advice of the Governor General to appoint either three or six additional senators with the qualification that the equality of representation between Ontario, Quebec and the Maritime provinces be preserved.

38. The definitive account of the history of the amending procedure up to the time it was written is Paul Gérin-Lajoie, *Constitutional Amendment in Canada* (Toronto: University of Toronto Press, 1950). See also Livingston, *Federalism and Constitutional Change,* Chapter 2.

39. *Reference re Legislative Authority of Parliament to Alter or Replace the Senate* (1980) I.S.C.R. 54.

40. The Honourable Guy Favreau, *The Amendment of the Constitution of Canada* (Ottawa: Queen's Printer, 1965), p. 15.

41. *Re Objection by Quebec to Resolution to Amend the Constitution* [1982] 2 S.C.R. 793.

42. For an account of United Kingdom involvement in the Canadian constitutional events of 1980–81, see generally Roy Romanow, John Whyte and Howard Leeson, *Canada Notwithstanding: The Making of the Constitution, 1976–1982* (Toronto: Carswell/Methuen, 1984), particularly Chapter 5.

43. An exhaustive legal analysis of the new amending formula is contained in Stephen A. Scott, "The Canadian Constitutional Amendment Process," in Paul Davenport and Richard H. Leach, eds., *Reshaping Confederation: The 1980 Reform of the Canadian Constitution* (Durham, N. C.: Duke University Press, 1984), pp. 249–282.

45. Whitaker, *Democracy and Canadian Constitution.*

46. Scott, *Canadian Constitutional Amendment Process,* p. 254.

47. For one of the few analyses of a provincial constitution, see Campbell Sharman, "The Strange Case of a Provincial Constitution: The British Columbia Constitution Act," *Canadian Journal of Political Science* 17, no. 1 (March 1984): pp. 87–108. It is significant that Sharman is an Australian because in that country, as in the United States, state constitutions are matters of serious concern, and there is a complex body of state constitutional law.

48. However, in *Reference re Initiative and Referendum Act,* 1919, A. C. 935, the Judicial Committee of the Privy Council invalidated Manitoba legislation which provided for the enactment and repeal of provincial laws without the participation of the lieutenant-governor. The Quebec government argued unsuccessfully in the *Blaikie* case decided by the Supreme Court of Canada in 1979 that the provincial legislature under its power to amend the provincial constitution might override Section 133 of the British North America Act which established English as an official language of the legislature and courts of Quebec. *A.-G. Quebec v. Blaikie,* (1979) 2 S.C.R., 1016.

49. Peter Russell, "Introduction" to Russell, *Leading Constitutional Decisions,* pp. 3–4.

50. For conflicting accounts of the origin of judicial review in Canada, see Russell, "Introduction" and also Jennifer Smith, "The Origins of Judicial Review in Canada," *Canadian Journal of Political Science* 16, no. 1 (March 1983): pp. 115–134.

51. Bora Laskin, "The Supreme Court of Canada: A Final Court of and for Canadians," in W. R. Lederman, ed., *The Courts and the Canadian Constitution* (Toronto: McClelland and Stewart, 1964), p. 143.

52. For an excellent analysis of these controversies, see Alan C. Cairns, "The Judicial Committee and its Critics," *Canadian Journal of Political Science* 4, no. 3 (September 1971): pp. 301–345.

53. *Report* by Parliamentary Counsel of the Senate on the British North America Act (Ottawa: King's Printer, 1939).

54. Louis-Phillipe Pigeon, "The Meaning of Provincial Autonomy," in Lederman, *The Courts and the Constitution,* p. 46. Reprinted with the permission of Carleton University Press.

55. Pierre Elliott Trudeau, "Federalism, Nationalism, and Reason," in Trudeau, *Federalism and the French Canadians* (Toronto: Macmillan of Canada, 1968), p. 198.

56. G. P. Browne, *The Judicial Committee and the British North America Act,* (Toronto: University of Toronto Press, 1967).

57. Corry, *Uses of a Constitution,* p. 7.

58. P. W. Hogg, "Is the Supreme Court of Canada Biased in Constitutional Cases?" *Canadian Bar Review,* 57, no. 4 (December, 1979): pp. 729–733.

59. Patrick J. Monahan, "At Doctrine's Twilight: The Structure of Canadian Federalism," *University of Toronto Law Journal* 34 (1984): p. 69.

60. J. R. Mallory, *Social Credit and the Federal Power,* reprint (Toronto: University of Toronto Press, 1976), p. 55.

61. Peter Russell, "The Supreme Court and Federal-Provincial Relations," *Canadian Public Policy* 11, no. 21 (June 1985): pp. 161–170.

62. On the Supreme Court of Canada, see generally James G. Snell and Frederick Vaughan, *The Supreme Court of Canada: History of an Institution* (Toronto: University of Toronto Press, 1985), particularly Chapter 10 on the 1975–1982 period.

63. J. Bruce Doern and V. Seymour Wilson, "Conclusions and Observations," in Doern and Wilson, eds., *Issues in Canadian Public Policy,* (Toronto: Macmillan of Canada, 1974).

64. Gilbert L'Écuyer, *La cour suprême du Canada et le partage du compétences 1949–1978* (Quebec: Ministère des affaires intergouvernementales, 1978).
65. Hogg, "Is the Supreme Court of Canada Biased in Constitutional Cases," LVII, *Canadian Bar Review*, No. 4, December 1979, pgs. 729–733.
66. Ibid., pp. 725–726.
67. Ibid., p. 739.
68. Paul Weiler, *In the Last Resort: A Critical Study of the Supreme Court of Canada* (Toronto: Carswell, 1974), Chapter 6, "The Umpire of Canadian Federation."
69. Ibid., pp. 173–174.
70. Ibid., p. 175.
71. Gerald Rubin, "The Nature, Use and Effect of Reference Cases in Canadian Constitutional Law," in Lederman, *Courts and the Constitution*, pp. 220–248.
72. See "A Symposium on the Appointment of Judges" in F. L. Morton, ed., *Law, Politics and the Judicial Process in Canada* (Calgary: University of Calgary Press, 1984), pp. 70–84.
73. Hogg, "Is the Supreme Court Biased?" pp. 724–726.
74. Russell, "Introduction" p. 23. See also Russell's excellent article, "Constitutional Reform of the Judicial Branch, Symbolic versus Operational Considerations," *Canadian Journal of Political Science* 17, no. 2 (June 1984): pp. 227–252.
75. There is a burgeoning literature on the Charter. An excellent collection of essays on specialized aspects of human rights in Canada just before the Charter came into effect is contained in Walter S. Tarnopolsky and Gerald-A. Beaudoin, eds., *The Canadian Charter of Rights and Freedoms: A Commentary* (Toronto: Carswell, 1982). On the Charter, see Peter W. Hogg, *Constitutional Law of Canada*, 2d ed. (Toronto: Carswell, 1985), Chapters 30–37 inclusive; Claire Beckton and A. Wayne Mackay, research co-ordinators, *The Courts and the Charter*, vol. 58, of the research studies prepared for the Royal Commission on the Economic Union and Development Prospects for Canada (Toronto: University of Toronto Press, 1985).
76. Bora Laskin, *Canadian Constitutional Law: Cases, Text and Notes on the Distribution of Legislative Power*, 3d ed. (Toronto: Carswell, 1966) and J. D. Whyte and W. R. Lederman, eds., *Canadian Constitutional Law: Cases, Notes and Materials on the Distribution and Limitation of Legislative Powers under the Constitution of Canada*, 2d ed. (Toronto: Butterworth, 1977). The Whyte and Lederman text does not even contain those sections of the Constitution not related to the distribution of legislative powers.
77. The Right Honourable Lester B. Pearson, *Federalism for the Future* (Ottawa: Queen's Printer, 1968).
78. Ibid., p. 8.
79. Alan Cairns, "Recent Federalist Constitutional Proposals, A Review Essay," *Canadian Public Policy* 5 (1979): p. 360. Reprinted by permission: *Canadian Public Policy — Analyse de Politiques*.
80. Mark Sproule-Jones, "The Enduring Colony? Political Institutions and Political Science in Canada," *Publius: The Journal of Federalism* 14, no. 1 (Winter 1984): p. 93.
81. Jennifer Smith, "Intrastate Federalism and Confederation," in Stephen Brooks, ed., *Political Thought in Canada* (Toronto: Irwin, 1984), p. 265.
82. Ibid., p. 269.
83. Sharman, "The Strange Case," p. 105.
84. *Report of the Royal Commission on the Economic Union and Development Prospects for Canada*, vol. 3 (Ottawa: Minister of Supply and Services Canada, 1985), p. 22.
85. Ibid., p. 91.
86. Ibid., p. 86. The conservatism of the Commission is in marked and depressing contrast to the bold views of the report of the McGrath Committee of the House of Commons on reform of the House published at about the same time.

Appendix to Chapter 2

AMENDMENT TO THE
CONSTITUTION ACT, 1867

Amendment to
Constitution
Act, 1867

50. The *Constitution Act, 1867* (formerly named the *British North America Act, 1867*) is amended by adding thereto, immediately after section 92 thereof, the following heading and section:

"Non-Renewable Natural Ressources, Forestry Resources and Electrical Energy

Laws respecting
non-renewable
natural
resources,
forestry
resources and
electrical
energy

92A. (1) In each province, the legislature may exclusively make laws in relation to

(a) exploration for non-renewable natural resources in the province;

(b) development, conservation and management of non-renewable natural resources and forestry resources in the province, including laws in relation to the rate of primary production therefrom; and

(c) development, conservation and management of sites and facilities in the province for the generation and production of electrical energy.

Export from
provinces of
resources

(2) In each province, the legislature may make laws in relation to the export from the province to another part of Canada of the primary production from non-renewable natural resources and forestry resources in the province and the production from facilities in the province for the generation of electrical energy, but such laws may not authorize or provide for discrimination in prices or in supplies exported to another part of Canada.

Authority of
Parliament

(3) Nothing in subsection (2) derogates from the authority of Parliament to enact laws in relation to the matters referred to in that subsection and, where such a law of Parliament and a law of a province conflict, the law of Parliament prevails to the extent of the conflict.

Taxation of
resources

(4) In each province, the legislature may make laws in relation to the raising of money by any mode or system of taxation in respect of

(a) non-renewable natural resources and forestry resources in the province and the primary production therefrom, and

(b) sites and facilities in the province for the generation of electrical energy and the production therefrom,

whether or not such production is exported in whole or in part from the province, but such laws may not authorize or provide for taxation that differentiates between production exported to another part of Canada and production not exported from the province.

"Primary production"

(5) The expression "primary production" has the meaning assigned by the Sixth Schedule.

Existing powers or rights

(6) Nothing in subsections (1) to (5) derogates from any powers or rights that a legislature or government of a province had immediately before the coming into force of this section.''

Idem

51. The said Act is further amended by adding thereto the following Schedule:

"THE SIXTH SCHEDULE

Primary Production from Non-Renewable Natural Resources and Forestry Resources

1. For the purposes of section 92A of this Act,
  (a) production from a non-renewable natural resource is primary production therefrom if
      (i) it is in the form in which it exists upon its recovery or severance from its natural state, or
      (ii) it is a product resulting from processing or refining the resource, and is not a manufactured product or a product resulting from refining crude oil, refining upgraded heavy crude oil, refining gases or liquids derived from coal or refining a synthetic equivalent of crude oil; and
  (b) production from a forestry resource is primary production therefrom if it consists of sawlogs, poles, lumber, wood chips, sawdust or any other primary wood product, or wood pulp, and is not a product manufactured from wood.''

The Canadian Constitution 1981: Reproduced with permission of the Minister of Supply and Services Canada.

III

The Continuing
Constitutional Agenda

In the period between the early 1960s and the proclamation of the Constitution Act, 1982 there was a vast amount of debate among Canadians about explicit reforms in the Constitution. This emphasis on constitutional change was unprecedented in Canadian history. Up until the 1960s all but a few of the Canadians seriously concerned with public affairs were constitutional conservatives in the sense that they did not believe that the values and interests they respectively espoused required explicit constitutional reforms. This was so even in the vigorous constitutional controversies during the decade of the Great Depression.[1] On the one side there were those who argued that the Constitution was a compact, either among the provinces or between English and French, and demanded that others adhere to the letter and spirit of the original federal bargain. The anti-compact forces argued from the position that Canada's constitutional difficulties were not the result of the British North America Act itself, but rather of the alleged misinterpretation of that document by the Judicial Committee of the Privy Council.

The emergence of widespread debate about the reform of the Canadian Constitution from the early 1960s onward was, for the most part, a resultant of the pressures emanating from the new Quebec and the response to these pressures.[2] In 1956 the Report of the Quebec Royal Commission of Inquiry on Constitutional Problems had elaborated the consensus among the then dominant elites of the province in the most elegant and detailed defence of Confederation as a French-English compact ever made. Less than a decade later the leader of the Union Nationale, soon to become premier, wrote in his book, *Égalité ou Indépendance,* "Ce que nous voulons, c'est plus que les provisions que nous accordant la constitution de 1867."[3] The response to the autonomist forces from Quebec embodied in demands for explicit constitutional change also took a constitutional form, most coherently and persistently elaborated by Pierre Elliott Trudeau both before and after he entered elective politics in 1965.[4]

Up until roughly the mid-1970s the constitutional debate was, to an overwhelming degree, monopolized by the competing visions and strategies of nationalist and federalist francophones from Quebec.[5] English-speaking Canadians were not, on the whole, deeply dissatisfied with the existing constitutional arrangements and were, to widely varying degrees, willing to contemplate seriously changes in these arrangements only as these were perceived necessary to sustain Confederation by meeting the new circumstances of French-English duality. However, there developed from the latter years of the 1970s onward a stream of pressures for constitutional reform, emanating mainly from Western Canada, which suggested that it was urgently necessary to undertake changes which would make the institutions of the central government more representative of and responsive to the values and interests of provincial governments and/or of citizens as residents of particular provinces or regions.[6]

It is unlikely that comprehensive constitutional reform will be on the Canadian political agenda in the next decade. The influence of Pierre Trudeau on the agenda during the period when he was minister of justice and later prime minister can hardly be exaggerated. Trudeau's disposition to emphasize constitutional matters was well honed prior to his entry into elective politics in 1965, and this penchant never weakened. Further, his rationalistic approach to this subject was influential in placing the discussion of constitutional matters within the framework of debate about the fundamental nature of the Canadian political community. Robert Stanfield in a 1985 address expressed a very different view and one which is likely to prevail in the foreseeable future:

> Canadians do not agree on what Canada is or ought to be. That does not worry me. I think it is great. Canada has evolved into something quite different than it was supposed to be. That is clear enough. Canada is still evolving and will continue to evolve as long as we do not agree on what Canada is. Fortunately that is likely to be a long time hence. I consider our recent constitutional exercise to have been a serious mistake, though not a fatal one. I hope we will resist future temptations to fasten our notions of our country upon our children.[7]

At any rate, Brian Mulroney views Canada through other than a constitutional prism as he said in a speech delivered in 1980:

> We have been studied to death. Our self-analysis would make Freud look like a choir-boy. We have developed our own peculiar cottage industry — highly paid and unproductive — in the field of constitutional reform. Imagine what might have been accomplished in, say, the field of medical research if the same amount of time and energy, talent and money had been available as in the field of federal-provincial relations. I became actively involved in the debate when I was nineteen and I can say with authority that I have played a peripheral role in erecting a monument to sterility.[8]

The incumbent prime minister has been an influential participant in forging the prevailing Canadian consensus that the country's major problems are economic and that the Constitution does not impose significant obstacles to economic reform.

Further, the new premier of Quebec, Robert Bourassa, has never been as disposed towards emphasizing constitutional change as most of his recent predecessors.

Despite what I have written above, specific matters of constitutional change remain on the political agenda. Two of these (the definition of aboriginal rights and the adherence of Quebec to the Constitution Act, 1982) are in a sense unfinished business from the constitutional settlement of November 1981. The constitutional status of the Yukon and the Northwest Territories are in rapid evolution. And, as I shall argue, the existing Canadian Constitution puts the country under considerable disability in conducting its international relations, something which will almost inevitably become evident if and when we come close to entering a comprehensive agreement on trade with the United States.

The Rights of the Aboriginal Peoples

The status of the aboriginal peoples of Canada is a highly complex matter,[9] and in the short discussion which follows only the federal dimensions of this status will be discussed, i.e., federal-provincial relations in respect to aboriginals and whether or not future advances in aboriginal self-government are likely to be embodied in federal forms.

Section 91(24) of the Constitution Act, 1867 — formerly the British North America Act, 1867 — confers on Parliament exclusive legislative jurisdiction in respect to "Indians, and Land Reserved for the Indians." A Supreme Court of Canada reference in 1930 determined that Eskimos (Inuit) came within the category of Indians under Section 91(24). In the 1981 census some 491 460 persons or about 2 per cent of the Canadian population identified themselves as Indians, Inuit or Métis. However, the anthropologist Michael Asch has estimated that there are a further 350 000 aboriginals, most of them Métis.[10]

Despite the exclusive legislative jurisdiction conferred on Parliament by Section 91(24), the provinces in both a legal and an administrative sense are very much involved with aboriginal Canadians. Métis and non-status Indians are in the same legal relationship with their respective powers as are other residents. Many of the unresolved territorial claims of the native peoples involve provincial Crown lands. Provincial laws of general application apply, with some few exceptions, to aboriginals, even in some cases those living on Indian reserves. Most crucially, perhaps, for the future of the native peoples, the provinces under the Constitution Act, 1982, are involved in the definition of aboriginal rights, and any proposed constitutional amendment to give expanded and/or more specific definition would require the agreement of the legislatures of seven of the provinces having in the aggregate half the population of all the provinces. If such amendments embodied a derogation from the powers of the dissenting provinces, these provinces would have the right not to be bound by these provisions.

Changes in the constitutional status of aboriginal peoples was a relatively late item on the Canadian constitutional agenda. In the period immediately after the Second World War, the formal apparatus of discrimination against Indians ended. They gained the right to vote, access to family allowances, a partial dismantling of the special status of Indian reserve communities and the increasing integration of Indian children into provincial school systems as the old state-church alliance in native education was phased out. The culmination of this general development so to speak was the issuance of a federal White Paper on Indian Policy in 1961. This document proposed the elimination of Section 91(24) by constitutional amendment, denied the validity of Indian land claims and suggested generally that the special status of Indians in Canadian society be ended. The native peoples' vigorous rejection of the assimilationist proposals of the White Paper caused the federal government to withdraw it within a year. However, throughout the next decade Ottawa forthrightly resisted the idea that the legal or constitutional status of any group of Canadian should be based on ethnicity, an idea contrary to many of the fundamental elements of Pierre Trudeau's political philosophy. A new element was the *Calder* case decided by the Supreme Court of Canada in 1973 in which a minority of the judges recognized the existence of certain land rights of the Nishga Indians of British Columbia.[11] Subsequent judicial decisions have tended to affirm that aboriginal land rights exist, although these can legally be modified by federal or provincial governments and legislatures. There was a further recognition of aboriginal land rights in the agreement concluded in 1976 between the government of Quebec and the Cree and Inuit of the James Bay region.

Bill C-60 for the amendment of the Constitution of Canada introduced into Parliament by the Trudeau government in June 1978 contained a provision that nothing in the proposed charter of rights "shall be held to abrogate, abridge or derogate from any right or freedom not declared by it that may have existed in Canada at the commencement of the Act, including, without limiting the generality of the foregoing, any right or freedom that may have been acquired by any of the native peoples of Canada by virtue of the Royal Proclamation of October 7, 1763." Douglas Sanders has described subsequent events:

> The constitution became the dominant political issue for Indians, Métis and Inuit in the years 1978 to 1982. They pursued a complex and expensive strategy which many politicians dismissed as naive and quixotic. They sought recognition as political actors within the Canadian state and piggy-backed the campaign on a legal issue not of their making. In the effort to block or transform patriation, they sought to change their roles within Canadian federalism.[12]

The focus on the Constitution was intensified after the introduction into Parliament of the Constitutional resolution in October 1980.[13] The major objectives of the leaders of the aboriginal groups was to ensure that any new constitutional settlement included an explicit recognition of native rights and that aboriginal groups would have a veto over any change in the Constitution directly affecting them. In London there was a vigorous campaign by native representatives to block the federal Resolution both by lobbying members of the UK Parliament and government and by appealing, unsuccessfully as it turned out, to British courts to decide that the UK authorities rather than those of Canada retained the continuing responsibility to protect native rights under the terms of the Royal Proclamation of 1763.

Three sections (25, 35, 37) of the Constitution Act, 1982 relate directly to the native peoples of Canada.

Section 25 provides that:

The guarantee in this Charter of certain rights and freedoms shall not be construed so as to abrogate or derogate from any aboriginal, treaty or other rights or freedoms that pertain to the aboriginal peoples of Canada including:

(a) any rights or freedoms that have been recognized by the Royal Proclamation of October 7, 1963 and

(b) any rights or freedoms that may be acquired by the aboriginal peoples of Canada by way of land claims settlement.

This section would appear to give some protection to aboriginal groups against adverse consequences from the application of the liberal and universalistic rights of the Charter. For example, persons who were not beneficiaries of a recognized land claim of some aboriginal group would not have the right otherwise recognized in the Charter "to move in and take up residence in any province and to pursue the gaining of a livelihood in any province" if the area involved was that of an aboriginal land claim.

Section 35 enacts that:

(1) The existing aboriginal and treaty rights of the aboriginal peoples of Canada are heretofore recognized and affirmed;

(2) In the Act 'aboriginal peoples of Canada' includes the Indian, Inuit and Métis peoples of Canada.

This section was embodied in the Constitution without regard to the circumstance that there was a great deal of unresolved disagreement about the question of what the "existing" rights of the aboriginal peoples actually were. Neither does the section specify who is to decide whether particular persons are Indians, Métis or Inuit.

Section 37 directed the prime minister of Canada to convene a First Ministers Conference within a year and that one item of the agenda of that conference should be "constitutional matters that directly affect the aboriginal peoples of Canada, including the identification and definition of the rights of these people to be included in the Constitution". The prime minister was directed to invite native representatives to participate in these discussions. This constitutional provision confers on the aboriginal communities and their leaders the right, not possessed by any other non-governmental groupings, to participate in constitutional deliberations of public authorities directly involving aboriginal rights.

One of the most persistent demands of Canada's native peoples is for an enhanced measure of self-government. This demand is closely related to the settlement of aboriginal land claims, for without a more secure economic base, measures towards self-government would have little real effect in diminishing the dependence of these peoples on decisions made by others.

There are two models of formative self-government congruent with Canadian political traditions. One is the municipal according to which the extent of autonomy possessed by native groupings would be delegated to them by some superior legislative authority, and (as is the case in the relation between local governments in Canada and their respective provinces) might be extended, limited or ended at the discretion of that authority. The other is the federal model in which the jurisdiction of native groups would be specified by the Constitution and could be changed only by some form of consent given by those groups themselves. There might of course be a regime in which some aboriginal groups had municipal status while the function of others was constitutionally entrenched. Such a situation might best include procedures embodied in the Constitution to determine how groups could pass from one status to the other.

The municipal and federal models are of course derived from the experience of peoples of European origin and may be irrelevant or worse to the needs and wishes of Canadian aboriginal peoples. There are barriers to communication of the most fundamental kind between natives and non-natives. For example, Menno Boldt and Anthony Long caution the leaders of the Indian movement against arguing the cause of self-government in terms of sovereignty.[14] Sovereignty to these leaders means the absence of external controls. However, as Boldt and Long argue, sovereignty in the European sense means not only that a community is free of external control, but also that power within that community is hierarchically ordered. The latter is quite foreign to Indian concepts of authority which are based on age-old custom rather than law and which are egalitarian in the sense that there is no dichotomy between ruler and ruled. Further, sovereignty in the European sense is inextricably related to spatiality with each sovereign unit occupying a particular part of the earth while, "Indian notions of territoriality were not conceived of in terms of precisely fixed territorial boundaries," although the present Indian emphasis on land claims "represents a concession to European-western political-legal influence".[15]

Some considerable progress towards an enhanced range of aboriginal self-government is likely in the foreseeable future. The leaders of the aboriginal peoples have not, however, spelled out or perhaps even agreed among themselves as to what would be acceptable measures to this end. This lack of precision is understandable because workable solutions must be tailored to the needs of groups in very different circumstances: to large units and small ones, to groups of settled and of nomadic peoples, to groups with considerable experience in decision making and policy implementation and to those less developed along these lines and so on. The failure of native leaders to spell out the precise nature of self-government has given the governments of the western provinces a plausible justification for resisting the demands for aboriginal autonomy.

Apart from the gross discrepancies in wealth, power and numbers between the native and non-native elements of the Canadian population and the challenge to important material interests inherent in aboriginal land claims, the following three circumstances may complicate progress towards further measures of aboriginal self-government:

1. Non-aboriginal Canadians and the federal and provincial governments can be expected to show some resistance to demands that political rights be based on ethnicity. The Canadian regime of rights as constitutionally recognized by the Charter is a complex net of universal rights some of which are available to all persons and others which adhere to persons only as members of a particular

group. In the first category are democratic rights (related to voting, elections and legislatures), fundamental rights (freedom of expression, religion, association, etc.), legal rights (respecting persons accused of or convicted of offences under the law) and mobility rights. The other class of rights belongs to persons as aboriginals, members of official language minorities, and Protestant minorities in Quebec and Roman Catholic minorities in certain of the other provinces.

Section 15 of the Charter dealing with equality rights contains clauses which can be advanced to protect both categories of rights outlined above.[16] Section 15(1) provides that, "Every individual is equal before and under the law and has the right to the equal benefit and protection of the law without discrimination and, in particular, without discrimination based on race, national ethnic origin, colour, religion, sex, age or mental or physical disability." This section embodies the universalistic thrust, persons are not to be denied "the equal protection and equal benefit of the law" because they belong to particular categories; the governmental regime is to be gender-blind, colour-blind, religion-blind and so on. However, Section 15(2) qualifies these universalistic imperatives: "Subsection (1) does not preclude any law, program or activity that has as its object the amelioration of conditions of disadvantaged individuals or groups including those that are disadvantaged because of race, national or ethnic origin, colour, religion, sex, age or mental or physical disability." This latter subsection along with Sections 25, 35 and 37 of the Constitution Act, 1982, gives constitutional sanction to public policies treating aboriginal peoples differently from other Canadians. However, despite such provisions, non-aboriginal Canadians are, to varying degrees, committed to universalistic premises and can be expected to offer some resistance to aboriginal self-government insofar as this is perceived to be contrary to such premises. One clash here will probably centre on the demands of the aboriginal community as such, and of particular groupings within it, to determine their own membership, and the stakes here will obviously increase as the benefits of aboriginal status are extended.

2. Aboriginal peoples are likely to be disadvantaged by the consensual nature of their traditional political structures as contrasted with the hierarchical structures of the federal and provincial governments with whom they must deal. J. Rick Ponting and Roger Gibbins see great hazards for Indians in relating themselves to the rest of the Canadian political community through the processes of executive federalism according to which federal and provincial governments can commit their respective jurisdictions without being concerned that their actions will not be ratified by Parliament or the provincial legislatures.[17] "If Indian governments were to join this intergovernmental process, they would have to negotiate on behalf of their constituents without having to worry about subsequent ratification from individual bands, tribal associations or provincial organizations. Thus the price of admission to executive federalism and effective participation in the intergovernmental process will be a substantial loss in local autonomy."[18] The aboriginal peoples can advance towards self-government only through bargaining between leaders of a small number of native associations and the federal and provincial governments. Those organizations themselves represent complex and not always consistent patterns of interests and aspirations. Yet the price of the effective advancement of native demands in respect to self-government and other matters

is a relatively centralized pattern of decision making within national and provincial groupings of aboriginals.

3. It is likely that some elements of the traditionally paternalistic stance of non-native Canadians towards aboriginal peoples will be perpetuated. The native peoples demand measures of self-government so that important elements of their lives will be determined according to their values. It is almost inevitable that, in governing themselves, native peoples will make choices which are not congruent with the basic values of other Canadians, specifically perhaps with the universalistic values which have already been mentioned and which are embodied in the Charter of Rights and Freedoms. When such conflicts occur, there will be strong impulses for the federal and provincial governments to influence the aboriginal authorities to conform to the core values of the wider Canadian community, and, in some circumstances, these impulses may be strengthened by the existence of divisions within the aboriginal groups themselves. A harbinger of this kind of conflict has arisen in the insistence of the government of Canada, supported no doubt by most Canadians, that there be eliminated those sections of the Indian Act which specify that Indian women who married non-Indians lose their Indian status while Indian status is acquired by non-Indian women who marry Indian men. What was at stake here was more than the impulse of many native groups to preserve male-dominated societies; it involved the fundamental question of whether aboriginal status was to be determined by the aboriginal peoples themselves or by others.

In general, the more precise definition and extension of aboriginal rights will require a very high degree of sympathetic imagination among Canadians of the dominant community, and among them and aboriginal peoples alike a high degree of ingenuity in devising and working new political and administrative forms.

The Adherence of Quebec to the Constitutional Settlement of 1981

It is of considerable importance that the provincial authorities of Quebec be brought to give their adherence to some variant of the constitutional settlement agreed upon between Ottawa and the other provincial governments in November 1981 and embodied in the Constitution Act, 1982. Despite its present weakness, Quebec nationalism is a persisting and recurrent phenomenon in that province, and unless some sort of constitutional accommodation is brought about, we can expect future Quebec nationalists and separatists to raise the 1981 theme of "betrayal" by English-speaking Canada. It is patently unsatisfactory that the two major elements of the 1981 settlement (the domestic amending procedure and the Charter of Rights and Freedoms) are regarded as illegitimate by a large though indeterminate section of the Quebec population. There are other adverse consequences of the existing situation.

First, the Parti Québécois government which left office in December 1985 asserted that it would refuse on principle its consent to any proposed amendment regardless of the government's judgement on substantive grounds as to the desirability of that amendment. So long as this position is maintained by the Quebec authorities, the 1982 amending formula is more rigid than its contrivers designed it to be. Although there are not a large number of proposed amendments "in the hopper," this Quebec position might frustrate changes in the short-term future related to the definition of aboriginal rights and restrictions on the powers of the Senate.

Second, according to legislation enacted by the national assembly in 1982, Quebec has taken the maximum advantage of the "notwithstanding" provisions of Section 33 of the Constitution Act, 1982. Thus, within Quebec the provincial bill of rights supersedes those provisions of the Charter in respect to the fundamental freedoms of Section 2 and the legal and equality rights of Sections 7 to 15 inclusive. Although there were conflicting expectations and preferences at work in the contriving of Section 33, it is reasonable to suppose that it was the intent that Parliament and the provincial legislatures would exercise this option only in respect to particular clauses of the Charter as judicially interpreted and not, as in the case of the Quebec action of 1982, to the maximum extent permitted by law. Quebec has thus provincialized what at least the federal supporters of the Charter believed would be a nationalizing instrument.

The Quebec Liberal party's policy committee in a statement issued in February 1985 said this:

> The following are the main conditions which would enable a Liberal government to seriously consider Quebec's acceptance of the Constitutional agreement of 1981: a preamble recognizing Quebec as a distinct society; a constitutional right in the matter of immigration; a stipulation providing for Quebec's participation in the appointment of judges to the Supreme Court; limitation of the federal spending power; and a full veto for Quebec written into the amending formula.[19]

It is the last of these conditions, i.e., changes in the amending formula itself, which is most likely to frustrate Quebec's adherence to the 1981 bargain. The Quebec Liberals have been consistently critical of the opportunism of the PQ in being willing to give up a Quebec veto over important constitutional amendments as part of the "gang of eight" provinces resisting Ottawa's resolution for constitutional change. Under the existing arrangements, amendments related to several consequential matters can be made by action of Parliament and two-thirds of the provinces having together at least half the population of the provinces and thus against Quebec's opposition: the principle of representation according to population in the House of Commons; the powers of the Senate and the method of choosing its members; provisions related to the Supreme Court of Canada and the creation of new provinces. On the other hand under Section 41(e) of the Constitution Act, changes in the amending formula itself require the consent of all the provinces. It may be difficult to get this consent. The existing amending formula embodies the principle of the equality of the provinces, and the adoption of this principle was, in the main, a victory for Alberta and British Columbia who are likely to resist such a fundamental change in the 1981 bargain.

The Mulroney government has strong political incentives for bolstering its position in Quebec by bringing the government of that province into a new constitutional accommodation. The rewards for the Bourassa administration for concluding such an agreement, at least on the terms likely to be made available to them, are less evident. The other provinces appear to have little desire to return to the process of constitutional review, and, in particular, unanimous provincial consent for changes in the amending procedure itself appears unlikely.

The Status of the Northwest Territories and the Yukon

In the past decade-and-a-half the Northwest Territories and the Yukon have become more important than ever before in national policies and in the awareness of Canadians outside the region. This may be attributed to two interrelated factors. The first is that the discovery of large supplies of petroleum on the Alaskan North Slope in 1968 projected the North into national prominence just at the beginning of a period when Canadians were experiencing new urgencies in energy and resource development. The second factor was the increasing sensitivity of the people and government of Canada to the status and position of the aboriginal peoples and the impact of resource development on these peoples. As Edgar Dosman has shown, in his book-length analysis of the 1968–75 period, national policies towards northern development were negotiated in secret between senior officials of the federal government and representatives of a few major resource corporations with little effective influence from Parliament, conservationists, the native peoples and other residents of the North and the governments of the region.[20] Many more actors are now involved, and in particular the status of the governments of the Northwest Territories and the Yukon is a matter of constitutional concern.

Like the area comprised in Alberta and Saskatchewan, the Northwest Territories and the Yukon have advanced from direct rule to responsible government in piecemeal steps.[21] The Yukon has developed somewhat further along this road than the Northwest Territories, although, in the latter, local government institutions are better developed. Gurston Dacks in 1981 outlined several of the ways in which the Yukon legislative assembly was limited: it had a narrower range of jurisdiction than the provinces (particularly in respect to land and national resources); it could not amend its own constitution without federal legislation; its bills might be disallowed by the federal cabinet; its plans for borrowing, lending and investment required federal approval, and it was under the continuing need to negotiate with Ottawa about money.[22] In both the Yukon and the Northwest Territories there is the emergent development of political parties which is a necessity of parliamentary responsible government as it is practised by Canadians and other peoples adhering to the Westminster model.

Recent years have seen two important advances in the status of the Northwest Territories and Yukon which are both symbolic and more than symbolic:

1. These jurisdictions received a limited recognition under Section 37 of the Constitution Act, 1982 which required the convening of a first ministers' conference on the Constitution within a year and Section 38 which required two subsequent such conferences, with the latter being not later than April 1987. It was specified that an item on the agenda of these meetings was to be "constitutional matters that directly affect the aboriginal peoples of Canada, including the identification and definition of the rights of these peoples." It was provided that selected representatives of the governments of the Yukon and the Northwest

Territories be invited to these conferences and be given the opportunity to participate in discussion on any matters which in the opinion of the prime minister
directly affected those jurisdictions.

2. At the First Ministers' Conference dealing mainly with economic matters
in February and November 1985, members of the governments of Yukon and
the Northwest Territories were present as representatives of these jurisdictions
rather than, as at previous such meetings, as observers or members of the federal
delegation. On both occasions leaders of these governments accepted the invi-
tation of Prime Minister Mulroney to address the conference.

Dacks in his admirable book on the North is pessimistic about the prospects
for residents of that region attaining significant control over their own destiny.[23]
Ottawa's primary concern in the North is with the development of energy, and
Dacks argues that the federal government will not surrender any significant degree
of control over this development or of public revenues resulting from it. The
power of the federal Department of Indian Affairs and Northern Development
(DIAND) in respect to development is in decline and the territorial governments
will take over some of these responsibilities. However, this declining influence
of DIAND — as well as of the Department of the Environment — in the North
will result in an "increasingly ideologically homogeneous federal government
struggling for control of northern development." Dacks concludes, "With the
lion's share of the political resources, Ottawa will not find it difficult to hold
off the territorial assault. Rather, the consequence of this protracted struggle will
be the continued colonial shape of the northern political agenda, with the attendent
waste of energy."[24] On the positive side, however, "northerners will become
more experienced in operating their maturing political institutions; hence the
administrative competence of these governments will grow."[25]

The Yukon and the Northwest Territories are unlikely to attain provincial
status in the foreseeable future. Gordon Robertson has made a powerful argument
that the granting of such status would be unwise.[26] His major point is that, in
the foreseeable future, the financial situation of these areas will make them
overwhelmingly dependent on federal transfers and that the existing federal-
provincial fiscal regime is quite inappropriate to these jurisdictions. The costs
of providing services in such a vast and remote area is exceedingly high, and
the resource base on which northern governments depend for independently-based
revenues is both narrow and subject to abrupt variations. Robertson's alternative
is that these jurisdictions receive constitutional status as "Autonomous Federal
Territories" with changes in such status possible only by action of the Parliament
of Canada and that of the legislature of the territory concerned.

The Constitution Act, 1982 erected an obstacle to the Yukon and Northwest
Territories' attaining provincial status which did not exist before, by the provision
in Section 42(1)(f) that new provinces can be established only by an amendment
to the Constitution requiring the approval of the Parliament of Canada and the
legislatures of two-thirds of the provinces having in aggregate half the Canadian
population. Prior to 1982, the federal authorities had the power to bring new
provinces into Confederation so long as this did not affect the boundaries of the
existing ones. Robertson perceptively points out that the new amending formula,
or more accurately, that part of the formula wich governs the federal-provincial

distribution of powers, allows any four provinces to block an amendment and thus gives a protection to the western and Atlantic regions which would be weakened if two or three new provinces were created.[27] Stephen Scott has written of Ottawa's willingness to surrender power to the provinces in this matter. "It is a fair guess that the Trudeau government did not resist the curtailment of federal legislative power to create new provinces because the federal authorities could henceforth more easily resist pressures for the creation of new provinces in the north."[28]

To the extent that residents of the North are to have a significant measure of control over their own governance, a number of significant questions arise. What kinds of public institutions are appropriate for governing an area of continental size inhabited by only 90 000 people? By what experiences of common learning can natives and non-natives with their vastly different cultures and interests come to operate common political and governmental institutions? To what extent are structures and processes (perhaps most crucially those related to local government) developed by and for Europeans appropriate to the circumstances of the aboriginal peoples of the North?

The Constitution and International Relations

Federal countries have difficulties in conduct of international affairs. Public international law and international diplomacy are for the most part premised on sovereign states being unitary actors; within this framework a nation is disadvantaged unless its national authorities speak with a single voice and have the capacity to implement international obligations. On the other hand, the territorial particularisms which sustain federalism require such states to give some protection to state/provincial interests to ensure that these will not be easily overridden by the national authorities under the guise of international action. This problem becomes increasingly more difficult as interactions among sovereign states have moved from the traditional concerns of trade and defence to encompass virtually every matter subject to governmental action: education, environmental pollution, human rights, scientific research and so on. In the Canadian context the federal dimension of international relations has now become acute in respect to trade policy.

The constitutions of federal states deal with the external affairs power in quite different ways. Under the constitution of the United States, all treaties concluded by the president and ratified by two-thirds of the senators at such a vote are, under Article VI(3), the "supreme law of the land" and thus override state jurisdictions. Recent decisions of the High Court of Australia appear to give the Commonwealth almost unlimited power to override the states in implementing international agreements under the central authorities' power over "External affairs" in Section 51(XXIX) of the constitution.[29] Similarly, in the Federal Republic of Germany Article 73(1) of the constitution gives the central legislature exclusive legislative powers over "Foreign affairs as well as defence including the protection of the civilian population." The Canadian Constitution as judicially interpreted is quite different.

The leading Canadian decision in respect to the external affairs power is the *Labour Conventions* case of 1937.[30] In effect the Supreme Court decided that the federal Parliament's legislative power could not be extended beyond the subjects enumerated in Section 91 by virtue of any international obligation entered into by the national government. Thus, international obligations incurred by Canada which involve provincial legislative jurisdiction can be implemented only with provincial consent. A major difficulty in this distribution of powers arose in respect to the Columbia River Treaty signed by Prime Minister Diefenbaker and President Eisenhower in 1961.[31] Subsequently, however, the government of British Columbia, which had the major responsibilities for carrying out Canada's responsibility under the treaty, dissented, and in a complex series of later developments, a new international agreement for the development of the Columbia was concluded in 1964 with the involvement of the national governments of Canada and the United States and the government of British Columbia. During the 1960s and 1970s there were ongoing conflicts between the federal and Quebec governments related to the participation of that province in organizations of French-speaking nations. In the conditions of the foreseeable future the difficulties are more likely to involve international trade policy.

As citizens of a nation heavily dependent on international trade, Canadians face very considerable constitutional disabilities in forging common policies in respect to such matters and in implementing international obligations in respect to trade. It is generally agreed that the most significant impediments to international trade are not explicit tariffs but non-tariff barriers (NTBs) erected by national governments and sub-national jurisdictions. In particular circumstances, it can plausibly be argued that any significant differences in public policies between or among trading nations constitute a NTB whether these relate to taxation, environmental pollution, policies to reduce regional economic disparities, welfare measures, measures to protect certain industries deemed essential to national distinctiveness, public procurement policies and so on. Many of the existing non-tariff barriers are erected by the Canadian provinces. Thus, Ottawa will need the consent of the provincial governments to conclude significant international agreements lessening the impediments to trade whether within the multilateral context of the General Agreement on Tariffs and Trade (GATT) or in bilateral relations with the United States. As this is written, it seems unlikely that the requisite degree of provincial consent can be obtained for a comprehensive Canadian-American agreement on trade.

But even if the federal government were able to obtain the consent of provinces to international agreements on trade, there would still be constitutional difficulties. Such consent would be embodied in formal agreements with the provinces and perhaps, in some cases, in provincial legislation, yet there are no constitutional or legal obstacles to the subsequent modification or elimination of such consent by provincial governments or legislatures. There are a very large number, perhaps thousands, of federal-provincial agreements, and although many of these are highly formalized, their legal status has not, so far as I am aware, been settled. According to the doctrine of parliamentary supremacy, no legislature can bind its successor, and, on this basis, it would appear that there are no legal or constitutional impediments to unilateral provincial changes in previous arrangements concluded with Ottawa. In any future negotiations between Canada and the United States related to a comprehensive agreement on trade, it is likely that the Americans will be very much aware of the constitutional disabilities under which the Canadians work.

The Report of the (Macdonald) Royal Commission on the Economic Union and Development Prospects for Canada made two constructive recommendations for removing the constitutional barriers to Canada as an effective international actor whether in respect to trade or other matters.[32] Two constitutional amendments are suggested:

1. There should be a procedure which would permit Parliament and the provincial legislatures to enter into intergovernmental agreements binding their successors.
2. Where a proposed international treaty contains provisions which affect matters within provincial jurisdiction or require implementation by the provinces, the relevant sections should be ratified by the provincial legislatures. Sections of a treaty imposing obligations on provinces would come into effect on the passage of such resolutions by two-thirds of the provinces representing at least half the population of the Canadian provinces.

Notes

1. For a comprehensive account of those controversies, see Alan C. Cairns, "The Judicial Committee and its Critics," *Canadian Journal of Political Science* 4, no. 3. (September 1971): pp. 301–345.
2. See generally, Edward McWhinney, *Quebec and the Constitution, 1960–1978* (Toronto: University of Toronto Press, 1978), and particularly Chapters 3 and 4.
3. Daniel Johnson, *Égalite ou indépendance* (Montréal: Éditions Renaissance, 1965), p. 120.
4. Pierre Elliott Trudeau, *Federalism and the French Canadians* (Toronto: Macmillan of Canada, 1968).
5. Donald V. Smiley and Ronald L. Watts, *Intrastate Federalism in Canada,* vol. 39 of the research studies prepared for the Royal Commission on the Economic Union and Development Prospects for Canada (Toronto: University of Toronto Press, 1985), Chapter 1.
6. See the important writings of Roger Gibbins about this matter: "Constitutional Politics and the West," in Keith Banting and Richard Simeon, eds., *And No One Cheered: Federalism, Democracy and the Constitution Act* (Toronto: Methuen, 1983), pp. 119–132; and *Regionalism: Territorial Politics in Canada and the United States* (Toronto: Butterworths, 1982), particularly Chapter 8.
7. Robert L. Stanfield, *National Political Parties and Regional Diversity* Institute of Intergovernmental Relations Discussion Paper (Kingston: Queen's University 1985), pp. 1–2.
8. Brian Mulroney, *Where I Stand* (Toronto: McClelland and Stewart, 1983), p. 57.
9. These recent books are helpful introductions: Leroy Little Bear, Menno Boldt and J. Anthony Long, eds., *Pathways to Self-Determination: Canadian Indians and the Canadian State* (Toronto: University of Toronto Press, 1984); and Michael Asch, *Home and Native Land: Aboriginal Rights and the Canadian Constitution* (Toronto: Methuen, 1984).
10. Asch, *Home and Native Land,* p. 3.
11. *Calder et al. v. Attorney General of British Columbia* (1973) SCR 313. For the significance of the *Calder* judgment, see Asch, *Home and Native Land,* pp. 64–68.
12. Douglas Sanders, "The Indian Lobby," in Banting and Simeon, *And No One Cheered,* p. 301.
13. Ibid., pp. 301–324.
14. Menno Boldt and J. Anthony Long, "Tribal Traditions and European-Western Political Ideologies: The Dilemma of Canada's Native Indians," *Canadian Journal of Political Science* 17, no. 3 (1984): pp. 551–553.
15. Ibid., p. 546.

16. F. L. Morton has argued vigorously that it will be impossible for the judges to make any principled reconciliation of individual claims for non-discrimination and of group rights under the Charter, particularly as these are embodied in Section 15. "Group Rights versus Individual Rights in the Charter: The Special Cases of Natives and Quebecois," in Neil Nevitte and Allan Kornberg, eds., *Minorities and the Canadian State* (Oakville: Mosaic Press 1985), pp. 71–85.

17. J. Rick Ponting and Roger Gibbins, "Thorns in the Bed of Roses: A Socio-political View of the Problems of Indian Government," in Little Bear, Boldt and Long, *Pathways to Self-Determination,* pp. 130–132.

18. Ibid., p. 131.

19. Statement of the Quebec Liberal Party's Policy Committee in February 1985, in Peter Leslie, ed., *Canada: The State of the Federation 1985,* (Kingston: Queen's University, Institute of Intergovernmental Relations, 1985), p. 81. See also the analysis of Quebec's new Minister of Intergovernmental Relations, Gil Remillard, "The Constitution Act, 1982; An Unfinished Compromise," *American Journal of Comparative Law* 32, no. 2 (Spring 1984): pp. 269–281.

20. Edgar Dosman, *The National Interest: The Politics of Northern Development, 1968–75,* (Toronto: McClelland and Stewart, 1975).

21. See Lewis Herbert Thomas, *The Struggle for Responsible Government in the North-West Territories 1870–97,* 2d ed. (Toronto: University of Toronto Press, 1978), Chapter 10 "Reflections on Territorial Government — 1897–1970."

22. Gurston Dacks, *A Choice of Futures: Politics in the Canadian North* (Toronto: Methuen, 1981), p. 92.

23. Ibid., pp. 196–197.

24. Ibid., p. 202.

25. Ibid., p. 203.

26. Gordon Robertson, "Autonomous Federal Territories," *Policy Options* 6 (September 1985): pp. 9–13. Robertson, a former deputy minister of northern affairs and natural resources and commissioner of the Northwest Territories, is completing a longer study of this issue under the auspices of The Institute for Research on Public Policy.

27. Ibid., pp. 11–12.

28. Stephen A. Scott, "The Canadian Constitutional Amendment Process," in Paul Davenport and Richard A. Leach, eds., *Reshaping Confederation: The 1982 Reform of the Canadian Constitution* (Durham, N. C.: Duke University Press, 1984), p. 270.

29. Koowarta v. Bjelke-Peterson (1982) 56 A.L.J.R. 625 and *The Commonwealth v. State of Tasmania* (1983) 57 A.L.J.R. 450.

30. *A.-G. Can. v. A.-G. Ontario* (1937) A.C. 326.

31. Neil A. Swainson, *Conflict over the Columbia* (Montreal and Kingston: McGill-Queen's University Press, 1979).

32. *Report of the Royal Commission on the Economic Union and Development Prospects for Canada,* vol. 3 (Ottawa: Minister of Supply and Services Canada, 1985), p. 473 and pp. 467–468.

IV

Executive Federalism

Canadians live under a system of government which is executive dominated and within which a large number of important public issues are debated and resolved through the ongoing interactions among governments which we have come to call "executive federalism." Of this latter dimension Michael Jenkin has written: "More than any other federation, Canada relies on intergovernmental negotiation to help resolve political differences."[1] These negotiations range from the involvement of federal and provincial officials in the grading of meat to the highly publicized first ministers' conferences dealing with constitutional reform or the fundamental aspects of economic policy. In the last two decades there has emerged a new kind of agency having direct responsibility for particular public services or programs with the mandate of conducting what Richard Simeon has called "federal-provincial diplomacy."[2] As we shall see later in this chapter, executive federalism in the past decade has raised fundamental questions concerning the nature of the Canadian Confederation.

Executive Federalism: The Parliamentary and Federal Dimensions

The executive consists of the federal and provincial cabinets and the appointed officials who within the framework of law and custom work under their direction. Such executives under the normal circumstances in which governments retain the continuing support of majorities in the House of Commons and the provincial legislatures have the five following powers:

    1. The executive not only carries out the terms of legislation, but also designs almost all bills which are presented to the legislature. Further, within the terms of legislation, the executive formulates orders-in-council and other statutory instruments with the force of law.

    2. Under Sections 53 and 54 of the Constitution Act, 1867 all bills for taxation and for the appropriation of public moneys must be introduced into the House

of Commons by a minister of the Crown. Similar provisions are in effect in the provinces.

3. The executive has unshared responsibility for relations with other governments, whether those jurisdictions are domestic or foreign. This has included the role of negotiations on the Constitution, the most crucial element of political action. The agreement between the federal government and the governments of all the provinces but Quebec which formed the basis for the Constitution Act, 1982 was concluded among first ministers, although in the events leading up to this other governmental actors had been involved: the Leader of the Opposition, members of the Senate-House of Commons Committee on the Constitution, the appellate courts of three provinces and the Supreme Court of Canada.

4. The executive controls its own internal organization. As we shall see later in this chapter, this organization has been a crucial determinant of the way executive federalism operates.

5. Many adjudicative functions are carried out within the executive.

As we saw in the last chapter, the bias of the Westminster model is towards "strength, order and authority" in government both in Ottawa and the provinces. A. H. Birch has written that "the most important tradition of British political behaviour is that the government of the day should be given all the powers it needs to carry out its policy."[3] Something the same can be said of Canada, and it is pointless to inquire whether this way of viewing government is a cause or a result of executive dominance.

Notwithstanding the thrust of the Westminster model toward strong and decisive government, the federal imperative is that territorially-bounded interests be given a strong influence in the governmental process. Some reconciliation of these two circumstances can be effected by conferring on the states or provinces constitutional jurisdiction over those matters in respect to which spatially based differences are most profound, while assigning to the central authorities control over matters where non-territorial cleavages are dominant. This is essentially what the Fathers of Confederation did in establishing the first political community which attempted to combine the Westminster model with federalism. The new Dominion incorporated federal elements only because the French-Canadian politicians from Lower Canada would not have it otherwise, and legislative jurisdiction was conferred on the provinces in respect to those matters in respect to which the interests and values of the English and French differed markedly: most importantly in respect to education; what we would now call health and welfare matters; municipal institutions and property and civil rights. A reading of the Confederation Debates also demonstrates that the Fathers had what now seems a naïve belief that a clear-cut distinction could be made between national matters and those which were, in the language of the day, of only 'local' incidence and concern.

The proximate reconciliation between the federal and parliamentary principles which was effected by the Confederation settlement of 1864–67 has long since broken down. As we saw in Chapter II, the British North America Act of 1867 did contain a number of quasi-unitary elements giving the Dominion authorities the power to encroach on matters within provincial legislative jurisdiction. However, quite apart from these elements and others like the spending/lending power later developed, the two orders of government are inextricably involved in one another's activities over a wide range of matters. Further, the general expectation of the Fathers of Confederation that matters under the jurisdiction of the federal government would not divide Canadians along provincial or French-English axes has proven unattainable. The result is a situation in which federal and provincial governments are both interdependent and autonomous and in which there is a relative lack of institutional machinery for effecting the authoritative resolution of conflicts between them.

Even in situations where the Constitution confers exclusive jurisdiction for some subject on one of the orders of government, the interests of the other may be directly involved. To take one important example, Parliament has the exclusive power to enact laws in respect to unemployment insurance; but the levels of unemployment benefits and the conditions under which those are paid have a direct and immediate impact on the demands for social assistance provided by the provinces and their constituent municipalities. Again, the provinces have exclusive jurisdiction over education, including training and re-training directly related to employment, but the demands on the Unemployment Insurance Commission will be intimately related to the effectiveness of this activity. Or, to take another case, Parliament has, under the Constitution, exclusive authority over banking, while trust and loan companies and other ''near banks'' are for the most part regulated under provincial legislation. However, the various kinds of financial institutions are related to one another in a complex way, and the health of the total credit-granting system depends on the strength and integrity of those under federal and those under provincial jurisdiction.

Under the Constitution, the provinces are not given the power to encroach on matters within federal jurisdiction in the way that Ottawa can involve itself in provincial matters through the spending power, reservation and disallowances, the declaratory power and other quasi-unitary features of the constitutional order. However, in recent years the provincial governments have, with some success, asserted their right to be consulted by Ottawa in respect to a range of matters like trade and tariffs and interprovincial transportation and communications where the federal authorities have exclusive legislative powers. Gordon Robertson, then secretary to the (federal) cabinet for federal-provincial relations, analysed and deplored this movement in a paper delivered in 1978. He attributed it in large part to the absence of ''an effective forum for open regional advocacy and broker-age within our institutions at the federal level of government.'' Robertson saw as a ''watershed'' in this evolution the Western Economic Opportunities Conference of 1972 consisting of representatives of the federal government and the governments of the four western provinces.[4] During the Tokyo Round negotiations on the General Agreement on Tariffs and Trade, the provinces were consulted by Ottawa[5], and the Mulroney government has recognized the right of the provinces to be consulted in whatever future negotiations take place with the United States about a comprehensive agreement on trade.

In general, then, the constitutional distribution of powers between Parliament and the provinces underlies a situation in which the two orders of government are highly interdependent but are not related to one another through hierarchical structures of power. This interdependence, as we have seen, occurs even in those situations in which the Constitution confers explicit power over particular matters on one order or the other. Thus, a continuous process of federal-provincial consultation and negotiation is at the heart of the Canadian federal system. It is not that the constitutional division of powers as interpreted by the courts is unimportant. The bargaining position of the participating governments will in large part be determined by this division. To take an obvious example, the provinces have direct interests in both unemployment insurance and the Canada Pension Plan (CPP). However, they can press these interests less effectively in respect to the former because the Constitution confers exclusive legislative jurisdiction on Parliament, whereas old age pensions are, under the Constitution, a concurrent field of jurisdiction with provincial paramountcy and under the legislation governing the CPP, it is provided that substantive amendments to it must be approved by two-thirds of the provincial governments representing at least two-thirds of the Canadian population.

In the article to which reference has been made, Robertson attributed the involvement of the provinces in matters within federal jurisdiction largely to the lack "of an effective forum for open regional advocacy and brokerage within our institutions at the federal level of government." The Westminster model in its Canadian variant has a pervasively majoritarian thrust. Thus, particular provinces and regions are often is a position in which they have little influence in the structures and operations of the central government. To remedy this perceived deficiency, there have been a number of recommendations for reform in the direction of what has come to be called "intrastate federalism" to distinguish this dimension of the federal system from the "interstate" distribution of legislative powers between Parliament and the provinces:[6]

1. To replace the existing Senate, there should be a reformed second chamber whose members would be chosen either by popular election or, alternatively, by the governments of the provinces.

2. The electoral system by which members of the House of Commons are elected should be changed with the object of having the regional composition of the parties in the House reflect better their voter support within particular provinces and regions.

3. Party discipline in the House of Commons should be weakened to permit MPs to be more effective — and open — advocates of the interests of their localities, provinces and regions.

4. Changes should be made in the structures and processes of the executive to allow provincial and regional interests to be articulated more effectively by the cabinet and the federal public service.

Many of the intrastate reformers argue that, because the central government is insufficiently representative of and responsive to spatially-based interests and values, the provincial governments have emerged as the almost exclusive articulators of these concerns with the consequent provincializing of the federal system to an inappropriate degree.[7]

In summary, the parliamentary and federal divisions of the Canadian system of government have proved difficult to reconcile. The result of this difficulty has been to extend the scope of intergovernmental conflict over an increasing number of matters and to have such conflicts waged by increasingly integrated structures of executive power within these respective jurisdictions.

Executive Federalism and the Internal Structures of Executive Power

The relations between federal and provincial governments are decisively influenced by the way in which that power is organized within the federal and provincial executives. One way to get at this complex question is to outline briefly the various forms that the federal cabinet has taken in successive periods of Canadian history and to relate these forms to relations with the provinces.

1. *The cabinet as a "chamber of political compensation"*   Jean Hamelin wrote of the first federal cabinet:

> It would have been wrong to suppose that Macdonald was leading a centralized party. He was rather the chief of a coalition of groups in which each obeyed a regional leader, rather than Macdonald himself. To keep the confidence of the majority, Macdonald knew that he must negotiate with these leaders. In this spirit the cabinet was to be, in a certain sense, a chamber of political compensation, where the provincial spokesmen traded their support for national policies in return for concessions to their regions.[8]

Frederick W. Gibson described the cabinet's role under the conditions which might, for purposes of convenience, be said to have ended in 1918 with the establishment of the merit system in the federal civil service:

> Since there was little government, the burdens of administration and lawmaking were light and the leaders of the political party in power, the cabinet, devoted most of their time and energy to the intricate task of holding together a majority in the legislature and of employing, for this purpose, the patronage role at the disposal of the government. . . . Patronage was a national currency of political life and the power to dispense it was what for the most part gave the cabinet minister the authority and prestige that he desired.[9]

The era of the cabinet as "chamber of political compensation" was one in which governmental activities were limited and in which each order, for the most part, confined its action to matters conferred on it by the Constitution. Thus, although we have few detailed studies of federal-provincial executive relations in this earlier period, it appears that these relations, in contrast with later years, were sporadic and confined to a relatively small number of matters.

2. *The departmental cabinet*   The movement towards a more active federal state meant that cabinet ministers and the officials working under their direction would be more involved than before in the administration of particular programs and policies as authorized by law. However, in the period from the end of the First World War until roughly the end of the 1950s, there was little co-ordination of departmental activities on a jurisdiction-wide basis. Thus, each department,

and often agencies within departments, had a relatively wide scope of freedom in carrying out their respective functions. This fragmentation within the federal executive was buttressed by the circumstance that senior appointed officials characteristically pursued their careers within single departments or even their sub-units and were carriers of the interests, traditions, skills and memories of these particularized bureaucratic organizations.

The departmental cabinet regime was compatible with a complex of relations between federal and provincial governments oriented around particular public programs with little overhead control or co-ordination of such activities on a jurisdiction-wide basis. From the Second World War until 1960, there developed a very large number of conditional grant programs in respect to fairly well-defined provincial activities in health, social assistance, hospital insurance, forestry, the building of the Trans-Canada Highway, housing and so on.[10] For the most part, such joint activities were characterized by federal-provincial co-operation. The officials from both orders shared common professional norms and were aware that the participation of both governments influenced higher levels of public expenditure on the aided service than if the provinces alone were involved. During this period, public revenues were buoyant, and, most importantly, there was little effective federal resistance to Ottawa's taking on new financial responsibilities. On the provincial side, budgetary co-ordination and long-range budgetary planning were at an embryonic stage and so there was little provincial concern about the financial distortions in expenditures inherent in the grant-in-aid device.

3. *The collegial cabinet*   From the early 1960s onward, there were developments in Ottawa and in several of the provinces away from the fragmented and unco-ordinated structures of executive power that had grown up in the previous period of relative departmental autonomy. This complex development had several interrelated roots. In part, there was a reassertion here of control by cabinet ministers over the appointed bureaucracy. There were also new currents of thought critical of the haphazard and incremental nature of public policy. These suggested that the activities of each jurisdiction be perceived and organized as an integrated system. This system would have as its purposes: the specification and ranking of public objectives and the development of actual and projected programs using the most precise measurements available to determine their efficiency and effectiveness.[11] In Quebec, interventionist governments came to assert provincial autonomy as a prerequisite to the survival and integrity of that community and to structure governmental power in a more integrated way than before in pursuit of such autonomy; the responses to the new Quebec by other governments led to parallel developments in these jurisdictions.

Within individual governments, there were several institutional manifestations of the new and more integrated structures of executive power. Ministers became involved in the activities of departments other than their own through cabinet as such and, even more importantly, through cabinet committees.[12] New central agencies with jurisdiction-wide responsibilities were established and previously existent ones became more powerful, restricting departmental autonomy in the process. Super-ministries and ministries of state were developed whose major or exclusive role was the co-ordination of a comprehensive range of programs.

The impact of the new structures of executive power on federal-provincial relations was crucial. Officials and agencies concerned with particular programs came increasingly to lose their autonomy in interacting with their professional counterparts in the other order of government; in a complex and uneven way conditional grants for very specific purposes (which were the essential element of executive federalism from the Second World War onward) gave way first to subventions for much broader purposes, then to block grants and finally to unconditional fiscal transfers to the provinces. New departments and agencies responsible for federal-provincial relations as such were established and these, of course, restricted the freedom of program departments in intergovernmental relations. First ministers became more involved in the process than before, and increasingly, matters formerly dealt with at less senior levels of government came onto the agendas of meetings at the summit of the federal system.

I have outlined the development of the structures of executive power in a schematic way which does not do justice to the complexity of the process and which disregards the continuing residues of former circumstances in the progression from one stage to another. For example, in the last years of the Trudeau government, three ministers — Axworthy from Manitoba, LeBlanc from New Brunswick, and MacEachen from Nova Scotia — were able to channel federal resources to their respective provinces in a manner reminiscent of the days when the cabinet was a chamber of political compensation. Also, various departments and their constituent units retained a significant degree of autonomy; Richard J. Schultz has argued that the control of operating departments by central agencies has often been exaggerated by observers and that the former, particularly in the possession of specialized expertise and power over the flow of information, have important resources to sustain their independence.[13] Despite these qualifications, the more integrated structures of executive power came to be important determinants of the workings of executive federalism.

There is fragmentary evidence of a partial return to departmental autonomy and a more fragmented system of executive power. There has been a weakening of the heady faith of the late 1960s and early 1970s in the possibility or even the desirability of perceiving the organization of executive power on a jurisdiction-wide basis. Several of the co-ordinating ministries and agencies have been abolished and the power of others limited. Perhaps just as importantly, it is now taken for granted by governments that the Canadian Confederation will survive for the forseeable future and thus federal and provincial interests are pressed in a less ideological way.

Cairns and "The Other Crisis of Canadian Federalism"

In 1979, Alan Cairns published an article entitled "The Other Crisis of Canadian Federalism." It presented an extraordinarily pessimistic view of the contemporary federal system.[14] The crisis, as seen by Cairns, was a crisis of big governments, and it was argued that, "contemporary Canadian federalism makes a distinct contribution to the growth of the governments whose competitive tendencies it cannot effectively restrain or control." Thus:

Like lumbering mastodons in tireless competition these governments are possessed of an infinity of weapons capable of wreaking deliberate and inadvertent harm on each other, but incapable of delivering a knockout blow.

The federalism of contemporary big government at both levels can best be understood in terms of the tendency of each government to seek to minimize the policy contradictions in its own jurisdiction and reduce the environmental uncertainty emanating from the conduct of other governments. . . . Each government, in brief, strains, to exaggerate somewhat, to attain and exercise the powers of a unitary state. This tendency is unavoidable as long as each views the conduct of the other government as threatening to its own pursuits.

It is logically impossible for each government simultaneously to succed in controlling the environmental uncertainties caused by its rivals.[15]

Cairns' Hobbesian universe of Canadian federalism was premised on three assumptions, none of them completely defensible:

First, it was assumed that, in federal-provincial relations, governments perform as unitary actors. This is true in some circumstances, but not in others. Richard Schultz, in his case study of the politics of highway traffic regulation between 1966 and 1973, describes a process in which power within both orders of government was fragmented and, in particular, in which there was a very complex pattern of relations between central agencies of the federal government and federal operating agencies concerned with traffic regulation.[16] On the other hand, in Richard Simeon's analysis of "federal-provincial diplomacy" related to fiscal arrangements, public pensions and constitutional reform in the same period, governments did in fact perform as unitary actors.[17] More generally, the Cairns position can be criticized from the viewpoint of the "bureaucratic politics" model:

"It [the governments-as-unitary-actors model] obscures the persistently neglected fact of bureaucracy." The 'maker' of government policy is not one calculating decision-maker but rather a conglomerate of large organizations and political actors who differ substantially about what the government should do on any particular issue and who compete in attempting to affect both governmental decisions and the actions of their governments.[18]

Whether or not federal and provincial governments perform as unitary actors is a matter for investigation in particular circumstances; there is nothing inherent in the dynamics of Canadian executive federalism that they should always do so. There were powerful influences at work in Ottawa and most of the provinces during the late 1970s encouraging governments to act generally in the way Cairns described: the integration of executive power; both orders of government bidding for the allegiance of Canadians in circumstances under which Confederation appeared to be at risk; the expansion of the public sector and so on. However, there seems not to be as close a connection between big government as such and virulent intergovernmental conflict as he suggested.

Second, Cairns assumed that federal-provincial interactions were inherently zero-sum games in which there were no rewards for co-operation. These would be the circumstances in which the dominant objective of all governmental actors was to preserve and expand their own sphere of autonomy and where the actions of other governments were the major obstacles to these objectives. However, in some instances government officials may have other goals, and these goals may best be realized through intergovernmental collaboration. For example, in the period of 1950s and 1960s when conditional grants were more widespread and important than they later became, there were often co-operative patterns of relations between federal and provincial officials concerned with specialized programs or activities.[19] Donald Wallace has analysed the collaboration between federal and provincial agencies outside Canada in the promotion of trade and investment.[20] Many other examples could be given to demonstrate that intergovernmental relations are not always zero-sum games.

Third, Cairns appears to have assumed that governments had an inherent disposition always to extend the scope of their activities. This is by no means always so; for ideological and other reasons governments are sometimes disposed to cut back their scope of action. While a regime of such restraint is capable of generating its own kinds of intergovernmental tensions, these would be somewhat different from those described by Cairns. In particular terms, his analysis does not permit any plausible explanation of the dismantling of the National Energy Policy by the Mulroney Conservatives.

Industrial Strategy and Executive Federalism: The Thorburn and Jenkin Studies

During the past two decades or so there has been an enormous amount of debate about a coherent industrial strategy for Canada. A significant element of this debate has been concerned with the implications of the federal-provincial distribution of powers and federal-provincial relations for the design and implementation of such a strategy.

Within the general framework of the Keynesian imperatives accepted by Ottawa at the end of the Second World War, the federal government for more than a decade proved able to ensure relative price stability and relatively full employment.[21] The major instrument of federal management of the national economy was fiscal policy, and the central authorities were able to sustain widespread prosperity without concerning themselves with coherent attempts to shape the industrial structure. These circumstances ended in the late 1950s.

In the decade after the petroleum crisis brought on by the OPEC in 1973, the government of Canada undertook successive industrial strategies based on the exploitation of natural resources. Peter Leslie has succinctly summarized the earlier elements of such developments which culminated in the adoption of the National Energy Policy (NEP) in the fall of 1980: "over a period of about eight years (1973 to 1981) a policy was put in place that in effect imposed federal controls on provincial revenues from oil and gas production — presumably to be used in the interests of the consumers and industries of central Canada."[22]

In the wake of vigorous protests from the producing provinces and producer interests, Ottawa in 1981 concluded bilateral agreements with the former which significantly increased the domestic prices of oil and natural gas. The stage was then set for the so-called "mega-projects strategy" based on the following premises:

> [T]he leading opportunities for economic growth lay in the development of natural resources. This would require massive government-assisted investments in productive capacity and transport systems. Manufacturing industry would supply machinery, equipment, and materials needed for resource development, and would extend the processing of resources beyond the primary stage. In other words, though some expansion of manufacturing would occur in high-technology goods, the principal strategy for strengthening Canadian manufacturing would henceforth lie in building up linkages with the resource sector. Thus resource development and manufacturing would become complementary rather than competing, harmoniously integrating Canada's diverse regional economies.[23]

The resource-based strategies from 1973 onward assumed that the world prices of raw materials, most critically of energy, would continue to rise indefinitely relative to the prices of manufactured goods. When the reverse proved to be the case, some alternative industrial strategy was required. By the fall of 1985 the Mulroney government had eliminated the last remaining elements of the NEP and had committed itself to seeking a comprehensive free trade agreement with the United States. Just prior to this, two important studies of Canadian industrial strategy had been published: Michael Jenkin's *The Challenge of Diversity: Industrial Policy in the Canadian Federation*[24] and Hugh Thorburn's *Planning and the Economy: Building Federal-Provincial Consensus*[25]. The major focus of both these studies was the federal-provincial dimension of industrial strategy, and both were concerned about the absence of a coherent strategy under the circumstances of vigorous international competition. Both studies also outlined in some detail the relatively coherent industrial strategies of some of the provinces.

Unlike many other observers, Jenkin took a relatively sanguine view of provincial activities in industrial policy: *"Perhaps the best way to deal with the more active industrial-policy role played by the provinces is to view provincial industrial strategies as an opportunity rather than a liability in the creation of a stronger and more aggressive response in restructuring the national economy."*[26] However, "We should be concerned at the lack of a continuing mechanism to encourage consultation on industrial-policy issues." Thus:

> To guard against . . . unproductive competition, the federal government and the provinces should move rapidly to re-establish regular meetings of industry ministers and senior officials responsible for industry. . . . If possible, this group should have a small, permanent and independent secretariat providing a basic organizational capability for the council and *acting as a resource group* to explore possible areas of intergovernmental collaboration on industrial policy. . . . The council would provide the necessary infrastructure to pursue intergovernmental initiatives and ensure that some

administrative pressure is brought to bear on the governments to pursue cooperation.[27]

Two particular areas in which "unproductive competition" had prevailed were in government procurement and research and development policy.

In his review of the record Jenkin saw few possibilities for Ottawa and the provinces' coming to agreement on a comprehensive and coherent national industrial strategy. Thus:

> There does . . . seem to be an inexorable logic to the whole nature of intergovernmental relations and industrial policy. That logic is simply that, to be effective, relations should *either* be based on specific issues where there is some acceptance of the need for a common policy, or be primarily bilateral in nature (between individual provinces and the federal government) in order to simplify the negotiations and limit conflict. That is not to say that other forms of collaboration (for example, federal-provincial ministerial meetings) do not have their place. Indeed, they foster the communication that allows cooperation to develop even though they often do not permit forceful and coherent action.[28]

Thorburn is much more concerned than Jenkin with the lack of co-ordination between Ottawa and the provinces in industrial strategy. In Thorburn's view, we must put our economic house in order within the context of the international competition of such nations as France, Japan and West Germany who have done so and by the instrument of a coherent national plan. His diagnosis of the Canadian situation is this:

> At the heart of our difficulties is the fact that we have developed a relationship of deadlock that has set the pace for other relations, especially between business and government. This has prevented us from agreeing on our economic goals. Instead our attention has been drawn to the struggle between our governments. . . . We have allowed this sterile process to prevent us from making rational allocations of our resources, to plan for the maximization of productivity in order to succeed in the scramble that the international market has become.[29]

Thorburn's prescription is for "an overall, master plan within which the lower levels of economic activity fit as part of a whole." We thus require a single planning agency "at the apex of our national governmental structure." He elaborates:

> The agency would have to be *federal-provincial;* that is, it would have to answer to *both* levels of government. The secretariat would have to be led by a person enjoying the confidence and trust of *both* levels of government, who would offer leadership and diplomatic skills. There would be a directing council for the body, nominated in *equal* numbers by both levels of government and answering to their principals. The professional staff would be employed on the basis of their expertise, with an adequate support staff to assure their capacity to do their jobs effectively.[30]

rn has an overweening faith in the possibilities of rational planning. les, in a 1980 essay on successive national energy policies between .980 and the studies on which they were based, took an opposite view. Nelles demonstrated that the premises of successive national energy policies had uniformly proved to be invalid within a very short time — from the projections of a 1945 royal commission that national energy requirements would continue to decline and be met largely from coal, to the 1957 assumption that Canada had enough conventional oil reserves to meet its soaring energy needs for several centuries to the almost catastrophic views of an influential federal document of 1978 about Canada's energy future.[31] (As we have seen, national energy policies of the early 1980s were premised on the assumption that world energy prices, most critically petroleum prices, would continue to escalate indefinitely). Nelles concluded that because of the inherent deficiencies in energy forecasting, and because of provincial jurisdiction over resources, a coherent national energy policy is unattainable. His point is well taken. If then it is not within our capacity to arrive at a defensible national policy in respect to energy, we are even less able to do so in respect to the even more comprehensive planning recommended by Thorburn.

Even if we accepted Thorburn's faith in the possibilities of rational planning, there is nothing in the history of governmental conduct in Canada to suggest that either Ottawa or the provinces would be willing to surrender to a central planning agency the powers conferred on them by the Constitution. Industrial strategies in Canada involve essentially political factors unsusceptible to resolution as if they were technical matters. Past industrial strategies (for example, the National Policy of 1878 and the NEP of 1980) and projected strategies such as a comprehensive free trade agreement with the United States are inevitably regionally discriminatory, or are at least perceived as being so by certain regions of Canada. And under the federal regime those parts of the country which feel themselves left out or disadvantaged are served by provincial governments with the jurisdiction and the will to oppose such policies. Despite the heavy economic penalties Canadians may pay for the absence of a coherent national policy in industrial matters, Thorburn's quest for a federal-provincial consensus is the pursuit of a mirage.

The Virtues of Federal-Provincial Competition: The Macdonald Report

Much of the recent analysis of executive federalism has been critical of conflict in federal-provincial relations and has sought to overcome it. A contrary view arguing the advantages of such conflict was presented in the Report of the Royal Commission on the Economic Union and Development Prospects for Canada, published in the fall of 1985.[32] Albert Breton in a long Supplementary Statement to the Report made a vigorous case for "competitive" as opposed to "co-operative" federalism.[33]

So far as economic management is concerned, the Macdonald Commission suggests: "Federalism seems to be the enemy of policy that is planned, comprehensive, coherent, uniform and consistent."[34] There is little reason to believe

that "coherent planning would result from centralization" because of the underlying economic and social differences among Canada's regions and differences
among economic policy makers in the federal government. Thus: "In a country
as diverse as Canada, centralization would be a recipe for paralysis." However,
federalism has several advantages for effective economic management:

> It provides greater stability for diffusing conflict and expectations through-
> out the system. It offers the opportunity to tailor economic policies to the
> specific needs and concerns of citizens in different parts of the country. It
> minimizes the ever-present danger of the spectcular failure that can result
> when all the eggs are put in one basket. In a world of uncertainty and
> rapidly shifting economic challenges, where there is little understanding
> of what is likely to work best, it provides the opportunity for experiment
> and learning, for flexibility and inventiveness. It enhances sensibility to
> different viewpoints and permits canvassing of multiple sources of infor-
> mation and intelligence in different settings. We can try different methods
> of improving labour relations, for integrating education and training, for
> stimulating the flow of investment, and for diffusing technology. *Indeed,
> economic development in federations is likely to exceed that in centralized
> states as a result of the beneficial effects of competition in the public
> sector.*[35]

The general thrust of the commission's prescription for the reform of executive
federalism is in the direction of clarifying and regularizing the relations between
federal and provincial governments rather than replacing competition by co-
operation.[36] Such regularization would, it is hoped, weaken the bitter intergovernmental conflicts of the recent past "based primarily on concern for status."
To these general ends, certain reforms were recommended:

1. There should be some clarification of the respective powers of Ottawa and
the provinces, although the commission rejects radical constitutional amendments
embodying a comprehensive redistribution of legislative powers. The commission's recommendation for a federal Universal Income Security Program, with
other income assistance benefits paid by the provinces, would rationalize the
Canadian welfare state and clarify the respective responsibilities of Ottawa and
the provinces in respect to income assistance. There should also be some disentanglement of responsibilities for regional development through the federal
government's withdrawing from all "explicit and direct regional employment-
creation programs" and confining its regional activities enhancing the productivity and the efficiency of the labour market.

2. There should be a constitutional amendment permitting Parliament and the
provinces to delegate legislative powers to one another by mutual consent and
further amendment permitting the two orders to enter into agreements binding
their successors.

3. There should be a constitutional amendment providing that parts of a treaty
imposing obligations on the provinces would come into effect on the passage of
appropriate resolutions in the legislatures of two-thirds of the provinces representing at least half the population of all the provinces.

4. There should be a regularization of federal-provincial relations. A constitutional amendment should require an annual meeting of first ministers. Such a conference should appoint a network of ministerial councils related to finance, economic development and social policy, "to support first ministers in their individual and collective responsibilities."

5. The federal and provincial governments should develop a "Code of Economic Conduct" whose major purpose would be to reduce barriers to the allocation of capital, labour, goods and services within Canada. There would be a Federal-Provincial Commission on the Economic Union working under the Council of Economic Development to ensure adherence to the Code.

Albert Breton in this Supplementary Statement went much further than the other commissioners in providing a rationale for what he designated as "competitive federalism." Breton made a direct attack on "co-operative federalism" and on the general notion that relations between the two orders of government should be collaborative. "Co-operative federalism does not necessarily eliminate federalist competition, but by moving it into executive offices and bureaucratic offices and corridors, it mutes its public manifestations and its effectiveness. The heart of co-operative federalism is secret deals, not the stuff on which a lively democracy thrives!"[37] Further, "Co-operative federalism, because it prescribes unilateral action, is . . . a disguised ploy to shackle the federal government, to prevent it from addressing the problems it alone can resolve and is constitutionally responsible for resolving."[38]

Like the regime of markets in the sphere of private economic activity, competitive federalism is "not co-operation and not anarchy." The market system contributes to the maximization of individual preferences and to the well-being of the community under certain limiting conditions: that there be a precise definition of property rights, a degree of mutual trust among competitors and the monitoring of the competitive process by the public authorities. Similarly, competition among public authorities can make the political system more responsive than otherwise to the needs and wants of citizens. Breton opts squarely for a regime of checks and balances in which "more barriers have to be open, more hoops jumped, more obstacles circumvented and more impediments negotiated in an effort to obtain the passage and implementation of a piece of legislation than would be the case in a system in which [checks and balances] played a lesser role."[39] This pluralistic distribution of political power contributes to democratic values by reducing secrecy in government and by stimulating political participation and the discussion of public affairs. Checks and balance's also work in the direction of the more efficient exercise of government power. There will be fewer policy reversals as a consequence of changes in government. A pluralistic regime enhances the legitimacy of the political process, and, by reducing the differences between majorities and minorities, leads to consensus which makes policies and their implementation more successful.

Breton's prescriptions follow from his premises. Federal-provincial consultation should follow rather than, as now, precede debates on those matters in Parliament and the provincial legislatures. Party discipline in legislatures should be weakened. More information should be made available to the public. An elected Senate should be established with the primary role of giving "saliency to the provincial dimensions of public policies in the affairs of the national government.

Breton appears to believe that his regime of checks and balances is compatible with the continuance of parliamentary responsible government. This, in my view, is doubtful. The Westminster model is flexible — otherwise it could not have survived so long and in so many political circumstances in Canada and elsewhere — but it is not infinitely so, and its tendencies towards majoritarianism and the integrated structure of executive power are irreconcilable with the pluralism Breton desires.

Conclusions

The period between the early 1960s and the ascent to power of the Mulroney government in 1984 was characterized by intense and bitter conflict in federal-provincial relations. There were two interrelated sources of this conflict:

First, the ambience of federal-provincial relations became intensely ideological. To a greater or lesser extent, representatives of governments came to press their claims in terms of relatively coherent and contradictory views of the essential nature of the Canadian political community — views categorized by David Elkins and Richard Simeon as nation-centred, Quebec nation-centred and province-centred.[40] In the polarizing process it is almost impossible to exaggerate the personal influence of Pierre Trudeau with his penchant for debating even the most particularized matters within the framework of generalized concepts about the nature of the Canadian Confederation and his demonstrated capacity to keep federal questions at or near the top of the Canadian political agenda.

For the time being, the intense federal-provincial conflicts of the recent past, characterized by strong ideological commitments of the participants to contradictory views of what the Canadian political community is and should be are over; the rhetoric of federal-provincial relations is phrased in much less combative terms than before. There is some fragmentation of the integrated structures of executive power both in Ottawa and the provinces. Of course the relatively durable and persisting interests of particular provinces remain, as well as the inevitable need of Ottawa to defend its own concept of the national interest, however reluctant the Mulroney government has been to articulate a coherent formulation of this interest.

Second, and as we have seen, there were developments towards integrated systems of executive power on a jurisdiction-wide basis in both federal and provincial governments. Some of the impulses towards such developments arose from the ideological conflict which I have mentioned above in which governments sought to maximize their power in defence of what were perceived to be the most fundamental of interests; others were a reflection of the disposition to reject piecemeal and incremental ways of policy making and policy implementation. The net result was to decrease the capacity of the federal system to arrive at intergovernmental agreements about specific matters.

The recent Canadian experience with executive federalism suggests the following:

First, agreement between Ottawa and the provinces is more likely if their relations are "factored" than if most of the important interactions occur at or near the summit. This factoring may involve interactions between Ottawa and individual provinces rather than all the provinces,[41] or it may consist of intergovernmental relations among officials concerned with very specific programs as against broader aspects of public policy.

Second, agreement is more likely when participants of both orders of government are in continuous communication. Such consultation will not always lead to agreement, but, at a minimum, those involved will have a reasonably accurate perception of one another's interests and motivations.

Most of the analytical literature of executive federalism deprecates conflict and extols co-operation and collaboration. Breton, however, is perceptive in questioning this choice. In certain dimensions of our governmental system we accept competition as a norm: in elections, in the continuing confrontation between government and opposition in Parliament, in the adversarial proceedings of our courts. It is by no means self-evident that collaboration rather than competition should be the norm in intergovernmental relations.

Breton quite accurately asserts that co-operative federalism challenges key democratic values, that the heart of the system is "secret deals." It has long been recognized that shared jurisdiction and federal-provincial collaboration in matters of joint concern is to a greater or lesser degree incompatible with the effective accountability of governments to Parliament and the provincial legislatures; in such circumstances the legislature is reduced to *post hoc* debate on decisions already negotiated in the intergovernmental context, but perhaps we should not make too much of this dimension. Even in circumstances where only one jurisdiction is involved, the House of Commons and the provincial legislatures have not as yet developed ways to make governments effectively accountable. A more important consideration here is that federal-provincial co-operation contributes to secrecy in the governmental process and to the frustration of public debate about important aspects of our common affairs. Breton points out that, "in the present [federal] Access to Information Act, federal-provincial communications are accorded a status equal to that of national security."[42] Reginald Whitaker has written: "Democratic federalism involves elite competition to mobilize support from overlapping electorates."[43] Obviously, when governments can come to agreement without the necessity of appealing to wider publics for the latter's support, such debate and discussion is frustrated.

The Macdonald Commission made a persuasive case for regularizing the structures and processes of executive federalism. An important element of our governmental system has grown up piecemeal, and efforts should be made to regularize its workings. Successful efforts to regularize this process would in themselves do something to depress the less constructive aspects of federal-provincial conflict.

Now, if only a variant of executive federalism, characterized by a high degree of federal-provincial competition, is compatible with democratic values, does this not mean that Canadians must choose between democracy and effective government? Only if we have the alternative of national public policies which are, in the words of the Macdonald Commission, "planned, comprehensive, coherent, uniform and consistent." However, this alternative is probably not available, or, if available, only at the price of federal-provincial conflict which might destroy Confederation. Advocates of planning have an overweening faith in the capacity of human beings to contrive and implement coherent and comprehensive schemes in a volatile world and a pronounced disposition to minimize the possibilities of piecemeal adjustments in such a world. Furthermore, at least so far as comprehensive economic strategies are concerned, almost any conceivable formulation of the national interest will be regionally discriminatory, or will be perceived as such by governments and residents of particular provinces.

In less abstract terms, the new era of executive federalism has been marked by the resignation or retirement of several of the most powerful actors from the preceding period. Pierre Trudeau resigned in mid-1984, and within less than 18 months the three most powerful first ministers involved in the events of the immediately preceding years also left office — William Davis, Peter Lougheed and René Lévesque. Similarly, several of the most powerful appointed officials in federal-provincial relations are now elsewhere — Claude Morin, Gordon Robertson, Peter Meekison and Thomas Shoyama. Executive federalism was and is significantly shaped by the complex interplay of human personalities, and a new group of dominant actors are now in place.

Notes

1. Michael Jenkin, *The Challenge of Diversity: Industrial Policy in the Canadian Federation* (Ottawa: Science Council of Canada, Minister of Supply and Services Canada, 1983), p. 101.
2. Richard Simeon, *Federal-Provincial Diplomacy* (Toronto: University of Toronto Press, 1972).
3. A. H. Birch, *Representative and Responsible Government,* reprint (Toronto: University of Toronto Press, 1969), p. 243.
4. Gordon Robertson, "The Role of Interministerial Conferences in the Decision-Making Process," in Richard Simeon, ed., *Confrontation and Collaboration — Intergovernmental Relations in Canada Today* (Toronto: Institute of Public Administration of Canada, 1979), pp. 78–88.
5. *Report of the Royal Commission on the Economic Union and Development Prospects for Canada,* Vol. 3 (Ottawa: Minister of Supply and Services Canada 1985), pp. 152–153.
6. For a detailed analysis see Donald V. Smiley and Ronald L. Watts, *Intrastate Federalism,* vol. 39 of the research studies prepared for the Royal Commission on the Economic Union and Development Prospects for Canada (Toronto: University of Toronto Press, 1985). The most persuasive case made for intrastate federalism in Canada is Roger Gibbins, *Regionalism: Territorial Politics in Canada and the United States* (Toronto: Butterworth, 1982).
7. The analysis in this section and, indeed, this chapter as a whole owes much to the imaginative essay by J. Stefan Dupré, "Reflections on the Workability of Executive Federalism," in Richard Simeon, research co-ordinator, *Intergovernmental Relations,* vol. 63 of the research studies prepared for the Royal Commission on the Economic Union and Development Prospects for Canada (Toronto: University of Toronto Press, 1985), pp. 1–32.
8. Jean Hamelin, *First Years of Confederation,* Centennial Historical Booklet, No. 3 (Ottawa: The Centennial Commission, 1967), pp. 3–4.
9. Frederick W. Gibson, "Conclusions," in Frederick W. Gibson, ed., *Cabinet Formation and Bicultural Relations,* studies of the Royal Commission on Bilingualism and Biculturalism (Ottawa: Queen's Printer, 1970), p. 171.
10. Donald V. Smiley, *Conditional Grants and Canadian Federalism* (Toronto: Canadian Tax Foundation, 1963).
11. For this kind of analysis see *Design for Decision-Making,* Eighth Annual Review, Economic Council of Canada (Ottawa: Information Canada, 1971) and *Report,* Committee on Government Productivity (Toronto: 1973).

12. See Thomas Hockin, ed., *Apex of Power: The Prime Minister and Political Leadership in Canada,* 2d ed. (Scarborough: Prentice-Hall Canada, 1977), essays by Pitfield, Sharp, Hockin, Doern, Szablowski and Schultz.

13. Richard J. Schultz, *Federalism, Bureaucracy and Public Policy: The Politics of Highway Transport Regulation* (Montreal and Kingston: McGill-Queen's University Press, 1980), pp. 182–186.

14. Alan C. Cairns, "The Other Crisis of Canadian Federalism," *Canadian Public Administration* 22, no. 2 (Summer 1979): pp. 175–195.

15. Ibid., pp. 191–192.

16. Schultz, *Federalism, Bureaucracy and Public Policy.*

17. Simeon, *Federal-Provincial Diplomacy.*

18. Gordon T. Allison and Morton Halperin, "Bureaucratic Politics: A Paradigm and Some Policy Implications," *World Politics,* 24, Supplement (Spring 1972): p. 42. Quoted in Schultz, *Federalism, Bureaucracy and Public Policy,* p. 5.

19. Smiley, *Conditional Grants and Canadian Federalism.*

20. Donald Wallace, *Provincial Control Agencies for Intergovernmental Relations and the Policy Process,* Unpublished doctoral dissertation, York University, 1985.

21. Robert M. Will, *Canadian Fiscal Policy 1945–63,* Studies of the Royal Commission on Taxation (Ottawa: Queen's Printer, 1966).

22. Peter M. Leslie, "The State of the Federation 1985," in Peter M. Leslie, ed., *Canada: The State of the Federation 1985* (Kingston: Queen's University, Institute of Intergovernmental Relations, 1985), p. 11. For an excellent analysis of the NEP see G. Bruce Doern and Glen Toner, *The Politics of Energy: The Development and Implementation of the NEP* (Toronto: Methuen, 1985).

23. Leslie, "State of the Federation," p. 11.

24. Jenkin, *Challenge of Diversity,* note 1.

25. Hugh C. Thorburn, *Planning and the Economy: Building Federal-Provincial Consensus* (Ottawa: Canadian Institute for Economic Policy, 1984).

26. Ibid., p. 172. Italics in original.

27. Ibid., p. 175.

28. Ibid., p. 143.

29. Ibid., p. 242.

30. Ibid., p. 213. Italics in original.

31. H. V. Nelles, "Canadian Energy Policy 1945–1980: A Federalist Perspective," in R. Kenneth Carty and W. Peter Ward, eds., *Entering the Eighties: Canada in Crisis* (Toronto: Oxford University Press, 1980), pp. 91–119.

32. *Report of the Royal Commission on the Economic Union and Development Prospects for Canada,* Vol. 3 (Ottawa: Privy Council of Canada, 1985), pp. 146–148.

33. Ibid., pp. 486–526.

34. Ibid., p. 147.

35. Ibid., p. 148. Reproduced with permission of the Minister of Supply and Services Canada.

36. Ibid., pp. 251–272.

37. Ibid., p. 493.

38. Ibid., p. 493.

39. Ibid., p. 498.

40. David J. Elkins and Richard Simeon, *Small Worlds: Provinces and Parties in Canadian Political Life* (Toronto: Methuen, 1980), pp. 299–309.

41. On bilateral relations between individual provinces and the federal government see Kenneth McRoberts, "Unilateralism, Bilateralism and Multilateralism: Approaches to Canadian Federalism," in Richard Simeon, research coordinator, *Intergovernmental Relations,* vol. 63 of the research studies prepared for the Royal Commission on the Economic Union and Development Prospects for Canada (Toronto: University of Toronto Press, 1985), pp. 78–93.

42. Ibid., p. 504.

43. Reginald Whitaker, *Federalism and Democratic Theory,* Institute Discussion Paper (Kingston: Queen's University, Institute of Intergovernmental Relations, 1983), p. 35.

V

Political Parties and the Federal System

It is only recently that scholars of federalism have turned their attention to political parties. Prior to the 1960s, a university course in Canadian federalism would in all likelihood have focused almost exclusively on two matters: the judicial interpretation of the BNA Act and the financial and administrative relations between the Dominion and the provinces. If anything at all were said about parties, it would probably have been to the effect that the Liberals and Conservatives by acting as brokers among divisive cultural and regional interests had played and were playing a nationally integrative role.

Parties and the Canadian Federal System: General Perspectives

In his book, *Federalism: Origins, Operations, Significance,* published in 1964, William H. Riker broke with previous scholarship by giving a political explanation for the establishment and maintenance of federal systems[1] According to Riker, the original federal bargains were hammered out among politicians who had conflicting but reconcilable dispositions towards territorial expansion without the use of military force and regional autonomy within the security of a larger union. However, once a federal bargain is concluded, will it be sustained in a centralized or a "peripheralized" form? This answer is given:

> The federal relationship is centralized or peripheralized according to the degree to which the parties organized to operate the national government control the parties organized to operate the constituent governments. This amounts to the assertion that the proximate course of variations in the degree of centralization (or peripheralization) in the constitutional structure of a federalism is the variation in the degree of party centralization.[2]

Riker's analysis is suggestive in turning our attention to the role of parties in shaping the forms in which federal systems are sustained, and on first reading it appears to be valid. For example, most informed observers agree that, because of the overriding powers of the Communist Party, the USSR is not a genuine federation despite some federal elements in its constitution. The centralizing thrust of the constitution of India has been buttressed by the capacity of the Congress and later the Congress (I) parties to control the parties and the governments of the same persuasion in the states. In the Canadian case, the growing strength and assertiveness of the provincial governments in the 1960s and 1970s coincided with the development of federal parties largely or wholly independent of their provincial wings. On the other hand, there is a relatively high degree of governmental centralization in Australia despite the strength of the extra-parliamentary elements of the state parties relative to the national parties.

Although it has a degree of plausibility, Riker's analysis is quite deficient in its neglect of the role which parties do play in federal systems; particularly the relation between the processes of centre-state partisan interactions and other processes such as judicial review and intergovernmental relations. In an article published in 1979, John Meisel outlined a complex of circumstances which, he argued, were leading to "the relative decline of parties in Canada"[3]: the shift in the locus of power from politicians to appointed public officials; the increasing involvement of interest groups in the making of public policy and the disposition of an increasing number of citizens to participate in politics through membership in interest groups rather than parties; "federal-provincial diplomacy"; and the rise of the electronic media. This kind of analysis is useful in alerting us to the roles which parties actually do perform.

There are four major elements in a party operating within a liberal democratic polity:

1. Those citizens who with greater or lesser degrees of intensity and continuity identify with the party,

2. Those elements of the extra-parliamentary party made up mainly of persons for whom partisan politics is a part-time activity,

3. The party professionals who have specialized skills in the measurement of public opinion, political advertising and voter mobilization and

4. Those members of the party who hold elective office in legislatures and/ or governments.

With only a few qualifications, the following four generalizations can be made about the division of labour among these elements in the Canadian political parties:

1. The Canadian electorate is volatile in its party allegiances. The record is summed up in a recent study: "[M]ost Canadians assess political parties in terms of transitory factors associated with elections (leaders, candidates, issues, performance in government, etc.) rather than basing their evaluations on longer-lasting perceptions of parties' ideologies or group linkages."[4] As we shall see, one dimension of this volatility is the disposition of a large proportion of the electorate to support one party in federal elections and another in provincial elections.

2. The extra-parliamentary elements of the party who serve for the most part on a part-time basis virtually monopolize the role of nominating candidates for election to the House of Commons[5] and provincial legislatures, and to national and provincial party leadership. These elements play an important role in electoral campaigning, although they have lost ground here to the professionals with specialized skills in these matters.

3. The political professionals are the newest of actors in partisan politics, and they have come to play an increasingly important role not only in the organization of election campaigns but also in advising government and opposition parties as to what positions they should take in respect to policy matters.

4. Those elected to public office almost monopolize the role of enunciating party policies. Although leaders of these parties will often manifest a degree of sensitivity to members of their respective caucuses, they have an enormous range of discretion in formulating and committing their parties to particular policies, a discretion largely unfettered by coherent ideological commitments or directives from the extra-parliamentary elements of the party.

Confederal and Integrated Party Systems: Ideal Types

Integrated

1. *Electoral dependence*   National and provincial parties of the same designation draw very largely on common voter allegiances. When there are shifts in voter support at one level, these are characteristically followed by shifts in the same direction at the other level in subsequent elections.

2. *The nominating function*   A common set of procedures is employed to nominate party candidates for national and provincial elective office and to choose national and provincial party leaders.

3. *The policy function*   There are effective procedures for committing the national and provincial wings of the parties to common policies.

4. *The campaign function*   A common party organization contests both national and provincial elections.

5. *Party careers*   Those who pursue elective careers characteristically move between provincial and national office.

6. *Party finance*   The financial resources at the disposal of the national and provincial parties are distributed by intra-party procedures between the national and provincial wings.

7. *Party ideology*   The national and provincial elements of particular parties share common ideologies which distinguish them from other parties in the political system.

8. *Party symmetry*   The same national and provincial parties are the major political competitors at both levels.

Confederal

1. *Electoral dependence*   National and provincial parties have significantly different bodies of voter allegiance. Changes in electoral support for parties characteristically arise from circumstances primarily at one level only and are thus not accompanied by changes in the same direction at the other level.

2. *The nominating function*   There are two autonomous sets of nominating arenas for national and provincial elective office and for national and provincial party leadership.

3. *The policy function*   The national and provincial parties of the same designation are committed to policies without the decisive influence of one over the other.

4. *The campaign function*   There are different party organizations for contesting national and provincial elections.

5. *Party careers*   Party careerists characteristically fulfil their ambitions by contesting elections at either the national or provincial level.

6. *Party finance*   The national and provincial wings draw their financial resources from sources independent of one another.

7. *Party ideology*   The national and provincial parties often differ in their ideologies.

8. *Party symmetry*   In some or most of the provinces the major party competitors are different from those at the national level.

   The analysis which follows applies these two ideal types to the Canadian party system with emphasis on the two major national parties.

Voting Behaviour and the Federal System

Federalism is about territorialism. One index of the extent to which territorially-based cleavages have yielded to those on other axes is the convergence or non-convergence in the voting behaviour in national elections of state or provincial electorates. Richard Johnston has thus summarized this dimension of voting behaviour in the United Kingdom and the United States: "In this century local and regional differences in these countries' voting patterns have diminished. Average differences between regions are now relatively small and respond to short-term political forces, the interelection swing relatively more uniform across locales."[6] According to evidence from federal elections in Canada between 1878 and 1974 inclusive, this kind of national integration has not taken place, and, in fact, the standard deviation as applied to the two major parties is greater than it was a century ago.

   In terms of the analysis of this chapter, the major variable is the integration of voting behaviour along federal-provincial lines. By this standard, an integrated party system in a federation would be one in which the major contenders in federal elections would be the major contenders in provincial/state elections and in which shifts in the voting behaviour of provincial/state electorates at one level would be reflected by changes in the same direction and of the same order of magnitude at the other. Johnston measures this latter dimension in Canada in the period 1908–1974 by what he calls an "Index of Dissimilarities" defined as "the minimum percentage of the province's electorate that would have to be relocated between parties to transform the provincial outcome into the federal one, or vice versa."[7] The evidence presented is very complex, but the conclusion reached is that, apart from Quebec and British Columbia, there has been a positive correlation between federal and provincial results, with such correlations being stronger among the New Democratic Party (NDP) and the Progressive Conservatives than the Liberals. So far as the latter party is concerned, the correlation which was very strong in the 1908–1945 period in all provinces but Ontario and Prince Edward Island weakened between 1949 and 1974, with the correspondence being strong in only Alberta and Manitoba.[8]

Johnston attempts an explanation of the differences in federal and provincial voting choices within the provinces. He rejects the hypothesis of "selective abstention" according to which most of these differences can be attributed to voters who cast their ballots at one level but do not vote at the other. Thus, these variations are, in the main, the result of the same persons changing their partisan preferences in federal and provincial elections. Who are the switchers? One line of thought suggests that most switchers are, politically, a bit apathetic and another that they are better informed, are more critical voters. Johnston's evidence denies both these contradictory hypotheses: "[P]olitical involvement has little obvious and interpretable effect on the magnitude of most federal-provincial differences. The citizens who create the aggregate vote differences within the provinces come from the most active and involved to the most apathetic."[9] Neither is the propensity to switch strongly correlated with particular occupational groups. Of all the usual demographic variables, religion is the best predictor of Canadian voting behaviour, although there is an ongoing debate among political scientists as to why this is so.[10] However, federal and provincial shifts are "differentiated by religion, but only to a modest degree," with these groups having the longest history of religious antipathy, Roman Catholics and Protestants, less disposed towards switching than those "groups whose arrival in Canada is more recent, or for whom the religious struggle has been irrelevant."[11]

Another way of examining the orientation of citizens to the federal-provincial dimension of the party system is through their identification with parties. In terms of evidence from three national samples taken in 1974, 1979 and 1980, Harold Clarke and his colleagues concluded: "Only a minority of respondents. . . report feeling the same degree of attachment to the same party at both the federal and provincial levels. Ignoring intensity, two-thirds of Canadians are consistent across level with regards to direction of partisanship alone."[12] There is, not surprisingly, a substantial variation in the degree of cross-level consistency (in both direction and intensity) varying from a low of 27 per cent in British Columbia to a high of 68 per cent in Prince Edward Island.

The voting behaviour and party identifications of Canadians thus inclines towards the confederal rather than the integrated form. Despite the fragmentation of the American party system and what many informed observers regard as the declining role of parties, the voter is faced with a single ballot including the names of national, state and party officials with the consequent complex patterns of interdependence among candidates for office at the three levels. In Canada this is not so, and elections for federal, provincial and local office take place at different times and under different administrative auspices. So far as federal-provincial voting and party allegiances are concerned, it may be conjectured that a large number of citizens perceive that there are discrete political arenas in which, almost coincidentally, autonomous federal and provincial parties bear the same designation. As we shall see, such a perception would not be totally inaccurate.

The Nominating Function

In Canada, as in other Western democracies, those who successfully contest elective office in governmental institutions are almost always persons with the franchise of an organized political party. Thus, the way that parties perform the nominating function is crucial, and in the context of this analysis, the relation of the federal and provincial wings of the parties is of great importance.

The extra-parliamentary elements of Canadian political parties come into their own, so to speak, in the nomination of candidates for seats in the House of Commons and the provincial legislatures and in their choice of federal and provincial party leaders.

The nomination process for seats in the House of Commons and in provincial legislatures is highly decentralized.[13] There have been deviations from this general norm: in the 1935 Alberta elections, potential Social Credit candidates chosen by local associations were screened by the party leader, and in the Smallwood era in Newfoundland, the premier himself selected federal Liberal candidates. Federal and provincial party leaders do, from time to time, attempt to influence constituency organizations in the choice of candidates, particularly in trying to secure nominations for notables or other persons which the leadership for one reason or other wants to be elected. However, it is not uncommon for such involvement to be resisted by local riding organizations, and those most successful in doing so will be, understandably, in ridings where the chances of the party's candidate being elected are greatest. Further, under federal legislation, candidates of parties are required to have the endorsement of the parties' national leaders, although this endorsement is, in almost all cases, a ratification of the choices made by the riding organizations.

There have not been, so far as I know, any systematic studies of the degree to which there is overlapping membership in the federal and provincial constituency organizations of the parties. It is reasonable to suppose that a considerable overlapping occurs, perhaps to a considerably greater extent in the NDP than in the other parties. However, the process at both levels is highly decentralized, and in particular, there are few, if any, effective channels for federal leaders or federal party organizations to influence the choice of party nominees for provincial elective office or the reverse.

Beginning with the Liberals in 1919 and the Conservatives in 1927, the major national parties have elected their leaders through national conventions.[14] The NDP selects its leader in the same way, and at each of its biennial conventions the party leader is elected or re-elected. The current provisions governing leadership review differ between the major parties. Section 14.01 of the constitution of the Libertal Party of Canada provides that: "A resolution calling for a leadership convention shall be placed automatically on the agenda of the convention [which must be held at least once every two years] next following a federal general election. If such a resolution is duly adopted by secret ballot, the national executive shall call a leadership convention to take place within one year from the date of the above-mentioned secret ballot." Sub-section 3 of Article II of the constitution of the Progressive Conservative Association of Canada provides: "At the first lawfully convened general meeting of the Association after a federal general election in which the Party did not form the government, and only at such a meeting [such meetings must be held every two years], the voting delegates shall be asked by secret ballot, 'Do you wish to have a leadership convention?' In the event that fifty per cent (50%) of the votes cast indicate desire for a leadership convention, the Executive Committee shall call a leadership convention at the earliest time." The Progressive Conservative conventions in effect deposed John Diefenbaker in 1967 and Joe Clark in 1983.

The most recent national leadership conventions of the Liberal and Progressive Conservative parties were each composed of nearly 3000 delegates. About three-fifths of these were chosen from local constituency associations; the rest were *ex-officio* delegates or those chosen by other organizations of the parties. The two parties differ significantly in the ways they provide for the representation of provincial party organizations. Under the Liberal constitution, the party leader in each province is to be a delegate, along with four members of the executive of each of the provincial associations and of those in the Yukon and Northwest Territories and also:

> The Liberal members of each provincial or territorial assembly and the Liberal candidates defeated in the last provincial or territorial election in each province or territory or new candidates nominated, acting jointly, shall have the right to select from among themselves a number of delegates equal to one-fourth of the total of each provincial or territorial assembly.

The Progressive Conservative constitution provides for the membership in conventions of: (a) all elected Conservative members of provincial or territorial legislatures and (b) "Presidents in each province and territory of the recognized Progressive Conservative association, Progressive Conservative Women's organization and Progressive Conservative Youth Organization."

The national party leadership conventions are perhaps the least federalized of Canadian political institutions; party influentials organized for success in the provincial electoral arenas are, in general, not the decisive participants in this process. In fact, the voting rules of the conventions — successive secret ballots with the expectation that it will require more than one ballot to select a leader — mean that it is extraordinarily difficult to build coalitions under the control of influential figures in the party, whether they are from the provincial arenas or otherwise. Furthermore, there are incentives for provincial leaders not to involve themselves too overtly in these processes and thus maintain harmony in their own governments and/or parties.

The provincial parties select their leaders by processes basically similar to those of the national conventions. Although these provincial conventions have not been systematically studied, it appears that party members and party influentials oriented mainly towards federal electoral competition do not play an important role in such conventions.

In general, then, the nominating process is a powerful influence in the confederalization of the Canadian political party.

The Policy Function

In Canada the two major parties do not have national organizations which commit them to common party policies at both the federal and provincial levels. The federal and provincial party leaders have a wide degree of freedom to formulate and enunciate policies; they are relatively unencumbered by the extra-parliamentary elements of the parties and completely without the need to take the party's fortunes at the other level into account.

The cross-cutting of party lines on an important set of policy issues was dramatically illustrated by the conflicts related to the introduction into Parliament of the resolution on constitutional reform by the Trudeau government in October 1980:

1. Support for the Resolution came from the Progressive Conservative governments of New Brunswick and Ontario.

2. The provincial "gang of eight" which opposed the federal measure included governments of no fewer than four partisan complexions: five Progressive Conservative, one Parti Québécois, one NDP and one Social Credit.

3. Although the NDP is the most integrated of the parties, the action of the federal caucus in supporting the resolution — with open opposition from some western MPs — was opposed by the NDP government of Saskatchewan and the provincial party in Alberta, and it received lukewarm support from the NDP opposition in British Columbia.

4. The resolution was opposed by the provincial Liberals in Quebec.

5. Although the Progressive Conservative Opposition in Parliament opposed the "unilateral" nature of the federal resolution, it diverged from the dissident provinces in concentrating its efforts on changing particular clauses in the Charter of Rights and Freedoms.

The Campaign Function and Party Organization

The two major Canadian parties were late in developing extra-parliamentary organizations. Up until the Second World War these were almost classically cadre parties, congeries of members of Parliament and the provincial legislatures related to local party activists through the glue of patronage. The more recent period has seen the ongoing modernization and institutionalization of the Liberals and Progressive Conservatives. Through the recent books of Reginald Whitaker,[15] Joseph Wearing,[16] David Smith[17] and Christina McCall-Newman[18], we now know a good deal about this process within the Liberal party, particularly in terms of the focus of this chapter, about the federal-provincial dimension of party organization. Much less analysis has been done of the Progressive Conservatives and the NDP. However, the circumstance that the Liberal party has formed the government of Canada for the better part of the twentieth century makes their experience crucial to understanding the interactions between the party system and Canadian federalism.

Until the past generation, persons other than members of Parliament or the provincial legislatures did not play a crucial role in party strategy or party organization. There were some exceptions to this: Richard Bell for the Conservatives and Norman Lambert and Vincent Massey for the Liberals. However, it was only in 1961, with the appointment of Keith Davey as the national director of the Liberal party, that an extra-parliamentary official came to play a central role in either of the major parties.

Under the older system, when a party was in office the prime minister, along with his cabinet colleagues from the various provinces and regions, dominated party organization and activity, including in many cases the affairs of the provincial wings of the party. Wearing describes these relations which were perpetuated among the Liberals through the St. Laurent period which ended in 1957:

> From the days of Laurier, a system had evolved whereby key cabinet ministers from the various provinces took responsibility for party matters in their own bailiwicks. The minister kept in touch with the MPs and defeated Liberal candidates in his province or region, looked for promising candidates, held nomination meetings, and was consulted by other ministers over the distribution of patronage in his area. Particularly in the later King ministries, these political lieutenants exercised formidable political power in their own right: such men as Fielding, Ralston and Ilsley from the Maritimes; Lapointe, Claxton and Power from Quebec; Murphy, Howe and Martin from Ontario; Dunning, Crerar and Gardiner from the Prairies.[19]

Wearing points out that under King this kind of ministerialist organization was supplemented by the party leader's informal network of personal contacts throughout the country which gave him a source of political information "very different from what came to him from the civil service, cabinet, or even caucus."

The defeats of the Liberals in the 1957 and 1958 general elections led to significant changes in the organization of the national party. Most of the powerful party figures who had been ministers in the St. Laurent government had passed from the political scene, and the new party leader, Lester Pearson, was both uninterested in party affairs and willing to give at least half-hearted support to those who wished to effect radical changes in party organization. The impetus for such reforms, as well as for the later attempts to democratize the party after its victory under Pierre Trudeau, came from a relatively cohesive group of Liberals from Toronto whose most influential figures were Walter Gordon, Keith Davey and Richard Stanbury.

The changes in Liberal party organization, which were well in place by the time of the 1962 election, were in the general direction of modernization and centralization of national campaign direction in the hands of those chosen by the party leader. In the affairs of the party there was now more emphasis on policy formulation than before and among the reformers a marked distaste for patronage or the promises of patronage as a method of gaining party support. There was a much-enhanced reliance on modern techniques of political organization as developed in the United States: the extensive use of opinion polling; campaign schools for party candidates; the more sophisticated use of advertising and more rationalistic methods of allocating campaign resources. In terms of the focus of this section, the most important reforms were those of putting federal campaign activity in each province under a chairman appointed by the party leader and a national campaign committee also appointed by Lester Pearson and responsible for the leader's activities and party policy matters. Of course, this centralized pattern of control left little decisive influence in federal campaigns for the provincial wings of the party. Davey and his supporters were able to frustrate any return to the former ministerialist patterns when the party came to power as a result of the 1963 election.

The second wave of party reforms was in the general direction of attempts to democratize the party after the 1968 election and was led by Richard Stanbury, national president of the party between 1968 and 1973. According to the analysis of Stanbury and his supporters, the party had to be radically reformed to make it a more effective register and transmitter of public opinion. The Liberal party had to extend itself to encompass a very large number of emergent 'publics' not traditionally involved in partisan politics. To accomplish these ends, a complex framework of provincial and local policy committees was established. A high point of this exercise was the Harrison Hot Springs Conference of 1969 bringing together experts and representatives of the riding organizations to discuss policy. In general, the attempt to democratize the party and to give it more of a voice in policy formulation was a failure, largely because of the refusal of the government to share this function with the extra-parliamentary party and the reluctance of local party organizations to become enthusiastically involved in policy matters.

By the time of the 1972 election, the control of Liberal campaign activity had come to reside largely in the Prime Minister's Office (PMO). After that election in which the party was reduced to a minority position in the House of Commons, Trudeau established a system in which each cabinet minister was given a designated number of ridings which he or she was to visit each six months, and a senior member of the minister's staff was to visit each non-Liberal riding at least every two months.[20] On the basis of this kind of party activity, ministers were required to submit bi-monthly reports to the prime minister on their assigned ridings. According to Stephen Clarkson, by the time of the 1979 elections, appointed officials of the PMO had come to supervise this political activity of ministers, with delinquents being "chided by the prime minister in personal audiences."[21] It is almost redundant to suggest that the regional party chieftains of a previous era would never have tolerated this kind of detailed supervision of their partisan activities by appointed officials or even perhaps by the party leader himself.

David Smith has made a detailed and persuasive case that the organizational reforms effected in the Liberal party in the 1960s and 1970s were instrumental in the decline of both federal and provincial wings of the party in the Prairie provinces.[22] In larger part this decline is attributable to the overwhelmingly urban preoccupations of the Liberal reformers and their insensitivity to the concerns of westerners for agriculture and resource development, but in a sense the displacement of ministerialism was also crucial:

> If it was true that the former 'barons' had adopted a narrow outlook on the nature of political rule, this perspective was not wholly without redeeming features. As intermediaries, cabinet ministers might complicate political strategy; they might even distort national priorities — for with them politics was never tidy — but they were nonetheless keen interpreters of the local scene and, in return, committed spokesmen for party policies. Vertical integration, with a federal cabinet minister lord of the organization, was never free from friction even where it worked well, as in Saskatchewan. Yet, there were reciprocal benefits at both levels, especially when the Liberals were in power in each. Even when the provincial party was in opposition, it could still claim a share of patronage as well as an influence over federal policy.[23]

The more rationalistic thrust of the new campaign strategies also resulted in the relative neglect of western concerns as appeals were made to larger concentrations of voters in central Canada. The attempted democratization of the party in accord with the Stanbury reforms also contributed to the decline of the Liberals on the Prairies:

> Participating democracy depended upon co-operation attained through agreement on ends. It assumed a community of interest which, between federal and provincial Liberals, proved difficult to achieve, especially at a time when the grasp of the provinces grew about as fast as their reach. Participating democracy depreciated the effects of federal-provincial rivalry, jealousy and conflict. Where Liberals wanted the partisan equivalent of Canada's increasingly decentralized federation, participatory democracy sought to bring them closer together. Local Liberals wanted greater freedom to manage their own affairs, a desire as basic to them as it was antithetical to those responsible for the health of the federal party.[24]

Within the Liberal party, a formal organizational separation of the federal and provincial wings has developed. This was accomplished in Quebec in 1964 under pressures from the new reform-minded Liberals in the provincial party, at a time when the national party was still dominated by the more traditional elements and when policy differences between the two Liberal governments were intense. The separation of the federal and Ontario Liberals came in 1976 under pressure from the provincial party, which had been reduced to third place in the legislature in the election of the preceding year and had become convinced both that the federal tie was a political embarrassment and that the national party had done little to assist its provincial counterparts. In Alberta, where the provincial Liberals are an insignificant political force, a separation on the Ontario-Quebec model was effected in 1977 under the urging of the new leader Nick Taylor to rid the party ''of the albatross of having to explain every asinine move Ottawa makes.'' The provincial Liberals in the other western provinces are very weak and although there is no formal organizational separation from the federal party, the relations between the two elements are not harmonious; the situation of these provincial parties is vastly complicated by the left-right polarization which is the major axis of political conflict in the politics of Manitoba, Sasketchewan and British Columbia. In the Maritimes there is a close integration of the federal and provincial Liberals.

Although there is little published information on this aspect of the modern Progressive Conservative party, there appear to have been few, if any, of the kind of pressures for the organizational separation of the federal and provincial wings which have been evident among the Liberals. The parliamentary and extra-parliamentary elements of the federal Progressive Conservatives are devoted almost exclusively to the pursuit of power at the national level. However, because the party is a significant political force in all the provinces but Quebec and British Columbia (and now forms the government in five of these provinces) the national party is dependent to a very large degree on the support of provincial Conservatives leaders and their party organizations in federal elections, and sometimes this assistance is forthcoming to only a limited degree.

Whatever the organizational relations between the federal and provincial wings of the party as such, there is at the riding level some differentiation of activity occasioned by the circumstances that elections take place at different times, constituency boundaries do not coincide, and under recent legislation, riding organizations have in most jurisdictions funds from the public treasury not available for partisan activity at the other level. Despite this differentiation, it appears that the parties draw from and rely on the same pool of activists for work in the ridings. Although this finding should not be generalized, George Perlin discovered that, at the annual meeting of the national Progressive Conservatives in 1971, in about three-quarters of the federal constituencies most of the executives held office in provincial riding organizations, and he suggested that "many federal constituency associations may be little more than dependencies of provincial associations."[25] Whitaker draws our attention to "the inevitable conflict in which two wings of the same party must engage for the available human resources."[26] When the federal and provincial wings are in open conflict, there are enormous complications for the parties at the local levels; for example, the struggles between the King and Hepburn Liberals in Ontario in the late 1930s; the supporters of the national leader George Drew and the B. C. Conservatives in the 1950s and the Pearson Liberals and the Saskatchewan wing of the party in the early 1970s.

Career Patterns

A crucial dimension of the party system in federal states is whether or not there is a disposition of those who contest elective office to move between levels of government. Jean Holmes and Campbell Sharman write of Australia: "In default of a comprehensive study it appears that state politicians predominantly start and finish their careers at state level, although this is less true of them at the federal level. At the start of 1977 ten members (8 per cent) of the House of Representatives and five senators (9 per cent) had held office in state parliaments."[27] On the other hand, despite the decentralized nature of the nominating system in the United States "the structure of political opportunities . . . is national in scope," and "the principal flow of public office personnel is from state to nation."[28] In his important study on American political careers published in 1966, Joseph A. Schlesinger argued that this pattern had consequences in reducing the power of the state authorities by depriving them of their most able leaders and by creating circumstances in which state officials with national ambitions were unlikely to be aggressive in limiting Washington's powers.[29]

In contrast with the United States, there has been in Canada an ongoing specialization of federal and provincial political careers. The 1984 *Parliamentary Guide,* compiled before the federal general election of that year, gives this information:

— Thirty-three of 282 MPs (11.7 per cent) had contested provincial elections.

— Fifteen (5.4 per cent) had sat in provincial legislatures, and one had been a member of the legislative assembly of the Northwest Territories.

— Five former MPs sat in provincial legislatures, and a further 16 had unsuccessfully contested federal elections (of the former MPs, all but one of the MLAs was a member of the B. C. legislative assembly).

The patterns of prior provincial electoral experience differs between the national leadership of the two major parties. Laurier served as a member of the Quebec legislative assembly between 1871 and 1874, but none of his five successors had ever contested a provincial election. Brian Mulroney was the first Conservative leader since Arthur Meighen's resignation in 1942 not to have contested a provincial election. Three of Meighen's successors (John Bracken, George Drew and Robert Stanfield) had been provincial premiers, while John Diefenbaker and Joe Clark had been unsuccessful candidates for provincial elective office.

The Senate contains persons with more previous provincial experience than does the House of Commons. In the past decade, no fewer than four former provincial premiers have later become senators (E. C. Manning, Louis Robichaud, Dufferin Roblin and George I. Smith). At the end of 1984, 22 (21.6 per cent) of senators had contested provincial or territorial elections, and of these, all but three had, at one time or another, been elected to provincial or territorial office. While the Senate has not emerged as a strong defender of provincial rights, its membership contains more provincial experience than does the Commons.

In general, those making a career of elective public office in Canada choose either federal or provincial service. Most importantly in federal-provincial relations, ministers who interact with one another have, in general, neither experience nor, it seems, ambitions related to elective office at the other level.

Party Finance

With respect to party finance, there is little detailed information available on the relations between the federal and provincial wings of the Liberal and Conservative parties prior to the Second World War, but the pattern appears to be one of centralized control. K. Z. Paltiel, the most respected student of Canadian party finance, has written:

> The traditional methods of financing the two old Canadian parties, the Liberals and the Conservatives, helped overcome the splintering effect of

the provinces and provincial party organizations. This was accomplished through a highly centralized system of party finance. This system rested on a common basis: the centralized corporate industrial and financial structures located in Montreal and Toronto. It is common knowledge that the two old parties were largely financed from the same sources. These corporate contributors numbered in the hundreds rather than in the thousands. Under this system, provincial and even municipal elections, as well as federal elections, could be and were financed from the central party funds and sources. The traditional system of party finance had important integrative effects which helped overcome the centrifugal forces in Canadian political life. This beneficial result was made possible by the highly concentrated nature of Canadian industry and finance.[30]

In the period since the end of the Second World War, the older situation of centralization has weakened. In some of the provinces, particularly those in which natural resource development was important, the provincial parties have found corporate donors. Paltiel described the situation as it existed in the late 1960s:

> [T]he British Columbia and Alberta wings of the federal Liberal and Conservative parties have become largely self-supporting and contribute on occasion to the support of the Saskatchewan wing. Manitoba in the heyday of the Winnipeg Grain Exchange was self-supporting but now is a net importer of election funds. The rest of Canada, as far as the two major parties are concerned, are beneficiaries of transfer payments; they are in part political colonies except when some grass-roots movement has swept a minor party into power or a traditional party can exploit the advantages of incumbency by using office to gain funds by means fair or foul.[31]

Federal legislation and legislation enacted in several of the provinces in the past two decades has provided for public regulation of party finance and public subsidies to recognized parties, and these new circumstances have contributed to the organizational separation of the federal and provincial wings of the parties.

The first Canadian jurisdiction to introduce comprehensive public regulation of party finance was Quebec which provided, under a 1963 law, that there be statutory limitations on spending by candidates and parties and a mechanism for the legal recognition of parties. This reform was effected by the Lesage Liberal government and preceded by just a year the formal separation of the federal and provincial Liberal parties in Quebec. In 1964 the government of Canada appointed a five-person Committee on Electoral Expenses whose 1966 report was strongly influenced by the new regime of party finance in Quebec, but went further than the Quebec scheme by suggesting a limit on the amount of advertising time available to parties on the electronic media, a limit on public subsidies for such advertising and a system of tax credits for contributors to political parties.

In 1974 Parliament enacted the Election Expenses Act along the general lines of the 1966 Barheau Report. In the 1970s several of the provinces enacted laws governing the publicity of contributions to parties and imposing limits on party and candidate expenditures in elections. Three provinces (Nova Scotia, Ontario and Saskatchewan) provided reimbursement from the public purse for some or all of the expenses incurred by local candidates.

The formalization and public regulation of campaign finance undoubtedly contributes to the organizational separation of the federal and provincial wings of the political parties. There are very complex procedures involved here for the registration of parties: the reporting of contributions and expenditures; reimbursement from public funds of the expenses incurred by parties and local candidates; the division of subsidized broadcasting time among the parties under federal law and so on. Almost by its nature, this regime of institutionalizing parties frustrates the older and more informal patterns of federal-provincial party relations and integration.

Party Ideology

Party ideology would provide a basis for federal-provincial integration of the parties if, throughout Canada, each of the parties was distinguishable from the others on the basis of its ideological commitments. However, both the Liberal and Progressive Conservative parties are ideologically inclusive in the sense that each contains persons (as well as fluid and non-institutionalized groupings) of divergent ideological viewpoints, and each attempts to appeal to voters of differing ideological persuasions. However, even such differences as do exist between the two national parties do not always, or even usually, distinguish between Liberals and Conservatives in the provinces. Ideological differences complicated the relations between the federal and Saskatchewan Liberals in the 1960s with the provincial wing monopolizing the right wing of the political spectrum, while from 1963 to 1968 the federal party was mildly progressive and relied for the maintainance its position as a minority government, on the support of the NDP in the House of Commons. At the same time, the Lesage Liberals in Quebec and the Robichaud Liberals in New Brunswick were putting into effect very comprehensive programs of economic and social reform. Most Progressive Conservative administrations, with the exception of the Lyon government in Manitoba, have been middle-of-the-road in social and economic matters and such ideological conflicts as have occurred within the party do not follow federal-provincial lines.

The ideology shared by most members of the NDP does provide for a higher degree of federal-provincial integration than is the case with the other parties, and this common commitment is manifested in party organization, party finance and party careers. There have, however, been disputes of a broadly ideological nature between the national NDP and its provincial wings: the recurrent tension between the national party and its weak and unstable Quebec wing over the nationalist question in the 1960s and 1970s; the expulsion at one time of the radical New Brunswick party; the conflict between the national party and its Saskatchewan elements over the Constitution in 1980–81. The most dramatic ideological conflict within the party in recent years involved the left-wing Waffle, which had a measure of support throughout Canada, although the Waffle was in fact ejected by the Ontario rather than the national executive of the NDP.[32]

Party Symmetry

Party symmetry is in a sense a residual category, and the degree of such symmetry in a federal system is both a cause and a resultant of the extent of confederalization or integration of its political parties. If the party system is symmetrical with the same parties as the major competitors in all sub-national political arenas and the national level, there are important influences towards integration. Conversely, asymmetry contains predispositions towards the confederal form.

In mid-1986 the Canadian party system had many elements of federal-provincial asymmetry. The Progressive Conservatives were in power in Ottawa and in Newfoundland, Nova Scotia, New Brunswick, Saskatchewan and Alberta. The Liberals governed Prince Edward Island, Quebec and Ontario; the NDP formed the government of Manitoba and Social Credit that of British Columbia. Since the Mulroney government came to power in 1984, Progressive Conservative provincial administrations have been defeated in PEI and Ontario, and in the Alberta election of May 1986 the PC government lost considerable ground to the NDP and the Liberals. On the other side, there are Liberal governments in power in the two largest provinces as well as PEI, and in both the Manitoba and Alberta elections Liberals demonstrated considerable strength. However, these rapidly changing fortunes of the provincial wings of the two major parties took place with little involvement by the national parties and asymmetry is so much accepted as a norm of Canadian political life that no one seriously suggests that such changes are decisive for these national parties.

The asymmetry of the Canadian party system may be contrasted with the situations of the United States and Australia. In the American case, there are very great differences in the circumstances of party competition among the 50 states, but in no state are the serious contenders other than Republicans or Democrats in national, state and local elections. The Australian party system manifests a larger degree of asymmetry because of the strength of third parties. In state politics the National (formely Country) Party is dominant in Queensland and is a considerable force in New South Wales. Because of the electoral system for that body, the Australian Democrats have recently elected members of the Senate from all the states except Tasmania. In the Commonwealth parliament the Liberal and National parties co-operate in opposition to Labor and when in power, govern as a coalition. Despite these evidences of asymmetry, in both national and state elections the Australian Labor Party (ALP) and the Liberals have significant strength in all states. In terms of the 1980 national elections and state elections between 1979 and 1981, inclusive electoral support for the ALP nationally ranged from 46 per cent in New South Wales, Victoria and Queensland to 42 per cent in Western Australia and in state elections, between 56 per cent in N.S.W. and 41 per cent in Western Australia.[33] Liberal support was also widely distributed: in national elections between 52 per cent in Tasmania and 27 per cent in Queensland, and in state contests between 48 per cent in South Australia and 27 per cent in Queensland. Further, the underlying and persistent cleavage of Australian politics is that of Labor and anti-Labor forces, a circumstance that exists in Canada only in British Columbia.

(Although it does not relate directly to this analysis, Maurice Pinard's suggestive theory of the rise of third parties in Canada may be mentioned parenthetically here for the light it sheds on party asymmetry.[34] He presents an impressive array of evidence from federal and provincial political history leading to the conclusion that where one party dominates a political system, effective opposition to that party is likely to find an outlet in a new party rather than in a resurgence of strength in the weak opposition party (or the strongest of many opposition parties). Also when an opposition party fails to return at least a third of the votes while in opposition, it tends to be replaced by 'third parties'.)[35]

Asymmetry has direct consequences for intraparty relations, most of these consequences working in the direction of what I have called the confederal form. The existence in particular provinces of parties which are oriented exclusively or mainly to competition at one level or the other, rather than both, means that large groups of voters either switch allegiances between federal and provincial elections or abstain from voting, and, probably, it also encourages citizens to believe that they live in two relatively discrete political systems rather than in an integrated system. Those seeking party careers will be predisposed by asymmetry toward service at one level rather than both in succession. At the extreme, an ambitious British Columbia Liberal is unlikely to be attracted to provincial politics, and a Saskatchewan socialist with the goal of being a cabinet minister will perforce look toward Regina rather than Ottawa. If we assume, as is reasonable, that an important determinant of the success of a party in soliciting campaign funds is its prospects of electoral success, donors will be predisposed toward giving to one wing rather than both under conditions of asymmetry. Parties that are weak at one level sometimes evolve toward ideological sectarianism and sometimes become little more than groups of those interested more in patronage than electoral activity, to the embarrassment in both cases of the more serious politicians at the other level.

The Parties and the Federal System: Conclusions

In terms of the indicators which were formulated early in this chapter, the Canadian party system has developed from the integrated form to confederalism. Several qualifications to this statement need, however, to be made. The Progressive Conservatives and the NDP are significantly less confederal than the Liberals. The organizational separation of the federal and provincial wings of the two major parties has progressed less far in the Atlantic provinces than elsewhere in Canada. Confederalism is most marked at the higher levels of party organization, and in the constituencies the same persons often carry out both federal and provincial party activity. With these caveats, the Canadian party system is significantly more confederal than that of any other federation with which I am familiar. However, the results of the federal general election of September 1984 have brought about a new situation which may have some consequences for future federal-provincial party integration.

The partisan dimension of Canadian federalism is very much complicated by the fact that the leaders of successful parties are also heads of governments. We can assume, at least for purposes of analysis, that these persons are motivated by a single-minded desire to retain office. In some circumstances this objective can best be pursued by having government(s) of the same partisan designation in power at the other level. However, this is not always so, and, as we have seen, both federal and provincial governments have been sustained by provincial electorates which have given relatively little support to the other wing of the party. Thus the stronger and more persisting aim of government leaders is to have administrations at the other level whose substantive policies are in harmony with the former's objectives.

In his admirable and detailed account of the organization and financing of the Liberal party of Canada between 1930 and 1958, Reginald Whitaker analysed how the party's activities became more conditioned by the exigencies of executive federalism than of partisan competition more narrowly defined.[36] Those decades saw the federal Liberals engage in a process which increasingly assimilated the party to the institutional structures of the government of the national state. The party was under the control of federal ministers, and in their governmental and bureaucratic roles, ministers preferred to deal with provincial governments of other partisan complexions. So far as federal-provincial relations were concerned, Whitaker wrote:

> The claims of party became a complicating factor, adding new levels of conflict which can be avoided when the problem is simply intergovern-mental. The intra-party dimension of federal-provincial relations is thus a matter of *additional* complexity. It is difficult to generalize beyond this from the limited time period which has been examined, but it does seem by some to conclude that a Government party will seek to avoid such compli-cations. They may opt, as the federal Liberals did in Ontario and Quebec, for underwriting the position of their provincial wings as permanent oppo-sition parties, thus keeping the party name before the provincial voters while at the same time minimizing their impact on the federal level. Thus the dominant strategy of the federal Liberals is confronting the organiza-tional problem in Ontario and Quebec was to downplay partisanship between levels of government.[37]

The ongoing assimilation of the Liberal party to the federal state continued under Pearson and Trudeau with the consequent influence towards the confederalism of the party system.

It is prudent to be very tentative about the prospects of federal-provincial party integration in the light of the ascent to power of the Mulroney government in 1984, the unexpected defeat of the Ontario Progressive Conservatives in 1985 and what appear to be likely changes in the partisan complexion of the admin-istrations controlling several of the provinces in the next two or three years.

So far as the Liberals are concerned, John Turner has shown some disposition to give his and his party's support to provincial Liberals. This offer has been explicitly rejected by the Quebec party, and in Ontario, Turner and his senior colleagues did not participate actively in the provincial election of 1985. In general, the provincial parties in the two largest provinces appear to have little to gain and much to lose from close association with the federal wing which is now weak and which may, in the next two years or so, be subjected to internecine struggles over party leadership. Meanwhile there are few immediate prospects for the resurgence of Liberalism in Western Canada.

In their evident determination to replace the Liberals as the long-term governing party in Ottawa, there would seem to be considerable advantages for the Mulroney Conservatives in maintaining a considerable distance from the provincial elements of the party. There is relative harmony between the federal government and the provinces, but it is unrealistic to expect that this will continue indefinitely and when conflicts do arise, one can, with reasonable safety, predict that, as with the Liberals in the past, the federal Conservatives will find that intraparty relations complicate intergovernmental relations and that, on balance, it is preferable to deal with provincial administrations of other partisan designations. The situations in the four largest provinces can be described briefly as follows:

1. During the 1984 federal election campaign Premier Davis of Ontario gave his vigorous support to the Mulroney Conservatives, and the provincial "Big Blue Machine" was actively deployed in the latter's behalf. This was in marked contrast to the situation in the latter years of the Clark leadership in which there was apparently little personal rapport between Clark and Davis and in which the provincial Conservatives openly sided with the Trudeau government on the crucial issues of the Constitution and energy policies.[38] A very limited reciprocation of this provincial support was made by Prime Minister Mulroney in the 1985 Ontario election campaign in which he made a brief appearance with Davis' successor, Frank Miller, before a closed-circuit audience of provincial Conservatives. There would seem to be little advantage for the federal Progressive Conservatives to associate themselves with the provincial party as it regroups after the adverse results of the 1985 Ontario election.

2. In Quebec, Prime Minister Mulroney has decided that the federal Conservatives will not support a provincial Conservative party prior to the next provincial election. The federal Conservatives, the PQ and the provincial Liberals share a common desire to oppose the federal Liberals in the province, and in the 1984 election Mulroney and his colleagues received organizational support in some ridings from the PQ, and in others from the Bourassa Liberals. Mulroney is on friendly terms with the leaders of both the provincial parties, and the federal Conservatives would seem to have few incentives to complicate future relations with either a PQ or a Liberal government by giving support to a provincial Conservative party.

3. So far as British Columbia is concerned, the federal Conservatives and the provincial Social Credit party rely on essentially the same base of elite and mass support. Social Credit does not, of course, participate in federal elections, and there would seem to be no overwhelming advantage for the federal Conservatives in splitting the anti-NDP vote by actively supporting the provincial Conservatives.

4. In Alberta the federal and provincial Conservatives are so dominant that there would not appear to be much incentive for either wing to integrate with the other. It can be noted that this dominance was established by each of the wings at different times. The position of the federal Conservatives as the leading

Alberta party dates from the Diefenbaker sweep of 1958, and in the ten general elections from 1958 to 1984 inclusive they have won all but 11 of the 182 seats at stake — losing 4 of them to the Liberals in 1968. The revival of the provincial Conservatives can be traced to Peter Lougheed's accession as party leader and his bringing the party to power in 1971.

In general, then, it is reasonable to expect the high degree of confederalization in the Conservative party to be perpetuated in the foreseeable future. One factor which might introduce a higher degree of party integration would be the ideological polarization of Canadian politics as has happened in both the United Kingdom and the United States. If the federal Progressive Conservative party and all or most of its provincial wings should become dominated by right-wing elements, it is at least possible that a basis for closer integration among the federal and provincial elements would be established. However, it seems to me such polarization is, for a number of reasons, unlikely, among them the poor showing of the Ontario party under Frank Miller (the most right-wing of the candidates for leadership in the convention of early 1985) in the May election of that year.

Appendix: The Pan-Canadian Response to the Confederalization of the Party System

Near the beginning of his brilliant, recent reinterpretation of the Canadian party system, David E. Smith writes: "The nexus between party and government which . . . is at the heart of Canadian politics remains unexplained in its details and the reciprocating influence of its parts has been underestimated."[39] He goes on: "The primary thesis of this paper is that party government, that is, the system of rule which places a party in government, has determined Canada's political development."[40] Under the Westminster model, the prize for which partisan contenders strive is the unshared power to govern. To attain this prize, however, party leaders must be able to dominate the governments they head and also the extra-parliamentary elements of the party whose effective functioning is necessary to the getting and keeping of power. Smith suggests that the role of parties is downplayed in studies of our political system because Canadians are "institutionalists" and parties are regarded as informal private groupings (for the most part not regulated by law) and because of the "blinkered scholarship" which has given us the brokerage theory of parties. One might also surmise that this neglect arises from the circumstance that the major partisan contenders in federal and provincial politics seldom offer the electorate choices which are distinctive in ideological or policy terms. Thus, for most citizens and for the national and provincial societies as such the consequences of alternative electoral outcomes are not very great. However, these outcomes are crucial for those directly involved in partisan competition — more so than for competitors in the car-rental business, surely — and the behaviour of these politicians cannot be understood except in terms of their unending quest for electoral support which is the coin of the political realm as profits are that of private business activity.

Smith traces the government-party nexus in three succeeding periods of Canadian history:

1. *The period of Macdonald and Laurier*   This was the era of territorial expansion and nation-building. To accomplish these ends in an emergent political community in which economic, social and cultural ties were weak, the party was essential. In general, what developed was a "party system both intensively local in its interests and profoundly personal in its management by the party leader."[41] Patronage which penetrated virtually every local community was the essential device of party management. Thus: "Macdonald and Laurier were the creators not only of modern Canada but of modern political parties in Canada. They learned to command the party in Parliament by dominating the party outside Parliament."[42]

Although Smith gives the 1911–1921 decade relatively little attention, John English describes the attempts by Borden and some of his supporters to restructure Canadian politics in a radical way.[43] Borden had neither the taste nor the talent for the kind of party management so successfully carried out by Macdonald and Laurier, and English writes: "In those earlier days when Borden was fashioning the Unionist coalition [of 1917] he believed he was fathering a party which would transcend the variety of Canadian political cultures, a party which would define and indeed represent a definable public interest. Harking back to a tradition as old as the English Civil War which declared party and public interest to be antithetical, Unionism proposed to abolish party by declaring itself the embodiment of the public interest." Despite these pretensions, "National government became, to too many Canadians, a symbol not of innovation and creativity but of domination by an arrogant majority." Thus the Unionists were succeeded by the Mackenzie King Liberals, and Canadians would thereafter prefer "the muddle, the contradictions and the ambiguities of brokerage and consensus politics."[45]

2. *The "accommodative" approach of Mackenzie King*   Smith writes: "From 1920 on, Ottawa began to lose control of organized forces in Canadian life: farmers first, then business and labour, and still later, the provinces." King was a skilful party manager, but he performed this role at one step removed from local communities, and the 1918 reforms in the civil service had denied the party leaders many of the opportunities to involve themselves in such affairs which their predecessors had enjoyed. In the King era there was a much greater reliance on provincial party organizations than before. The linkage between these organizations and the national party was through regional ministers like James G. Gardiner, C. D. Howe, Ernest Lapointe and Angus Macdonald. Despite the power of these regional chieftains, King himself did not hesitate to override their judgement in constituency and other partisan matters when, in his view, the welfare of the party dictated such action.

King's successor, Louis St. Laurent, had little interest in party management. Under his leadership the extra-parliamentary elements of the party atrophied. Meanwhile, the increasing assimilation of the party to the federal bureaucracy proceeded apace and as did the consequent insensitivity to the wishes of the electorate which led to the Liberal defeat of 1957.

3. *The "pan-Canadian approach" of Diefenbaker, Pearson and Trudeau*[46]
Smith designates as the pan-Canadian approach the appeal of recent national party leaders to individual Canadians "regardless of where they lived or what

language they spoke." Diefenbaker was the first to emphasize such appeals. When he came to power in 1957, the Conservative extra-parliamentary organization was in some disarray, and Diefenbaker made little sustained attempt to rebuild it. Members of his cabinets did not have the linkages either with the federal bureaucracy or with provincial party organizations as had their counterparts in the King–St. Laurent period. Diefenbaker saw himself as leader of the Canadian people and had little disposition for consensual politics. Thus:

> Mr. Diefenbaker's concept of his country was not a community of communities but, as he repeatedly avowed, 'One Canada'. The Bill of Rights, the national development policy (with its vision of the North, its Roads to Resources and National Energy Board), the extension of hospital insurance and the creation of the Royal Commission on Health Services . . . these and other national policies revealed a pan-Canadian approach to political leadership which, in its explicitness went far beyond the actions of the St. Laurent government before him.[47]

The pan-Canadian approach was accepted and extended to new areas by Pearson and Trudeau: the Canada Pension Plan, medical insurance, energy, constitutional reform, the Charter of Rights. Also, as we saw earlier in this chapter, there were attempts to reform the extra-parliamentary elements of the party by cutting its ties with the provincial wings and creating a new mass party of individuals.

Although Smith does not emphasize this dimension, the pan-Canadian approach can reasonably be regarded as an attempt by federal party leaders to come to grips with the circumstances of both the confederalization of the party system and powerful and purposeful provincial leaders who control sophisticated bureaucracies and autonomous party organizations. By reaching out to individual citizens wherever in Canada they lived and by creating cleavages which do not coincide with provincial boundaries, national leaders have, to an extent, relegated the provinces to the sidelines.

The pan-Canadian approach has, however, been only partially successful in overcoming provincial cleavages. Quebec did not join the Canada Pension Plan and, much more importantly, has remained outside the constitutional settlement which came into effect in 1982; national energy policies pitted the petroleum-producing provinces against the others. Further, even in circumstances where national policies appear not to be accommodations of conflicting provincial demands, these policies have very different impacts on particular parts of Canada.

For example, Keith Banting has demonstrated how "the centralization of responsibility for income security in the post-war period has transformed it into a major instrument of inter-regional equalization, equal in importance to the much more publicized equalization grants."[48] Thus, in 1978 income security payments as a proportion of total personal income ranged from 29.4 per cent in Newfoundland to 10.7 per cent in Alberta, while in 1976–77 net income security benefits per capita were $378 in Newfoundland and − $155 in Alberta and net equalization grants per capita $364 and − $104 respectively.[49]

Again federal support for cultural activity — book publishing, films, broadcasting, and so on — appears on the surface to have no provincial incidence.

However, a disproportionate amount of this activity is centred in Montreal and Toronto.

Notes

1. William H. Riker, *Federalism: Origin, Operation, Significance* (Boston and Toronto: Little, Brown and Company, 1964), particularly Chapter 2.
2. Ibid., p. 129.
3. John Meisel, "The Decline of Party in Canada," in Hugh Thorburn, ed., *Party Politics in Canada,* 4th ed. (Scarborough: Prentice-Hall Canada, 1979), pp. 119–135.
4. Harold D. Clarke, Jane Jenson, Lawrence Le Duc and Jon H. Pammett, *Absent Mandate: The Politics of Discontent in Canada* (Toronto: Gage, 1984), p. 74.
5. Robert H. Williams, "Candidate Selection," in Howard R. Penniman, ed., *Canada at the Polls, 1979 and 1980* (Washington: American Enterprise Institute, 1981), pp. 86–120.
6. Richard Johnston, "Federal and Provincial Voting: Contemporary Patterns and Historical Evolution," in David J. Elkins and Richard Simeon, eds., *Small Worlds: Provinces and Parties in Canadian Political Life* (Toronto: Methuen, 1980), p. 141.
7. Ibid., p. 155.
8. Ibid., pp. 155–157.
9. Ibid., pp. 165–166.
10. See the debate between Johnston and William P. Irvine, "The Reproduction of the Religious Cleavage in Canadian Elections" and "Comment on 'The Reproduction of the Religious Cleavage in Canadian Elections'," *Canadian Journal of Political Science* 18, no. 1 (March 1985): pp. 99–118.
11. Johnston, *Federal and Provincial Voting,* p. 172.
12. Clarke et al., *Absent Mandate,* p. 70.
13. Williams, "Candidate Selection."
14. For a book-length analysis, see John C. Courtney, *The Selection of National Party Leaders in Canada* (Toronto: Macmillan of Canada, 1973). On the 1983 Progressive Conservative convention see Patrick Martin, Allan Gregg and George Perlin, *Contenders: The Tory Quest for Power* (Scarborough: Prentice-Hall Canada, 1983). Perlin's book *The Tory Syndrome: Leadership Politics in the Progressive Conservative Party* (Montreal and Kingston: McGill-Queen's University Press, 1980), contains valuable analyses of the 1967 and 1976 PC leadership conventions.
15. Reginald Whitaker, *The Government Party: Organizing and Financing the Liberal Party of Canada 1930–1958* (Toronto: University of Toronto Press, 1977).
16. Joseph Wearing, *The L-Shaped Party: The Liberal Party of Canada 1958–1980* (Toronto: McGraw-Hill Ryerson, 1981).
17. David E. Smith, *The Regional Decline of a National Party: Liberals on the Prairies* (Toronto: University of Toronto Press, 1981).
18. Christina McCall-Newman, *Grits: An Intimate Portrait of the Liberal Party* (Toronto: Macmillan of Canada, 1982).
19. Wearing, *L-Shaped Party,* pp. 9–10.
20. Georges Radwanski, *Trudeau* (Toronto: Macmillan of Canada, 1978), pp. 272–273.
21. Stephen Clarkson, "The Defeat of the Government, the Decline of the Liberal Party, and the (Temporary) Fall of Pierre Trudeau," in Penniman, *Canada at the Polls,* p. 160.
22. Smith, *Regional Decline of a National Party.*
23. Ibid., p. 52.
24. Ibid., p. 88.
25. Perlin, *Tory Syndrome,* p. 22.
26. Whitaker, *Government Party* p. 416. Because of the relative scarcity of human resources at the local level, "an increasing separation and insulation of the two wings of the party at the level of parliamentary leadership was never matched by an equivalent separation of the membership at the constituency level."

27. Jean Holmes and Campbell Sherman, *The Australian Federal System* (Sydney: George Allen and Unwin, 1977), p. 104.

28. Joseph A. Schlesinger, *Ambition and Politics: Political Careers in the United States* (Chicago: Rand McNally, 1966), p. 201.

29. Ibid., pp. 203–204.

30. K. Z. Paltiel, "Federalism and Party Finance: A Preliminary Sounding," in *Studies in Canadian Party Finance,* Committee on Election Expenses (Ottawa: Queen's Printer, 1969), pp. 4–5. See also K. Z. Paltiel, *Political Party Financing in Canada* (Toronto: McGraw-Hill of Canada, 1970).

31. Paltiel, "Federalism and Party Finance," p. 11. Material quoted is reproduced with permission of the Minister of Supply and Services Canada.

32. For an account of the expulsion of the Waffle, see J. T. Morley, *Secular Socialists: The CCF/NDP in Ontario: A Biography* (Montreal and Kingston: McGill-Queen's University Press, 1984), pp. 211–219.

33. Figures from Dean Jaensch, *The Australian Party System* (Sydney: George Allen and Unwin, 1983), p. 152. Figures are percentages of first-preference votes.

34. Maurice Pinard, *The Rise of a Third Party: A Study in Crisis Politics* (Englewood Cliffs, N. J.: Prentice-Hall, 1971).

35. Ibid., p. 37.

36. Whitaker, *Government Party* pp. 406–421.

37. Ibid., p. 419.

38. For an account of the strained relations between federal and Ontario Conservatives during the Clark government's period in office, see Jeffrey Simpson, *Discipline of Power: The Conservative Interlude and the Liberal Restoration* (Toronto: Personal Library, Publishers, 1980), particularly pp. 189–192.

39. David E. Smith, "Party Government, Representation and National Integration in Canada", in Peter Aucoin, research co-ordinator, *Party Government and Regional Representation in Canada,* vol. 36 of the research studies prepared for the Royal Commission on the Economic Union and Development Prospects for Canada (Toronto: University of Toronto Press, 1985), p. 2.

40. Ibid., p. 2.

41. Ibid., p. 17.

42. Ibid., p. 18.

43. John English, *The Decline of Politics: The Conservatives and the Party System, 1901–1920* (Toronto: University of Toronto Press, 1977), Chapters 6–11.

44. Ibid., p. 228.

45. Ibid., p. 229.

46. Ibid., pp. 25–33.

47. Ibid., p. 27.

48. Keith G. Banting, *The Welfare State and Canadian Federalism*, (Montreal and Kingston: McGill-Queen's University Press, 1982), p. 97.

49. Ibid., p. 101 and p. 105.

VI

French-English Duality and Canadian Federalism

The Dominion of Canada was established as a federation in 1867, albeit a federation of a highly centralized kind, because the French-Canadian politicians of Lower Canada would not agree to a new constitutional settlement on any other basis. The federal system was subsequently shaped in a profound and decisive way by the circumstances of French-English duality. In fact, during the 1960s and throughout most of the next decade many of the most influential participants and observers of Canadian federalism were, at best, totally preoccupied with duality as the central federal problem according to "the view which holds that the most significant cleavage in Canada is the line dividing English from French, and which defines as the major challenge to domestic statecraft the establishment of harmonious and just relations between English-speaking and French-speaking communities of Canada."[1] This view was not accepted by all anglophone Canadians and the differences between those who espoused it and those who rejected it resulted in a significant degree of conflict in this period. During the latter half of the 1970s the insistent pressures from provinces with English-speaking majorities, particularly those in the West, gave rise to a new variant of conventional wisdom expressed in these terms by the Pepin-Robarts Task Force on Canadian Unity in its 1979 Report:

> We believe that the heart of the present crisis is to be discovered in the intersecting conflicts created by two kinds of cleavages in Canadian society and by the political agencies which express and mediate them. The first and more pressing cleavage is that old Canadian division between "the French" and "the English". . . . The second cleavage is that which divides the various regions of Canada and their populations from one another.[2]

French-English Duality and the Confederation Settlement

The Confederation settlement negotiated among the politicians of British North America between 1864 and 1867, and facilitated and given final legal form by the authorities of the United Kingdom, was, in large part, a response to the circumstances of French-English duality in the United Province of Canada. The Act of Union of 1840 was an attempted British solution to Canadian duality, Confederation an almost entirely British North American one. Under the 1840 measure, Lower Canada was deprived of its legislative assembly which had been established under the Constitutional Act of 1791. The French were to be reduced to a permanent minority under the provision that each of the two sections was to have an equal number of members in the assembly of the new province, although at that time Lower Canada had a larger population, according to the expectation that the English-speaking members from Upper Canada would unite with their cultural and linguistic compatriots from the other section to render the French a permanent minority. There was some hope here that, by fastening this status on the French-Canadian minority, its members would, according to Lord Durham's view, opt for assimilation into the wider English-speaking society.

However the assimilation of the French was not to be. As often happened in subsequent periods of Canadian history, the French Canadians demonstrated a higher degree of political cohesion than their English-speaking counterparts and thus came to play a decisive role in the affairs of the United Province of Canada.[3] Sometime in the period between the attainment of responsible government in 1848 and Confederation there emerged in that province a regime which modern students of politics would designate as consociationalism. There developed the practice of double-headed ministries led by politicians from each of the two sections. There was considerable bifurcation on the executive side of government, with a different administrative apparatus for Upper Canada and Lower Canada. There was some recognition of the double-majority rule, according to which legislative measures impinging directly on one of the sections could be carried only by a majority of the members of the assembly from that section.

The consociational response to French-English duality proved unworkable. In constitutional terms, the majoritarian dispositions of the Westminster model of parliamentary government and consociationalism are not easily reconcilable. More fundamentally perhaps, the British North American politicians opted for consociationalism or majoritarianism as their interests in respect to particular issues directed them.[4] To take an important example with continuing consequences for contemporary Ontario politics, the double-majority rule was put aside for majoritarianism in the Scott Act of 1863 which increased the privileges of Roman Catholic separate schools in Upper Canada by the action of a majority in the legislative assembly from Lower Canada and the opposition from Upper Canada. By the mid-1860s there were four relatively cohesive political groupings in the legislature — bleus from Upper Canada and Lower Canada, Upper Canadian Reformers and Lower Canadian rouges — and the province had experienced a rapid succession of unstable and short-lived ministries. There were increasingly insistent pressures from Upper Canada, which now had a larger population than the other section, for representation by population in the Legislative Assembly, and although the French-Canadian politicians were understandably unwilling to concede this, the more perceptive of them, along with their bleu political allies from Upper Canada, knew that such pressures could not be resisted indefinitely. In short, Confederation was in large part a response to political deadlock in the United Province of Canada, and this deadlock was a result of the circumstances of French-English relations.

The following five elements of the Confederation settlement bore directly on cultural, linguistic and religious duality:

1. The provinces received exclusive legislative jurisdiction over those matters in respect to which the two linguistic and cultural communities differed most markedly, while for the most part the powers of the Dominion were those perceived not to have such incidence. Among the most important subjects of provincial jurisdiction was education. The British North America Act also ratified the concession made to the French-speaking community by the Quebec Act of 1774 by giving the provinces exclusive jurisdiction over property and civil rights, thus permitting Quebec to retain its system of private law based on the European civil code. In terms of the same kind of recognition of duality, the provinces were given the powers over municipal government, what we would now call health and welfare matters and the solemnization of marriage. With some few exceptions (divorce, Indian affairs, perhaps the criminal law), the powers of the Dominion related to defence and to economic matters, these being perceived as not impinging directly on the distinctive values and interests of the two communities.

2. There was a very limited constitutional recognition of the rights of the French and English languages. Under Section 133 of the BNA Act of 1867 these might be used in the debates of Parliament and the legislature of Quebec. The records and journals of both these bodies were to be printed in both languages, and either French or English could be used in the courts of Quebec and in any court established by Parliament. The French language had thus no constitutional status in the operations of the other federating provinces. Section 133 duplicated the circumstances of linguistic duality which had prevailed in the United Province of Canada under an amendment to the Act of Union in 1848.

3. The Confederation settlement envisaged a situation in which Quebec would come to have a more extensive sphere of legislative jurisdiction than the other provinces. Under Section 94 of the BNA Act it was provided in effect that the Parliament of Canada might make laws providing for the uniformity of laws relating to property and civil rights in the provinces of Ontario, New Brunswick and Nova Scotia when such laws were agreed upon by these provinces in the traditions of the English common law.[5] It was expected then, that there would soon come about an assimilation of the private law systems of these provinces into a uniform Dominion-wide code which would exclude Quebec.

4. The provisions of the BNA Act dealing with the protection of minority rights in education related to those of religious denominations rather than of French and English language groups. Under Section 93, an appeal against provincial restrictions on the rights and privileges of minority denominational schools existing by law at the time of union, or subsequently established, might be made to the Governor in Council, and if the wrong was not thereby righted, Parliament

might enact "remedial laws." This provision was enacted at the initiation of Alexander Galt specifically to protect the Protestants of Quebec, and, as A. T. Silver has shown, the dominant opinion among the French Canadians of Quebec was that it was an inappropriate restriction on provincial power over education.[6]

5. The English-speaking minority of Quebec received special protection. As we have seen, the English language was given a limited protection in Quebec provincial institutions under Section 133, and the Protestant school system of Quebec was also protected. Section 80 of the Act provided, in effect, that the boundaries of certain legislative districts for the election of the members of the Quebec legislature (those which were predominantly English-speaking) could not be altered without the approval of a majority of the members of the legislature from these districts. Sections 22 and 23 provided that senators from Quebec would be appointed from the 24 districts into which the province was divided by the Act, and the English-speaking groups who dominated in certain areas of the province were protected by the stipulation that a Quebec senator must either be a resident or have $4000 of real property in the district from which he was appointed. Unlike Ontario, Quebec was to have, under the BNA Act, a legislative council which, it was expected, would be an effective channel for the interests of the English-speaking minority. Thus, as well as being part of a majority in the affairs of the Dominion as a whole, the powerful Anglo-Protestant minority of Quebec received important constitutional protections for their interests against possible challenges by the French-Canadian majority of that province.

In more specifically political terms, the Confederation settlement permitted the dominant indigenous elites of French-speaking Canada — most decisively the Roman Catholic clergy — to control those elements of the province's cultural and religious life deemed most necessary to the integrity and survival of the French-Canadian community. At the same time it vastly enhanced the powers of the Anglo-Protestant political leaders and their allies in the business community to create a new transcontinental economic nation.[7] As we have seen, the English-speaking community of Quebec received a number of very specific constitutional safeguards for its interests which had no parallel in respect to the 150 000 or so French-speaking persons who lived outside Quebec. And despite the legislative powers conferred on the provinces by the BNA Act, the Macdonald government chose the first premier of Quebec and up until the defeat of that government in 1873, exerted a very direct influence over Quebec provincial affairs.[8]

French-English Relations: Confederation to 1960

Confederation did not eliminate conflict between the French and English communities. In the period between 1867 and the ascent to power of the Duplessis government in Quebec in 1936, the most bitter of these conflicts involved two concerns: Canadian orientations in external affairs as a member of the British Empire/Commonwealth and the position of French and Catholic minorities outside Quebec.

So far as external relations were concerned, the "little Englandism" which had prevailed at the time of Confederation gave way in the latter years of the nineteenth century to a militant Anglo-Saxonism and, as Carl Berger has demonstrated, English-speaking Canadian nationalists were for the most part imperialists.[9] French Canadians were obviously resistant to this kind of sentiment, and conflicts with their English-Canadian compatriots were particularly intense during the Boer War and in the years before and during the First World War. In respect to the second concern, the position of French and Catholic minorities outside Quebec, Silver's recent research has shown that at the time of Confederation the French-Canadian Fathers were preoccupied with provincial rights but that by the end of the century, dominant sentiment in French Quebec had come to associate that community with French-speaking minorities elsewhere in Canada.[10] In respect to both external orientation and minority rights, the English-speaking majority when mobilized as such got its way.

Despite the conflicts mentioned above, there were certain patterns of French-English relations which developed to make Canada, prior to the 1960s, one of the most stable of Western nations:

1. *The federal division of legislative powers*   As we have seen, the basic rationale of the division of legislative powers in the BNA Act of 1867 was to vest in the provinces control over those matters in respect to which French and English communities diverged most markedly, while Dominion powers were regarded as having no such incidence. Up until the First World War, the major activities of the federal government related to national economic development, and in respect to those policies, the interests of French and English were not perceived to be in opposition. On the other side, Ottawa, for the most part, did not involve itself in those matters of provincial jurisdiction believed to be crucial to French language and culture.

2. *Institutional self-segregation*   From the Conquest onward, there was sustained in Quebec what one might call a French counter-culture with its own justifying system of political, economic and religious thought. In 1954 Pierre Trudeau wrote: "[A]gainst the English, Protestant democratic, materialist, commercial and later industrial world, our nationalism worked out a defensive system in which all the opposite forces were stressed: the French language, authoritarianism, idealism, rural life and later the return to the soil."[11] In its comprehensive account of the Canadian experience, the 1956 Report of the Quebec Royal Commission on Constitutional Problems juxtaposed two homogeneous societies, one of French and one of English origin, each manifesting its own specific genius.[12] In general terms, the French-speaking counter-culture did not in any direct way challenge Anglo-Saxon political and economic power either in Quebec or Canada as a whole, and as individuals most anglophones and francophones could pursue their occupational and other objectives without coming into conflict with members of the other group. An interesting embodiment of institutional segregation occurred at the level of the federal cabinet where francophones tended to be disproportionately appointed to portfolios with a heavy patronage orientation (the Post Office, Public Works and Justice, for example), while anglophones monopolized appointments to departments concerned with economic matters.[13]

3. *Mediation at the summit*   Traditionally, the most important anglophone-francophone relations were mediated by leaders of the elites of the two commu-

nities. In federal politics, anglophone party leaders had their Quebec lieutenants or (as was the case with the Conservatives for most of the time after the death of Georges-Etienne Cartier in 1873) were trying to find someone to play that role effectively. Although the Quebec lieutenant was by no means a co-prime-minister, he normally had a wider scope of discretion in Quebec affairs than did ministers from the other provinces in respect to these areas.[14] This kind of mediation was facilitated by the fact that, at the time of Confederation and for some decades after, Montreal was the site of the dominant interests of the Canadian business community. Sheila McLeod Arnopoulos and Dominique Clift wrote with only a little exaggeration: "Historically, it has been the role of the English community of Quebec to bring together the diverse and competing elements of Canadian society and to formulate some national purpose to which all could subscribe."[15] From the coming to power of the Laurier Liberals in 1896 onward, the function of mediation was, for the most part, performed by the Liberal party which, in Arnopoulos' and Clift's words, was unique among Canadian public institutions "in having accepted in its internal operations a practical sharing of power between French and English."[16] In Quebec provincial affairs, there was a complex pattern of elite accommodation between leaders of the two communities, and in the cabinet there was usually an anglophone — often the minister of revenue — representing English-Canadian business interests.

4. *The traditional French-Canadian distrust of the state*   During most of its existence, the francophone community of Quebec has distrusted government, even governments in which members of this community were a numerical majority. According to Trudeau's analysis, because French Canadians received democratic institutions not through their own efforts but by the will of the English-speaking community, they came to value democracy not for itself but as an instrument of ethnic survival.[17] Ralph Heintzmann has evolved an alternative explanation. Quebec politics was based overwhelmingly on the distribution of patronage, and the patronage system was "rooted in Quebec's unresolved unemployment problem, including the lack of employment and career opportunities for the Quebec middle class."[18] However, "if the patronage system encouraged a climate of strong party loyalties, it produced a simultaneous impulse in the opposite direction, a profound cynicism about politics and politicians, and deep anxiety about the corroding influence of politics on many areas of national life."[19] Thus: "It was commonly assumed that politics ruined everything it touched, therefore activities of importance to the nation should be kept 'above' politics, or insulated in some way from the political process."[20] Heintzmann traces these efforts "to remove politics from government" in respect to several matters: education, agriculture and colonization, municipal affairs and welfare. This traditional distrust of the political process was, of course, congruent with the dominant position of the Church in many important aspects of Quebec life.

5. *The defence of historic, prescriptive rights*   Prior to the 1960s, French-Canadian leaders saw the welfare and integrity of their community in terms of an unyelding defence of historic prescriptive rights, particularly as these rights were embodied in the Confederation settlement. From the 1880s onward such interests were defined in terms of the theory of Confederation as a compact either

among the provinces or between the English and French communities.[21] The corollary of course was that the terms of the Confederation settlement, as these were given constitutional form in the BNA Act of 1867, must be fastidiously observed, and these terms could be changed only with the consent of the contracting parties. In short, the French Canadians were constitutional conservatives.

6. *The demographic balance*   The proportion of the Canadian population of French ethnic origin remained at a stable 30 per cent over a long period of Canadian history: 30.0 per cent in 1881 and 30.4 per cent in 1961, with a decline to a low of 27.9 per cent in 1921 after the very high immigration to Canada in the previous decade.[22] During this period there was a steady decline in the proportion of British origin from 58.9 to 43.8 per cent. However, in terms of linguistic usage and community identification, persons of non-British origin tended overwhelmingly to associate themselves with the English-language element while the French compensated by a higher birth rate.

Taken together, the circumstances outlined above gave a degree of stability to English-French relations and to Canadian federalism. Institutional differentiation based on contrary structures of values made the individual and group objectives of the two communities relatively compatible. The mediation of community relations by their respective elites provided a procedure for managing the demands of each group on the other. Anti-statism in Quebec facilitated the economic domination of the province by English-speaking business interests and (particularly between 1945 and 1960) the extension of federal powers in harmony with the preferences both of Canadians outside Quebec for national leadership and inside Quebec for public action to meet social needs to which the provincial authorities were not responding. Adherence by French Canadians to one version or other of the compact theory of Confederation was an affirmation of the continuing legitimacy of the federal system. While the demographic balance between the two communities was a continuing source of tension, with the French fearful of immigration and the English of the French "revanche du berceaux," the fact that this process resulted in a constant proportion of the French community being francophones was, in a sense, a stabilizing factor.

Quebec after 1960 and the Quiet Revolution

Each of the stabilizing elements discussed above was abruptly challenged by the so-called Quiet Revolution of Quebec from the early 1960s onward. Many years before the death of Maurice Duplessis in 1959, the traditional institutions of Quebec and their justifying ideologies had become progressively less relevant to the circumstances of an industrialized community exposed to a modernized and modernizing world. The formulations of the Duplessis era and post-1960 Quebec nationalism differed in many important respects, but both were of course based on the Quebec governmental authorities' need for autonomy, and both equated French Canada with Quebec (this was shown by their indifference to the interests of French-speaking Canadians outside the province). On the other hand, the older nationalism was primarily defensive, the newer currents of thought and policy much less so. In turning from "survivance" to "épanouissement," the new Quebec leadership decisively altered the older patterns of relations between the anglophone and francophone communities of Canada and exposed the federal system to the severest strains to which it had ever been subjected:

1. *Conflicts over the federal division of legislative powers*   By the 1960s, the original division of legislative powers according to which the provinces were given control over most matters perceived to bear directly on culture had broken down, mainly through the exercise of the federal spending power. Ottawa was now directly involved in health, welfare, post-secondary education, vocational training and other such matters largely or wholly within provincial jurisdiction. The Duplessis government had forthrightly resisted such involvement, and, in some cases, the province had foregone federal moneys which would have been available to it through participation. However, the Union Nationale had a somewhat negative approach to provincial autonomy and had little disposition to act constructively in the fields of jurisdiction it defended. From 1960 onward, the situation was otherwise when federal measures restricted the discretion of successive Quebec administrations with more positive aims.

2. *Institutional self-segregation*   What Guindon has called "a new middle class" has developed in Quebec in response to urbanization and industrialization.[23] During the Duplessis period this emergent class had been rendered impotent both by the traditional political and religious leadership and by the anglophone centres of corporate power. The new groups were committed both by ideology and individual and collective self-interest to the modernization of Quebec and of the provincial authorities' taking the lead in this process. Their frame of reference was secular, materialistic and technocratic. Because corporate business at the higher levels of decision was an Anglo-Saxon preserve, the new middle class turned to public institutions and, in the main, to the government of Quebec. Until roughly the mid-1970s, a high degree of institutional selfsegregation persisted, albeit with francophones now pressing their individual and collective interests through the increasingly modernized and effective state apparatus of the province of Quebec but with anglophone control of the private corporate sector basically unchallenged. However, with decreasing opportunities for employment in the public institutions of Quebec came new francophone challenges to the private sector mainly, as we shall see, through provincial legislation related to language.

3. *An end to anti-statism*   After the election of the Lesage administration in 1960, the dominant currents of thought and policy in Quebec turned away from the older suspicion of the state and came to see the provincial government as the major instrument by which Quebec society might be reformed.[24] The interests of the new middle class lay in the expansion of the public sector and in the bureaucratization of public and private institutions. This led inevitably to the displacement of the Church in health, education and welfare and to more government intervention than before in what had hitherto been the private sector.

4. *Complications in elite accommodation*   From 1960 onward there was overt conflict among the Quebec francophone elites which inhibited the older kinds of elite accommodation between francophones and anglophones both within

Quebec and outside. During the early 1960s, a frequent question asked by English-speaking Canadians was, "What does Quebec want?" The meaning was undoubtedly, "Who speaks authoritatively for Quebec?" and confusion was made worse because, as one French-Canadian scholar pointed out in 1968, "Actually too many individuals among the elite are speaking in the name of the whole French-Canadian population."[25] The overt and vigorous conflicts within the francophone society of Quebec became more salient for the relations between the two communities as an increasing number of anglophone Canadians came to interest themselves in Quebec affairs, and within Quebec a very large number of alternatives from revolutionary separatism to co-operative federalism were vigorously expounded. The complications in elite accommodation became even more severe after the PQ victory in the 1976 Quebec elections, with the political elites of the province in Quebec City and Ottawa polarized along separatist and federalist axes. These complications were compounded by some groups in English-speaking Canada accepting the supporters of Quebec nationalism as the authoritative representatives of Quebec society[26] while other anglophones regarded federalists as the only authentic representatives of Quebec interests and values.

5. *The turning away from historic, prescriptive rights*   There was little disposition in Quebec from 1960 onward to defend any version of the compact theory of Confederation. A crucial event here was the 1965 publication of the book *Égalité ou Indépendance* by Daniel Johnson, then leader of the Union Nationale opposition and from 1966 to his death in 1968 premier of Quebec.[27] He wrote "Ce que nous voulons, c'est plus que les pouvoirs que nous accordait la constitution de 1867,"[28] and he based Quebec's demands on the right of nations to self-determination rather than historic, prescriptive rights. Johnson, it should be remembered, had been a cabinet minister under the Duplessis government which had vigorously articulated Quebec's claims in terms of a prescriptive theory of Confederation.[29]

6. *The alteration in the demographic balance*   In the 1960s, there was a precipitous decline in the Quebec birth rate — from 26.1 births per thousand of population in 1961 to 14.8 in 1971.[30] Largely because the Quebec birth rate had declined to below the Canadian average, the proportion of the Canadian population of French ethnic origin declined from 30.4 per cent to 28.7 per cent in this decade.[31] Within Quebec, the proportion of persons of French ethnic origin declined from 80.6 per cent to 79.0 per cent between 1961 and 1971,[32] and there was a pronounced tendency among Quebecers of neither French nor English ethnic origin to assimilate themselves into the English-language community.

Responses to the New Quebec

During the 1960s, there developed among supporters of the federal system, both English-speaking and French-speaking, the judgement that under the new circumstances of Quebec the survival of Confederation dictated a much-enhanced and more explicit recognition of French-English duality in the Canadian community as such. More than in the past, particularly among anglophones, the dualistic dimension of Canada was emphasized. Ramsay Cook pithily summed up this perspective in the Introduction to his *Canada and the French-Canadian Question* published in 1966: "Canada and the French Canadian question is really the Canadian question."[33] The Terms of Reference of the Royal Commission on Bilingualism and Biculturalism defined "the Canadian Confederation" as "an equal partnership between the two founding races." And certainly Pierre Trudeau, whose importance in shaping Canadian political debate in the period when he was prime minister is almost impossible to exaggerate, articulated a dualistic view of the country both before and after his entry into elective politics.

Apart from ideological redefinitions, there were other responses to the new circumstances of duality which developed from 1960 onward:

1. *Accessions to Quebec's demands for an enhanced scope of fiscal and administrative autonomy*   On several occasions Ottawa was willing to respond positively to Quebec's demands for a wider scope of fiscal and administrative discretion. In 1965, Parliament enacted the *Established Programs (Interim Arrangements) Act* which permitted the provinces to contract out of certain established grant-in-aid programs with full fiscal compensation. On several occasions prior to 1966, the federal authorities extended the scope of provincial "tax room" and increased the scale of unconditional fiscal subsidies to the province. After lengthy negotiations between the federal and Quebec governments, it was decided that the Canada Pension Plan should not apply to Quebec. Two other programs, student loans and youth allowances, which elsewhere in the country were funded and administered by the federal authorities, were, in Quebec, undertaken by the province with full fiscal compensation from Ottawa. From 1971 onward, there have been agreements between the federal government and Quebec permitting a more extensive Quebec role in relation to immigration than that wished by the other provinces. In response to persistent Quebec demands for control over family allowances and other aspects of social policy, Parliament in 1973 enacted legislation allowing provinces to determine, within certain limits, the levels at which family allowances would be distributed among different categories of beneficiaries. It was Ottawa's general position in the kinds of matters outlined above that, in formal terms, the options to enhance provincial autonomy should be available on the same conditions to all the provinces. However, that these options were made available at all was almost exclusively a response to the circumstances of Quebec, and, in most cases, only Quebec took advantage of these options.

2. *Constitutional review and reform*   The process of constitutional review begun by the 1967 Confederation for Tomorrow Conference was a direct response to the emergent circumstances of Quebec. While the negotiations leading up to the November 1981 agreement between Ottawa and the nine provinces with English-speaking majorities isolated Quebec, the impetus for the renewal of the constitutional review process in the summer of 1980 was a direct result of the federal Liberals' promise in the referendum campaign earlier that year that a "No" verdict would result in what Prime Minister Trudeau designated as "renewed federalism."

3. *Reform in the federal public service*   In April 1966, Prime Minister Pearson announced a new linguistic regime in the federal public service.[34] This

was the first such federal policy related to this matter, although from a 1938 amendment to the Civil Service Act onward, there had been a requirement that in recruitment to local positions the Civil Service Commission should ensure that a successful candidate had a knowledge of either English or French if this was the language "of the majority of the persons with whom he is required to do business."

The prime minister's statement so enunciated the new policy:

The government hopes and expects that, within a reasonable period of years, a state of affairs will be reached in the public service whereby

(a) it will be a normal practice for oral or written communications within the service to be made in either official language at the option of the person making them, in the knowledge that they will be understood by those directly concerned;

(b) communications with the public will normally be in either official language having regard to the person being served;

(c) the linguistic and cultural values of both English-speaking and French-speaking Canadians will be reflected through civil service recruitment and training.

In the Report of the Royal Commission on Bilingualism and Biculturalism, published in 1969, a section on "The Federal Administration" made a detailed analysis of the participation of anglophones and francophones in the public service as well as of linguistic usage in the operations of the bureaucracy.[35] The commission attributed the "precipitous decline" in the French-speaking proportion of the public service between 1918 and 1946 — from 22 per cent to 13 per cent — to the workings of the merit principle adopted in the former year. According to the report, "both Francophone and Anglophone federal politicians and public servants accepted the prevailing orthodoxies linking unilingualism with rationality and efficiency,"[36] and "the Civil Service Commission and the departmental chiefs did not relate language use and participation to the goal of bureaucratic efficiency." In 1965 some 21.5 per cent of federal departmental civil servants had French as their mother tongue but it was reported that:

Only in two of the 22 larger departments and agencies did (persons with French mother-tongue) make up 22 per cent of the staff earning $10,000 or more — the departments of the Secretary of State and the Post Office (26 and 45 per cent respectively). At the level earning less than $10,000 a year, 10 of the 17 departments and agencies for which data were available had staffs that were more than 22 per cent of French mother tongue. They were obviously concentrated in the lower levels of the federal administration.[37]

Outside Quebec, and most importantly in Ottawa itself, English was the working language of the civil service, and the commission asserted: "Ability and willingness to work in English appear to be conditions of advancement in the Public Service for those of French mother tongue."

In June 1973, Parliament confirmed the general principles of the 1966 policies by a resolution which directed the government to identify the official-language requirements of all positions in the departmental civil service and to ensure a greater use of French at all levels in the service. On November 21, 1974 the President of the Treasury Board tabled a statement in the House of Commons[38] to the effect that language requirements had been established for 281 664 positions in the departmental public service:

Sixty per cent of positions were defined as those which English was essential, 13 per cent French essential, 19 per cent bilingual, and in 8 per cent either language might qualify.

In the National Capital Region 45 per cent of 79 939 positions required bilingual capacities.

The bilingual positions were so described by occupational category:

Category	Number of Positions	Per cent of Category Bilingual
Executive	963	93
Administrative and Foreign Service	16 805	37
Scientific and Professional	7 002	27
Technical	4 137	15
Administrative/Support	19 482	25
Operational	4 835	5

By 1975, the way in which the federal bilingualism program had been implemented was under attack by both the Commissioner of Official Languages and in a massive report prepared for the government under the direction of Dr. Gilles Bibeau of the University of Montreal. The major thrust of the Bibeau Report was that the 53 000 bilingual positions which existed in 1973–74 had been so classified without any detailed evaluation of the needs for the second language on the job, and the recommendations were made that the number of bilingual positions be reduced by relating these more closely to functional needs, but that the standards of competence in the second language be raised. In his 1975 report the Commissioner of Official Languages published a survey made by the Treasury Board secretariat of some 3762 graduates of courses in English and French which showed that, of 2670 graduates of French-language courses, 83 per cent spent less than 20 per cent of their working time in that language and 61 per cent less than 10 per cent of such time.[39] The commissioner questioned pointedly whether the estimated expenditure of $9150 on the linguistic education of each of these persons was justified.[40]

Partly no doubt in response to the kinds of criticism outlined above, the President of the Treasury Board issued in September 1977 a statement of revised government policies in respect to the official languages in the public service. Among the more important changes were these:

The less discriminating approach to bilingual classification was to be replaced by a principle which would "base the language requirements of positions on the specific and actual work-related need for one or both languages to carry out the duties of each position."

Under broad guidelines set by the Public Service Commission, the responsibilities for language classification and for second-language training formerly assumed by the commission were to be devolved on the departments and agencies.

Most of the federal Crown corporations were to be included in the linguistic regime prevailing in the departmental public service.

By 1983 the government was to end its policies of "appointments of unilingual persons to bilingual positions conditional on these persons acquiring the capacity in the second language, language instruction at public expense, and salary bonuses for bilingual employees."

4. *The legal and constitutional recognition of the official languages*   The Official Languages Act, 1969 and important changes in the Constitution which came into effect in 1982 gave increased recognition to the equality of French and English in the operations of the federal government and, in the case of the 1982 amendment, in the government of New Brunswick as well.

In 1967, the Royal Commission on Bilingualism and Biculturalism published its Report on The Official Languages, and in 1969 Parliament enacted The Official Languages Act. Article 2 of the act declared: "The English and French languages are the official languages of Canada for all purposes of the Parliament and Government of Canada, and possess and enjoy equality of status and equal rights and privileges as to their use in all the institutions of the Parliament and Government of Canada." The major thrust of this legislation was to ensure that citizens could communicate with the government of Canada in whichever of the official languages they chose, at least in places and situations where there was a sufficient demand for English or French to make this feasible. In order to police the operations of the act a Commissioner of Official Languages was appointed during good behaviour and for a seven-year term. The Supreme Court of Canada in a 1974 decision upheld the constitutionality of the Official Languages Act as a valid exercise of Parliament's power to legislate for the "Peace, Order, and Good Government of Canada."

It is difficult to measure exactly the increased capacity of the federal government to communicate with francophone Canadians brought about by the 1969 legislation and concurrent measures to increase the number of French-speakers in federal departments and agencies, even though successive annual reports of the Commissioner of Official Languages give invaluable and detailed accounts of such progress as well as obstacles encountered in attaining it. The ability of federal institutions to communicate with citizens in the French language and the levels of francophone participation in these institutions are related in a complex way. In a formal sense the bilingual requirement might be met by a public service made up wholly of anglophones who were fluent in French. However, in practical terms, bilingual positions have continued to be filled disproportionately by those whose mother tongue is French. This general disposition to enhance francophone participation seems to explain the government's rejection of the major recommendations of the Bibeau Report on official languages in the public service which suggested that the number of bilingual positions be restricted to those in which there was a functional justification for bilingual capacities.

The reforms which came into effect in 1982 gave the two languages a much more extensive constitutional recognition in the affairs of the federal government than had been contained in the provisions of Section 133 of the BNA Act of 1867.[41] In general terms, Section 16(1) of the Constitution Act, 1982 provided: "English and French are the official languages of Canada and have equality of status and equal rights and privileges as to their use in all institutions of the government and Parliament of Canada." As well as re-stating the provisions of Section 133 related to Parliament and courts established under Parliament's jurisdiction, Section 20(1) went on to provide:

> Any member of the public in Canada has the right to communicate with, and to receive available services from, any head or central office of an institution of the Parliament or government of Canada in English or French, and has the same right with respect to any other office of any such institution where
>
> (a) there is a significant demand for communication with and services from that office in such language, or
>
> (b) due to the nature of the office, it is reasonable that communications with and services from that office be available in both French and English.

Section 23 of the Constitution Act, 1982 provided educational rights for official-language minorities where the demand for such services so warranted. This was the first constitutional recognition in Canadian history of such rights based on language.

The Constitution Act, 1982 also established New Brunswick as an officially bilingual province. Not only is the equal status of English and French guaranteed in the legislative assembly and in the provincial courts, but also the right of any citizen to communicate with and receive services from "any office of an institution of the legislature or government of New Brunswick" with no restrictions on a where-numbers-warrant basis as prevails in respect to federal institutions.

Judicial review of the Constitution has in general supported the thrust towards the enhanced recognition of the two official languages.

In 1974, the Supreme Court of Canada upheld the validity of the Official Languages Act of 1969 as an exercice of federal power over federal governmental and parliamentary institutions stemming from the peace, order, and good government power of Section 91.[42] In the same case the Court upheld a section of the New Brunswick Official Languages Act providing for the use of both languages in provincial courts as a valid exercise of provincial power over the administration of justice.

In 1979, the Supreme Court of Canada invalidated the Official Language Act of Manitoba enacted in 1890 which provided that only the English language should be used in the legislature and courts of the province.[43] When the province was established, the Manitoba Act, 1870 provided that the status of the two languages should be the same as that of Quebec under Section 133 of the BNA Act of 1867. In effect, the 1979 judgement returned the province to the 1870 situation.[44]

In 1984, a decision of the Supreme Court of Canada overturned the "Quebec clause" of Quebec's Charter of the French Language which restricted admission to English-language schools in Quebec to children whose parents had been educated in English in Quebec.[45] The Court declared in this judgement that Quebec law contravened Section 23(1)(b) of the Charter of Rights and Freedoms which provided that minority-language education must be available to children whose parents were educated in that language anywhere in Canada.

5. *"French power" at the senior levels of political decision*   Provincial representation in the first cabinet of the new Dominion was a crucial element of the Confederation settlement. As agreed upon by the British North American politicians in 1866, the first Executive Council was to have five ministers from Ontario — including the prime minister — four from Quebec, and two from each of the Maritime provinces. This provincial balance was, in aggregate terms, perpetuated in succeeding decades, and between 1867 and 1965 some 30.4 per cent of cabinet ministers had come from Quebec, a proportion very close to that province's persistent proportion of the Canadian population.[46] However, such aggregates give an inaccurate indication of francophone influence: in particular with respect to departments having responsibilities for economic policy — where French-speaking persons were denied leadership. Pierre Trudeau wrote in 1962 that "with the sole exception of Laurier, I fail to see a single French Canadian in more than three-quarters of a century whose presence in the federal cabinet might be considered indispensable to the history of Canada as written — except at election time."[47] The later composition of Trudeau's own cabinets reversed all of that, and by the time he had left office in 1984, francophones from Quebec had held all the economic portfolios; at one time in 1982 such persons headed what might reasonably be considered the three most important economic departments of finance, energy and transport.

6. *The symbolic recognition of the two languages in federal affairs*   From the early 1960s onward there were efforts to give symbolic recognition to linguistic duality in the federal government. As there were efforts in Quebec to make the province "visually French," so there were corresponding attempts to make the central government visually bilingual. Fastidious attention was given to the design of government stationery, the translation of documents, and the presence of the two languages on federal buildings. Several federal departments and agencies were renamed to make the two languages in a sense inter-changeable — Air Canada, Environment Canada, Transport Canada, and so on.

Nineteen eighty-four appears to have been a watershed year in the symbolic (perhaps more than symbolic) recognition of the French language at the highest levels of partisan political life in Canada. In that year, John Crosbie's campaign to become leader of the Progressive Conservative party was very much compromised because of his lack of competence in French. There was also a nationally televised debate among the leaders of the three political parties wholly in the

French language. On the basis of these developments, it is unlikely that, in future, any national party will choose as its leader a person without considerable fluency in French.

7. *Closer Canadian ties with the francophone world*   Canadian foreign policy since 1960 has given more attention to the French-speaking world than in the past.[48] The Canadian government has been active in francophonie, the association of French-speaking nations, and in the Third World there has been an enhanced Canadian presence in francophone Africa in contrast with the earlier preoccupation with Commonwealth nations. In February 1986, Prime Minister Mulroney led the Canadian delegation to the first meeting of the heads of government of the 41 French-speaking nations. He was accompanied by the premiers of Quebec and New Brunswick. According to the agreement worked out among the three participating governments from Canada, the premiers would speak on matters outside provincial jurisdiction only with prior federal approval. Although francophonie had developed as a kind of French-speaking commonwealth from the 1960s, domestic Canadian problems about the status of Quebec in this organization had, it seems, obstructed a meeting at the level of heads of government.

Apart from the measures to increase the autonomy of the political authorities of Quebec, the responses outlined above also embodied a relatively coherent view of Canada and the kind of solutions needed to preserve Confederation under the new circumstances of French-English duality. In broad terms, a vastly enhanced recognition of such duality in national institutions and in those of the provinces with significant francophone minorities was urgently necessary. Ottawa as well as Quebec City could legitimately speak for francophones both in domestic and international affairs. Language alone rather than broader culture was the distinguishing characteristic of the French-speaking and English-speaking elements of the Canadian population; citizens as individuals were related to one or other of these linguistic communities, and it was urgently necessary to sustain the position of official language minorities in the provinces.

There was, of course, dissent from the general thrust towards recognition of duality in the Canadian community as such. These responses obviously did not win the support of those who believed that the integrity of the francophone community of Quebec required its establishment as a sovereign state, in some sort of economic association with Canada or otherwise. Writing from a perspective that was not separatist, the sociologist Hubert Guindon in a 1978 article made an attack on the Royal Commission on Bilingualism and Biculturalism's recommendations on the two official languages and the policies of the federal government based on these recommendations.[49] According to Guindon, the "central concern" of an appropriate federal policy towards language "should have been not to try to shore up the collapsing language frontiers upholding vanishing French communities outside Quebec, but to break down the unacceptable language frontiers preventing the expanding Québécois elites from penetrating both the federal state's own corporations and the private corporate world in Quebec." On this basis "the federal state has . . . followed a language policy that can only be described as a political irritation for English Canada which is entirely politically irrelevant to a modernizing Quebec." What was required, claimed Guindon, was the renegotiation of Confederation so as "to facilitate the full participation of *Québécois* in their political economy." He went on: "There is a price for a new political consensus in Canada. And certain groups will have to play this price. Those two unfortunate groups are the French outside Quebec and the English in Quebec."

There was also opposition to federal policies from many sources in English-speaking Canada. At one level, these were expressions of the most distasteful variety of anti-French bigotry. However, there was more principled dissent. In a book privately published in 1967 and which received little notice at the time, Richard J. Joy demonstrated from census materials that there was an ongoing linguistic segregation of French and English in Canada with the former confined to the area between Moncton and Sault Ste. Marie and, in Quebec, the English confined to the Montreal region.[50] Although federal policies from the 1960s onward emphasized official language minorities, Joy concluded: "The historical evidence printed indicates that two languages of unequal strength cannot co-exist in intimate contact and that the weaker must, inevitably, disappear."[51] In several of his later writings, Donald Creighton advised resistance both to demands for enhanced Quebec autonomy and to measures which would enhance the recognition of French in the wider Canadian community.[52] Using historical evidence, Creighton attacked the view that Confederation had been a French-English compact and the recent orthodoxy which "grotesquely exaggerated the importance of language and culture . . . [and] absurdly minimized the importance of everything else."[53] Creighton defended the continuing relevance of essentials of the Confederation settlement with its assertion of the dominant power of the central government and predicted that if Canada were re-established to emphasize cultural and linguistic values, the end would be "the creation of a separate or, virtually separate, Quebec." Thus:

> The French language has survived for one reason only: because Canada has survived. The Fathers of Confederation reached a settlement which gave the French language the best chance it will ever have on this continent. And if we try to improve on that settlement, we do so at our peril.[54]

Writing from a still different perspective, the Honourable J. T. Thorson, formerly a Liberal cabinet minister and after that President of the Exchequer Court of Canada, gave his views in a book published in 1974:

> The choice is between *a dual French-English Canada,* such as that which the Trudeau government is attempting to establish, with its continuing domination by its Quebec members and supporters, and the discord and dissention that result from the constant disputes between the leaders of Quebec and the Trudeau government; or *a Single Canada,* such as that which Canadians of many origins have been trying to build, in which the prime concern is for its individuals and all Canadians stand on the footing of equality with one another, both in the enjoyment of their rights and the fulfilment of their duties, without any preference to the members of any component of the Canadian nation.[55]

Constitutional and Legal Recognition of Language

As we have seen, the central element of federal strategies for combatting Quebec nationalism was the enhanced recognition of the French language in the Canadian community as such. This response was based on a combination of principled and expedient considerations.

On the basis of principle, the federal view of Canada — most coherently articulated by Pierre Trudeau both before and after his entry into elective politics in 1965 — was that of a country in which citizens were members of one or the other of the linguistic groups as individuals sharing a common allegiance to Canadian laws and political institutions. In Trudeau's opinion, the enemy was the national state, the political community whose will was the embodiment of the values and interests of only one cultural, ethnic or linguistic group.[56] According to this view, a rapid enhancement in the recognition of the French language in the affairs of the Canadian community outside the boundaries of Quebec was urgently necessary to combat Quebec nationalism and to strengthen the allegiance of francophone Quebecers to Canada.

On more expedient grounds, an emphasis on enhancing the status of the French language as a response to Quebec nationalism allowed Ottawa to avoid coming to grips directly with other pressures towards constitutional reform directed towards enlarging the powers of the provincial authorities of Quebec, either through changes which would give Quebec a special status or which would increase the powers of all the provinces.

Up until the 1960s the Quebec legislature enacted almost no laws directly related to language. In 1910 it was provided that public utilities should serve customers in French as well as English. A law enacted in 1937 provided that French had priority in the interpretation of provincial laws and regulations, but under pressure from the anglophone community this legislation was repealed a year later. In the late 1960s a crisis erupted in the St. Leonard suburb of Montreal over the demands of Italian-speaking parents that their children be educated in English rather than French. The Union Nationale government responded to this crisis by the enactment of Bill 63, giving parents the choice of having their children educated in French or English. The resultant hostility to this measure among francophones led the government to appoint a Commission of Inquiry on the Position of the French Language and Language Rights in Quebec. The Gendron Commission reported in 1972, and its work was the inspiration for Bill 22 sponsored by the Bourassa Liberal government and enacted by the national assembly in 1974. Bill 101 sponsored by the PQ government became law in 1977.

Both Bill 22 and Bill 101 were directed towards establishing the primacy of the French language in important aspects of the governmental affairs and economic life of Quebec. William D. Coleman has made a detailed analysis of the differences between these two enactments and the premises underlying them:[57]

1. Bill 22 permitted English to be used in "local municipal, school and social service institutions"; Bill 101 was much more restrictive in this respect. Coleman explains the difference in terms of the Liberal conviction that Quebec was and should be a part of Canada and that, on this basis, the English-speaking community of the province was part of the national majority group, whereas the PQ

viewed Quebec as an "embryonic nation state" with the English community being a "national minority" therein.

2. Bill 22 permitted a free choice in the language of education for children who could demonstrate a sufficient knowledge of English and French to receive an education in the preferred language, and it imposed an upper limit on the total number who could be educated in English; Bill 101 was more restrictive. Under the latter law, English-language instruction was available to only four groups:

(i)   Children who had a parent who had received primary education in Quebec in English.

(ii)   Children whose father or mother lived in Quebec at the time Bill 101 was enacted and who had received primary schooling in English outside Quebec.

(iii) Children who in the previous year had been legally enrolled in English-language schools of Quebec.

(iv)   Younger siblings of those in category 3.

3. In restricting the use of other languages than French in advertising, on store fronts and so on, Bill 101 went much further than did Bill 22 in its attempt to make Quebec "visually French."

In general terms, the progression from Bill 22 to Bill 101 represented a move away from a vision of Quebec as a bicommunal society to a pluralist community whose members were united rather than differentiated by language. Coleman has concluded:

> [T]he policies on language pursued by [Quebec] governments beginning in the mid-1960s had the effect of undermining the French language as a cultural foundation. The policies developed have transformed French as an informal language not used in several key spheres of economic life into a standard language helping to integrate the French-Canadian community into the dominant culture of North America. French, which had been one of the several barriers restricting contacts between les Canadiens français and les autres, has become the policy instrument for beaking barriers among the several cultural communities in Quebec.[58]

What is being played out in Quebec and in the wider Canadian context is a complex set of realignments between language and culture and between language/culture and citizenship in its fullest sense. George Etienne Cartier in the Confederation Debates spoke of Canadians under the projected Dominion forming a "political nationality with which neither the national origin nor the religion of any individual would interfere." Thus the ties of citizenship and allegiance would be purely political. Cartier's noble vision has never been fully realized in Canada and has been realized to any significant degree only since the Second World War. Older living anglophones were raised according to the imperative, "To be Canadian, we must remain British" — an assertion of the superiority of those of British (and Protestant) origins and of their continuing allegiance to the British Empire/Commonwealth. It must be emphasized that Anglo-Saxondom included much more than the English language and that even Canadians who were fully fluent in English were denied access to status and opportunities if they were not perceived as belonging to the dominant charter group.

As in Anglo-Saxon Canada, membership in the francophone community of Quebec has, until very recently, been defined in dimensions broader than language. This definition was most coherently and eloquently made by the Royal Commission of Inquiry on Constitutional Problems in its report to the government of Quebec in 1956.[59] According to the Tremblay Commission, "the whole Canadian problem" is the relation between two cultural groups each with an "almost monolithic homogeneity." Each group manifests a particular national genius; "those of French origin and those of English origin represent two distinct temperaments, two casts of mind, two distinct geniuses which differ as profoundly in their ways of understanding life and of practising it as they differ in their ways of expressing themselves."[60] Underlying this whole formulation was an emphasis on the distinctiveness of the two communities based on their Catholic and Protestant foundations respectively. The chief role of the state according to the Tremblay formulation was the "conservation and fruition" of the cultural values of the nation, the sustenance of a homogeneous "ethnic environnement."

It was implicit in the definition of Quebec nationhood made by the Tremblay Commission that membership in that community be restricted to those who traced all or part of their lineal descent to the 60 000 or so francophones who lived in New France in 1759. Thus, being a member of the Quebec nation was something like being a Jew. This nation in its struggle to preserve its integrity and homogeneity was not assimilationist in its dispositions, and in Quebec until the late 1950s at least, persons of non-francophone origins were encouraged to have their children educated in the Protestant school system whatever their religious, cultural and linguistic roots.

During recent years, and most dramatically since the PQ came to power in 1976, there has been a redefinition of the Quebec community and the relation of language to that community. In a book published in 1968, René Lévesque spoke of *québécois* in these terms: "Being ourselves is essentially a matter of keeping and developing a personality that has survived for three and a half centuries. At the core of this personality is the fact that we speak French. Everything else depends on this one essential element and follows from it or leads us infallibly back to it."[61] This is a definition of nationhood very different from that advanced by the Tremblay Commission.

Much of the impetus behind Bills 22 and 101 came from the strong tendency of immigrants to Quebec from outside Canada to have their children educated in English rather than French and to join the English-speaking community. This tendency, combined with a rapidly declining birth rate among francophones, gave rise to fears among *québécois* of a demographic balance within Quebec unfavourable to the French-speaking element of the population. Thus, it was believed urgent that the public authorities take decisive action to secure and extend the dominance of French in the governmental, educational and economic life of the province. However, to the extent that such efforts were successful, there was the implication that the French language, rather than being a crucial element in differentiating the two societies of Quebec, should become a unifying factor in that community. This result has been only partially realized, but it appears inevitable that when persons of non-*québécois* origins come fully to terms with a regime in which the language of public communication is French — with the public now defined to include most areas of economic life — such persons will strive to advance themselves individually in areas of life hitherto almost exclusively reserved by birthright to *québécois* (for example, in the provincial public service) and to exercise a measure of control over institutions which in the past have served *québécois* interests almost exclusively. Such a development is what Sheila McLeod Arnopoulos and Dominique Clift have called the "Trojan horse" of Quebec language policies.[62] The movement is by no means complete, and, in specific terms, the confessional nature of the educational system — buttressed by constitutional guarantees dating from Confederation — provides a continuing obstruction towards advancing in the direction of what Coleman designates as a "pluralist" society operating (for all but private purposes) in the French language and away from the older bicommunal framework. However, the general thrust in Quebec towards pluralism appears irreversible, and the decline of the Catholic religion along with other modernizing trends in the province have rapidly decreased the differences in values and lifestyles between *québécois* and other Canadians. Language is in the process of becoming an integrating factor within Quebec itself and the only important differentiation between Quebec and the wider Canadian community.

The regulation of language by the federal authorities and those of Quebec have had very different objectives. The measures undertaken by Ottawa have been directed primarily at minorities — whether of francophone minorities outside Quebec or of francophones as a minority in Canada as a whole. Those within in Quebec have been taken in the interests of the numerically dominant group. Federal actions have had an individualist thrust; those of Quebec a more collective orientation. Ottawa's policies have involved almost exclusively the governmental sphere of activity; Bills 22 and 101 have dealt with language usage in private business activity. However, both kinds of linguistic regulation have had as their objectives the enhancement of the position of the French language and the opportunities available to those competent in French. Both also differentiate between the anglophone and francophone communities on the basis of language alone, rather than the older distinctions based on lineage and/or a definition of culture broader than language. Because it is possible for a person to acquire competence in a language which is not his or her mother tongue, the boundaries of the two communities are more porous than before. We are, perhaps, in the process of realizing Cartier's vision of a political nationality with which neither the national origin nor the religion of an individual will interfere or, perhaps more correctly so far as Quebecers are concerned, two compatible political nationalities, one focussed on the French-speaking pluralistic nation of Quebec and the other on Canada.

Language and the public regulation of language remain matters of intense political conflict in Canada. A large part of this conflict relates to the educational and other rights of official-language minorities in Manitoba, New Brunswick, Quebec and Ontario.[63] Under the present constitutional arrangements the rights of these minority groups are different. In all cases, the provinces are under a constitutional obligation to provide educational services to official-language minorities on a where-numbers-warrant basis. Under the 1982 constitutional arrangements, New Brunswick is committed to providing all provincial and local services in both languages. In Quebec and Manitoba, the constitutional rights related to education in the official-language minority are supplemented by the continuance in effect of the original provisions of Section 133 of the BNA Act of 1867 and the Manitoba Act of 1870 which guarantee the rights of both languages in the legislature and in provincial courts. Ontario, unlike New Brunswick, has up to now refused to support the entrenchment of French-language rights in respect to matters within provincial jurisdiction, and although progress has been made in respect to such matters as education and judicial facilities in the French language through legislation and administrative action, these do not have a constitutional base except for the provisions of the Charter related to education. [64]

Another issue, largely hidden but potentially explosive, relates to the opportunities available to bilingual as against unilingual anglophones in national institutions. During his campaign for the leadership of the Progressive Conservative party in 1984, John Crosbie lashed out at those who had been critical of his inability to speak French: "[T]here are 20 million of us who are unilingual English or French. . . . I don't think that the 3.7 million who are bilingual should suddenly think of themselves as some kind of aristocracy and only leaders can come from this small group." [65] Crosbie in the next few days apologized for his intemperate remarks about language, although his own unilingualism seriously compromised his leadership campaign. Despite the issue's being effectively defused at this time, there remains in some anglophone quarters a smoldering resentment among those who perceive their opportunities for advancement to be limited by their lack of competence in French. And because in anglophone Canada it is the more prosperous parents who are most insistent about their children's becoming bilingual, the issue has the potentiality of dividing English-speaking Canadians along class lines.

The Referendum of 1980

With the coming to power of the Parti Québécois in November 1976 and the collective self-confidence this event gave to even those in the *québécois* community not committed to sovereignty, it was reasonable to forecast that a majority of the members of that community could be rallied to support independence in the near future. In a book published in 1978, the political scientist, André Bernard, marshalled the evidence for such a forecast: "In 1970, the Parti Québécois had a majority in the 18–24 age group; in 1973, it had a majority in the 18–30 age group; in 1976, it had a majority in the 18–35 age group. In 1980, if the trend is maintained, it will have a majority in the 18–40 age group, and probably also in the 40–45 age group, with a good showing (40 per cent) in the 45–55 category: this will make for a solid and absolute majority of the whole Quebec electorate." [66] Further, in the 1976 election the PQ had received the support of 50 per cent of all Québécois voters — 70 per cent of these with 12 years or more of schooling — and 20 per cent of bilingual English-speaking Quebecers. Surveys had shown that the PQ generally retained the support in subsequent elections of those who had once voted for it. Apart from support for the Parti Québécois, there had been, since early in the 1960s, a steadily increasing support for sovereignty-association. On the basis of these factors, Bernard concluded: "Support for Quebec independence has gradually increased with time, and, in my view, is likely to increase further because of the demographic trends which favour the Parti Québécois and because of the greater propaganda effect that can be put behind the idea now that the Parti Québécois is the Quebec government."[67] Not only did the PQ have the propaganda advantage to which Bernard referred but is also had the discretion to determine when the referendum on independence was to take place — within the limit imposed by the party itself of having such a ballot within its first term in office — the law under which the referendum would be conducted, and the question to be put to the voters.

The PQ leadership gave an enormous amount of attention to the framing of the question to be submitted to the Quebec electorate, and the following was finally adopted:

> The government of Quebec has made public its proposal to negotiate a new agreement with the rest of Canada based on the equality of nations.
>
> This agreement would enable Quebec to acquire the exclusive power to make its laws, administer its taxes and establish relations abroad — in other words, sovereignty — and at the same time, to maintain a common currency.
>
> Any change in political status resulting from these negotiations will be submitted to the people through a referendum.
>
> On these terms, do you agree to give the government the power to negotiate the proposed agreement between Quebec and Canada?
>
> YES
>
> NO

The question was very "soft" in the sense that it was deliberately contrived to elicit the support of voters not committed to Quebec sovereignty. The electorate was, after all, being asked to vote not for independence but only to give the government the "mandate to negotiate" some new form of economic association with Canada, and it was made explicit in the question itself that changes in Quebec's status would come into effect only after ratification in a subsequent referendum. Both before and during the referendum campaign, the PQ took great pains to reassure the electorate that the transition to sovereignty could and would come about without significant economic dislocations.

The Parti Québécois embarked on its referendum strategy on the optimistic assumptions that a majority of the Quebec voters would support its mandate to negotiate some form of continuing association with Canada and that Canada would have no alternative but to accept such an association. There was, it seems, no fall-back position to deal with other possible results:

First, if, as happened, a majority of the electorate voted NO, the PQ government would be placed in an extremely weak position in its dealings with Ottawa and the other provinces. From 1960 onward, Liberal and Union Nationale governments in Quebec had possessed a bargaining power attendant on their being the only alternative to independence, and they had pressed this advantage skillfully and aggressively. A NO verdict would and did eliminate this leverage. To be blunt, if a majority of the Quebec voters could not be rallied to support even the softest sovereignty option, separatism was decisively demonstrated to be a paper tiger. In its dealings with the federal government and those of the other provinces, the PQ administration was in a very weak position and the constitutional settlement which came into effect in 1982 demonstrated this weakness by further restricting Quebec autonomy which, in its fiscal and administrative dimensions, had been expanded under the previous Liberal and Union Nationale regimes.

Second, if a YES verdict had been rendered and the federal government had refused to negotiate economic association, or at least any association acceptable to Quebec, the PQ government would have been forced either to reject sovereignty outright or to convince the majority of the Quebec electorate in a subsequent referendum of the desirability of sovereignty without economic association. Premier Lévesque, in a statement to the Quebec national assembly in October 1978, had affirmed: "We have no intention of obtaining sovereignty and then negotiating an association. We do not want to end, but rather to radically transform, our union with the rest of Canada, so that in the future our relations will be based on full and complete equality. Sovereignty and association should therefore be attainted concurrently without any rupture, once the people of Quebec have given us our mandate in the referendum." There was here the assumption that once a YES verdict had been returned, the Canadian authorities would have no realistic alternative to negotiating an economic association with Quebec, and it was even suggested that, once they came to consider the matter seriously, they would find advantages for themselves in such an arrangement. During the referendum campaign the PQ asserted that the statements of Prime Minister Trudeau and the premiers of several of the provinces that they would refuse to negotiate an economic union with Quebec was nothing more than a ploy to influence the Quebec electorate to vote NO. However, although such a judgement is obviously impossible to prove, it seems to me unlikely that Ottawa would have responded to a YES verdict by entering into negotiations leading to sovereignty-association. I have argued elsewhere that the kind of economic association proposed by the PQ would not have been in the interests of Canada-without-Quebec and that, faced with the inevitability of Quebec sovereignty, the remaining Canadians would have preferred to deal with this new power through the normal procedures of international relations without submitting the most crucial of Canadian economic policies to a Quebec veto.[68] Furthermore, it seems unlikely that any administration headed by Pierre Trudeau and with half the government MPs coming from Quebec would have entered into such negotiations. To repeat, as in the case with a possible NO verdict, the PQ proceeded without a fall-back position, and if the federal authorities had failed to act as the separatist leaders predicted, Premier Lévesque and his colleagues would have faced the unpalatable alternative of a forthright retreat from sovereignty or of attempting to convince the Quebec electorate that sovereignty *sans* association was desirable.

There appears to have been considerable confusion and disagreement among the Quebec voters about both the meaning of the question put before them on the referendum ballot and the "renewed federalism" promised by Prime Minister Trudeau and the NO forces. In general, however, the latter alternative, as Trudeau had predicted it, had always meant patriation of the British North America Act and a charter of rights.

What was clearly put aside as a result of the referendum verdict was the version of a reformed Canadian federalism propounded by the Ryan Liberals in Quebec. Early in 1980 the provincial Liberals published *A New Canadian Federation* — a document which came to be known as the Beige Paper — proposing a more provincially dominant regime which would, among other things, vest residual powers in the provinces, clarify and extend provincial powers generally and replace the Senate with a "Federal Council" made up of persons chosen by and taking their instructions from the provincial governments.[69] According to Graham Fraser, Claude Ryan had been persuaded by Trudeau not to campaign on the Beige Paper proposals in the referendum "for the sake of federalist unity," with Ryan apparently gambling on three things: that the federal Liberals would wait until after the next Quebec provincial election before moving towards constitutional change, that the Quebec Liberals would win this election and that the Beige Paper reforms would then be on the constitutional agenda.[70] As it happened, this formulation of a renewed federalism did not influence subsequent constitutional evolution, and Ryan collaborated with the PQ leadership in drawing up a resolution passed by the National Assembly in September 1981 — with nine Liberals breaking ranks — condemning the Trudeau government for proceeding unilaterally with constitutional reform.

The referendum was a decisive event in the history of French-English duality in Canada, although it is perhaps still too early to assess its significance more than tentatively. The Quebec community displayed a very high degree of political maturity in debating and peacefully resolving the fundamental question of its collective political future. The campaign was the climax of the debate which had preoccupied the province since the early 1960s, and the verdict was a prelude to a decline in the vigour and intensity of this debate and to the rapid decline of Quebec nationalism.

How Can the Decline of Quebec Nationalism Be Explained?

The Quebec general election of 1985 was the first since 1940 in which the national question was not of some importance. Even in the immediate aftermath of the 1980 referendum few observers of Quebec affairs would have predicted that nationalism as a significant force in the internal politics of that province and in its relations with the rest of Canada would have disappeared within five years. How did this all come about?

Paradoxically, the importance of the national question in Quebec provincial politics led to the involvement of other Canadians in Quebec affairs. This involvement took its most direct form in the provincial election of 1939 in which the federal Liberals under Mackenzie King intervened successfully to defeat the Union Nationale government.[71] As Quebec elections from 1960 onward revolved largely about the national question, other Canadians perceived themselves to have a considerable stake in these contests. By 1985, this had ceased to be so because, for the time being at least, the PQ had turned its back on Quebec independence as an attainable or even desirable objective. In the provincial election of that year, the Mulroney government was overtly neutral — although its political opponents accused it of favouring the PQ — while the Bourassa Liberals, it seems, refused whatever aid their federal counterparts were willing to give. Thus, the disentanglement of the federal and provincial partisan/political system which was analysed in Chapter V has come to include Quebec in a fuller sense than before.

From its establishment in 1969, the Parti Québécois was the almost exclusive instrument of Quebec nationalism. In one sense, the collapse of Quebec nationalism can largely be explained in terms of the failure of the PQ to reconcile what the late Walter Young, in his analysis of the Co-operative Commonwealth Federation (CCF), designated as the conflicting claims of party and movement.[72] The test of a party is to win elections; a movement is oriented towards comprehensive social, economic and political reform. Sometimes the party-movement contradiction is resolved in favour of party as happened with the Union Nationale after 1936, Alberta Social Credit from the early 1940s onward and the Parti Québécois in the mid-1980s. In other circumstances, as with the CCF and NDP, the two impulses remain in permanent tension, with neither winning a decisive victory over the other.

The party-movement contradiction in the PQ was particularly difficult to deal with for two reasons:

First, from the beginning the Parti Québécois' support for Quebec independence was a significant electoral liability. This circumstance put the party's *raison-d'être* and its chances of gaining or retaining political power in direct conflict.

Second, despite the PQ's unconvincing attempt to make it appear otherwise, the attainment of sovereignty by Quebec was, by its very nature, a non-incremental matter. So far as democratic socialist parties are concerned, the conflicting impulses of party and movement can to a greater or lesser degree be resolved by more or less emphasis on public ownership or income redistribution or economic planning. Sovereignty was inherently otherwise: at some specific time Quebec would cease to be a province within the Canadian Confederation and would pass to membership in the international community of sovereign nations.

The PQ leadership appears to have handled the party-movement contradiction ineptly prior to the mid-1980s when almost all the ''movement'' elements were put aside. In the 1976 election, the party campaigned, and of course came to power, on the commitment that a referendum on sovereignty would be held during its first term of office and, as we have seen, the referendum question submitted to the voters in 1980 was a very soft one which promised that if a YES verdict were given, steps towards independence would be taken only after another referendum. The provincial election of 1981 took place less than a year after the referendum, and the sovereignty issue was put aside while the PQ campaigned on a much more conservative platform than before which saw its majority increased with significant growth in its electoral support from rural and small-town Quebec.

At the PQ convention in December 1981, following closely the humiliation of the Lévesque government in the first ministers conference the previous month, the party endorsed one motion turning its back on the association element of sovereignty-association and another to the effect that independence would be declared if in the next general election the party had a majority in the national assembly. However, these motions had been passed against the strenuous objections of René Lévesque, and he subsequently brought about an internal party referendum which reversed these hard-line positions and won the support of 95 per cent of the party membership which voted.[73] By the time Lévesque stepped down in 1985, many thousands of PQ members, most committed to independence, had resigned from the party, including several members of the National Assembly and some of Lévesque's most able cabinet ministers. In the 1985 general election Quebec sovereignty had become, in the words of the PQ's new leader, Pierre-Marc Johnson, no more than an "insurance policy."

The PQ in power faced other unresolved problems:

1. To the extent that the Quebec electorate perceived the PQ as governing effectively, the urgency of independence was weakened. This appears to have been particularly important in respect to linguistic matters. To the extent that the dominance of French was secured and that new occupational opportunities for francophones were created through provincial action, the removal of Quebec from Confederation appeared less urgent to *québécois*.

2. The PQ's stance towards the rest of the Canadian community caused the Lévesque government to be ineffective in defending Quebec's interests within Confederation. This was very important in respect to constitutional matters. From the beginnings of the Quiet Revolution onward, successive Liberal and Union Nationale governments had a degree of leverage in making demands on Ottawa and the other provinces in asserting that in the domestic context of Quebec politics they were the moderates. The PQ did not have this leverage. In their desire to frustrate Ottawa's constitutional resolution of 1980, the PQ had collaborated with seven other provinces in a common position which did not include a Quebec veto over future constitutional amendments, a veto which the Trudeau government tried (in the end unsuccessfully) to have incorporated into the new amending formula. The constitutional settlement which came into effect in 1982 did not include such a veto, and in respect to linguistic matters, it restricted Quebec's powers more than under the previous arrangements.

3. In respect to energy matters also, the PQ's disposition towards provincialism caused it to be an ineffective supporter of Quebec's interests. Although the interests of the province would have been served if the government had, along with Ontario, given general support to the National Energy Policy (NEP), the Lévesque government, because of its autonomist ideology, stood aside in the conflict.[74] Unlike its predecessors, the PQ government made almost no gains in federal-provincial relations, and in respect to the Constitution it sustained heavy losses.

4. In its response to pressures towards fiscal restraint, the PQ government alienated the most fervent members of its constituency. The party's ideology was social democratic, and, in particular, it favoured the state sector which had had such a decisive role in modernizing the province. Yet like other jurisdictions in Canada, the Lévesque government, from the time it came to power, was under considerable pressure to restrain public expenditures, and, in particular, to restrain growth in the number of government employees and the size of the government

payroll. In late 1982 and 1983 the national assembly enacted draconian legislation imposing agreements on public sector employees and forcing the province's striking teachers back to work.[75] Thus, the party incurred the hostility of that part of its natural constituency most aggressive in its support and in many cases in its commitment to Quebec independence.

It is reasonable to suppose that Quebec nationalism has been undermined by shifting ideological currents. Dominique Clift has suggested that at some times in their history *québécois* have been disposed towards collectivist goals, and at others, individualistic impulses have been dominant.[76] During the years of the Quiet Revolution, collectivist influences were dominant, but by the early 1980s:

> There is among certain segments of Quebec society a growing resistance to the idea of subordinating personal expectations to the collective goals identified with nationalism and with cultural and even ethnic solidarity. A substantial number of people feel excluded and marginalized by those who wield political power and those who benefit by it. Others are apprehensive about the cultural isolation which might result from a complete and overwhelming victory of nationalism.[77]

In the development of anti-nationalism, Clift gives a very prominent place to Claude Ryan's campaign for the leadership of the Quebec Liberal party and to Ryan's subsequent influence on the ideological development of the province.[78]

Quebec was not, of course, isolated from the increasing strength of neo-conservatism in the Western world. In both the United Kingdom and the United States neo-conservatism and nationalism are closely allied. It is otherwise in Canada, whether the context is Canada as such or Quebec alone. During the Quiet Revolution, the francophones of that province underwent profound changes in collective definition: from French Canadians to *québécois*, from minority to majority, from *survivance* to *épanouissement*. A new dominant ideology appears to be emerging asserting individualism and the primacy of business values and the private sector in Quebec development.

What, then, of the importance of the response of Ottawa and, to varying degrees, of the other provinces to the new circumstances of French-English duality in contributing to the decline of Quebec nationalism? One can only conjecture. In the absence of persuasive evidence one way or the other, my own disposition is to emphasize developments within Quebec itself in explaining the weakening of nationalism as a political and ideological force in that province. However, it seems plausible to suggest that the efforts made in the direction of the enhanced recognition of French-English duality outside Quebec has had at least a marginal impact on this development.

Notes

1. David R. Cameron, "Dualism and National Unity," in John H. Redekop, ed., *Approaches to Canadian Politics* (Scarborough: Prentice-Hall Canada, 1978), p. 237.
2. *A Future Together,* report of the Task Force on Canadian Unity (Ottawa: Minister of Supply and Services Canada, 1979), p. 21.

3. See the superb account of the political history of this period, Jacques Monet, S. J., *The Last Cannon Shot: A Study of French-Canadian Nationalism, 1837–1850* (Toronto: University of Toronto Press, 1969).

4. J. M. S. Careless, *The Union of the Canadas: The Growth of Canadian Institutions, 1841–1857*, (Toronto: McCelland and Stewart, 1967), particularly Chapter 12, "The Pattern of Discussion 1856–1857."

5. Frank Scott, "Section 94 of the British North America Act" in Frank Scott, *Essays on the Constitution* (Toronto: University of Toronto Press, 1977), pp. 112–130.

6. A. I. Silver, *The French-Canadian Idea of Confederation 1864–1900* (Toronto: University of Toronto Press, 1982), pp. 55–66.

7. Hubert Guindon wrote of the "social contract" of Confederation as a bargain between the Catholic clergy of Quebec and Anglo-Canadian and British capital. Thus "The trade-off for the preservation of language and religion was the complete institutional and educational autonomy of the English, and exclusion (of the French) from partnership in the industrial capitalist enterprise." "Quebec and the Canadian State," in Daniel Glenday, Hubert Guindon and Allan Turowetz, eds., *Modernization and the Canadian State* (Toronto: Macmillan of Canada, 1978), p. 236.

8. Brian Young, "Federalism in Quebec: The First Years after Confederation," in Bruce W. Hodgins, Don Wright and W. H. Heick, eds., *Federalism in Canada and Australia: The Early Years* (Waterloo: Wilfred Laurier University Press, 1978), pp. 97–108.

9. Carl Berger, *The Sense of Power: Studies in the Ideas of Canadian Imperialism 1867–1914* (Toronto: University of Toronto Press, 1970), particularly "Conclusions."

10. Silver, *French-Canadian Idea of Confederation,* particularly Chapters VII–IX.

11. Pierre Elliott Trudeau, (éditeur), *La grève de l'amiante* (Québec: Université Laval Presse, 1954), p. 12. My translation.

12. *Report of the Royal Commission of Inquiry on Constitutional Problems,* (Quebec: 1956), Vol. 1, Chapter II, "The Canadian Cultures."

13. Frederick W. Gibson, "Conclusions", in Frederick W. Gibson, ed., *Cabinet Formation and Bicultural Relations,* Studies of the Royal Commission on Bilingualism and Biculturalism (Ottawa: Queen's Printer, 1970), pp. 161–172.

14. Ibid., pp. 155–161.

15. Sheila McLeod Arnopoulous and Dominique Clift, *The English Fact in Quebec* (Montreal and Kingston: McGill-Queen's University Press, 1980), p. 67.

16. Ibid., p. 68. The analysis in this chapter, "The Mediation of the Federal Liberal Party," pp. 67–69, is very acute.

17. Pierre Elliott Trudeau, *Federalism and the French Canadians* (Toronto: Macmillan of Canada, 1968), "Some Obstacles to Democracy in Quebec," pp. 103–123.

18. Ralph Heintzman, "The Political Culture of Quebec, 1840–1960," *Canadian Journal of Political Science* 16, no. 1 (March 1983): p. 36.

19. Ibid., p. 18.

20. Ibid.

21. Ramsay Cook, *Provincial Autonomy, Minority Rights* and *The Compact Theory, 1867–1921,* Studies of the Royal Commission on Bilingualism and Biculturalism (Ottawa: Queen's Printer, 1969). See particularly Chapter V, "Compact of Cultures?"

22. Rejean Lachapelle and Jacques Henripin, *The Demolinguistic Situation in Canada* (Montreal: Institute for Research on Public Policy, 1982), Chapter 2, "Size and Distribution of Ethnolinguistic Groups since 1871."

23. Hubert Guindon, "Social Unrest, Social Class and Quebec's Bureaucratic Revolution," *Queen's Quarterly* 71 (Summer 1964): pp. 150–162. For another analysis of the new middle class theory, see Kenneth McRoberts and Dale Posgate, *Quebec: Social Change and Political Crisis,* 2d ed. (Toronto: McClelland and Stewart, 1980), pp. 98–103. There is a vigorous critique of this theory in William D. Coleman, *The Independence Movement in Quebec 1945–1980* (Toronto: University of Toronto Press, 1984), pp. 5–11.

24. McRoberts and Posgate, *Quebec: Social Change Political Crisis,* Chapter 6, "The 'Quiet Revolution': The New Ideology of the Quebec State."

25. Fernand Ouellett, in *Quebec: Year Eight,* Glendon College Forum (Toronto: CBC Publications, 1968), p. 80.

26. One of the puzzles, to me at least, was the sympathetic sensitivity of the English-Canadian nationalist left to Quebec separatism in this period.

27. Daniel Johnson, *Égalité ou Indépendance* (Montréal: Éditions Renaissance, 1965).

28. Ibid., p. 120.

29. See particularly the *Report of the Royal Commission of Inquiry on Constitutional Problems.*

30. Richard Arès, *Les positions-ethniques, linguistiques et religieuses – des Canadians français à la suite du recensement de 1971* (Montréal: Les éditions Bellarmin, 1975), p. 14.

31. Lachapelle and Henripin, *Demolinguistic Situation in Canada,* p. 331.

32. Ibid., p. 334.

33. Ramsay Cook, *Canada and the French-Canadian Question* (Toronto: Macmillan of Canada, 1966), p. 2.

34. For a general discussion, see V. Seymour Wilson, "Language Policy," in G. Bruce Doern and V. Seymour Wilson, eds., *Issues in Canadian Public Policy* (Toronto: Macmillan of Canada, 1974), pp. 253–285.

35. *Report of the Royal Commission on Bilingualism and Biculturalism,* Book III, *The Work World* (Ottawa: Privy Council of Canada, 1969).

36. Ibid., p. 111.

37. Ibid., pp. 211–213. Reproduced with permission of the Minister of Supply and Services Canada.

38. *Official Languages in the Public Service of Canada, A Report by the Honourable Jean Chrétien President of the Treasury Board,* Nov. 21, 1974. (mimeo)

39. (Ottawa: Information Canada, 1976), p. 8.

40. Ibid., p. 7.

41. For the present constitutional status of the two official languages in Canada, see Peter W. Hogg, *Constitutional Law of Canada,* 2d ed. (Toronto: Carswell, 1985), Chapter 36, "Language."

42. *Jones v. A.-G. N.B. (1974),* (1975) 2 S.C.R. 182.

43. *A.-G. Man. v. Forest* (1979) 2 S.C.R. 1032.

44. Bruce G. Pollard, "Minority Language Rights in Four Provinces," in Peter M. Leslie, ed., *Canada: The State of the Federation 1985* (Kingston: Queen's University, Institute of Intergovernmental Relations, 1985), pp. 208–216. See also *Hogg, Constitutional Law of Canada,* pp. 812–814.

45. *A.-G. Que. v. Quebec Protestant School Board,* (1984) 2 S.C.R. 66.

46. Richard J. Van Loon and Michael S. Whittington, *The Canadian Political System* (Toronto: McGraw-Hill of Canada, 1971), pp. 346–350.

47. Pierre Elliott Trudeau, "The New Treason of the Intellectuals," in Trudeau, *Federalism and the French Canadians,* p. 166.

48. Louis Sabourin, "Canada and Francophone Africa," in Peyton V. Lyon and Tareq Y. Ismael, eds., *Canada and the Third World* (Toronto: Macmillan of Canada, 1976), pp. 133–161.

49. Hubert Guindon, "The Modernization of Quebec and the Legitimacy of the Canadian State," in Glenday, Guindon and Turowetz, *Modernization and the Canadian State,* pp. 212–246.

50. Richard J. Joy, *Languages in Conflict* (Toronto: McClelland and Stewart, 1972).

51. Ibid., p. 135.

52. See particularly Donald Creighton, *Towards the Discovery of Canada* (Toronto: Macmillan of Canada, 1972), "The Myth of Biculturalism," pp. 256–270.

53. Ibid., p. 257.

54. Ibid., p. 270.

55. J. T. Thorson, *Wanted: A Single Canada* (Toronto: McClelland and Stewart, 1973), p. 149.

56. Trudeau, *Federalism and the French Canadians,* particularly "The New Treason of the Intellectuals," pp. 151–181, and "Federalism, Nationalism and Reason," pp. 182–203. Trudeau leaves a certain ambiguity by using the term "nation state" somewhat loosely to describe both the national state and the multinational sovereign political community. His opposition to the latter is not evident, although he writes somewhat imprecisely that "functionalism" may come to replace nationalism (p. 203). To repeat, Trudeau's target is the sovereign state which is the embodiment of the will and interests of a single nation defined by culture, ethnicity, language or a combination of these.

57. William D. Coleman, "From Bill 22 to Bill 101; The Politics of Language under the Parti Québécois," *Canadian Journal of Political Science* 14, no. 3 (September 1981), pp. 463–482.

58. William D. Coleman, *The Independence Movement in Quebec 1945–1980*, (Toronto: University of Toronto Press, 1984), p. 19.

59. *Report of the Royal Commission of Inquiry on Constitutional Problems*, particularly Vol. III, Part III.

60. Ibid., p. 42.

61. René Lévesque, *An Option for Quebec* (Toronto: McClelland and Stewart, 1968), p. 14.

62. Arnopoulos and Clift, *English Fact in Quebec*, "Epilogue: The Trojan Horse", pp. 191–202.

63. Bruce G. Pollard, "Minority Language Rights in Four Provinces," in Peter M. Leslie, *Canada: The State of the Federation 1985* (Kingston: Queen's University, Institute of Intergovernmental Relations, 1985), pp. 193–222.

64. It was announced early in 1986 that a bill providing for francophone language rights would be introduced into the Ontario legislature.

65. Quoted in Patrick Martin, Allan Gregg and George Perlin, eds., *Contenders: The Tory Quest for Power* (Scarborough: Prentice-Hall Canada, 1983), p. 120.

66. André Bernard, *What Does Quebec Want?* (Toronto: James Lorimer, 1978), p. 111.

67. Ibid., p. 112.

68. Donald V. Smiley, "The Association Dimension of Sovereignty-Association: A Response to the Quebec White Paper," Discussion Paper (Kingston: Queen's University, Institute of Intergovernmental Relations, 1980).

69. The Constitutional Committee of the Quebec Liberal Party, *A New Canadian Federation*, (Montreal: 1980).

70. Graham Fraser, *René Lévesque and the Parti Québécois in Power* (Toronto: Macmillan of Canada, 1984), p. 228.

71. The Quebec Liberal cabinet ministers committed themselves to resigning office if the Union Nationale were not defeated, thus removing what was perceived as the most effective obstruction between French Canadians and conscription for overseas military service.

72. Walter D. Young, *The Anatomy of a Party: The National CCF* (Toronto: University of Toronto Press, 1969), "Introduction."

73. Fraser, *René Lévesque and the Parti Québécois*, pp. 311–313.

74. G. Bruce Doern and Glen Toner, *The Politics of Energy: The Development and Implementation of the NEP* (Toronto: Methuen, 1985), pp. 281–282. "The question of who governed Quebec energy policy in the post-NEP period was answered by the Quebec government by their very refusal to enter into the national energy debate.", p. 282.

75. Fraser, *René Lévesque and the Parti Québécois*, pp. 328–336.

76. Dominique Clift, *Quebec Nationalism in Crisis* (Montreal and Kingston: Queen's-McGill University Press, 1982), particularly Chapters 2 and 7.

77. Ibid., p. 116.

78. Ibid., pp. 112–115.

VII

The Centre and the Peripheries

In 1977 David Jay Bercuson, an historian at the University of Calgary, edited *Canada and the Burden of Unity,* a collection of essays by scholars from the Prairie and Maritime provinces.[1] In his introduction, Bercuson took issue with the central Canadian view of Confederation which equated "national unity" with a centralized regime giving dominant place to the interests of Ontario and Quebec. He wrote: "This book is also about unity, but its perspective is different. This is anti-national history: the dominant theme of these essays is that the sacrifices called for in the name of 'national unity' have taken a heavy toll in the hinterland regions and no real national unity can be attained until national priorities have been rearranged."[2]

The approach taken by Bercuson and his colleagues is a recurrent one among those writing from the viewpoint of Canada's peripheries: to attack the "Laurentian thesis" (most coherently supported in the writings of Donald Creighton[3]) and the National Policy which is the embodiment of the Laurentian thesis, and to find allies among Canadians whose interests are allegedly subordinated to those of the central provinces. Writing from the University of Manitoba in 1946, W. L. Morton examined the "three decisive fields of Canadian historical interpretation" as "the French survival, the dominance of Ontario, and the subordination of the West."[4] He criticized the Laurentian thesis in these terms:

> For Confederation was brought about to increase the wealth of central Canada, and until that original purpose is altered, and the concentration of wealth and population by national policy in central Canada ceases, Confederation must remain an instrument of injustice.

> As long as the cause of sectional injustice remains, and as long as the French feel that they are not admitted to equality in Confederation, there can be no commonly acceptable interpretation of Canadian history. . . .

For indeed the sectionalism of the West is, in different terms, as justified as the French nationalism of Quebec of the British nationalism of Ontario.[5]

Regions or Provinces?

As we saw in Chapter I, the term regionalism is loosely used in Canadian political discourse. In some circumstances regions are defined so as to serve the polemical and political purposes of some individual or group. Bercuson wrote:

> The power of Quebec votes and the necessity of the federal government to pay as much heed to Quebec as it does to Ontario reveals the existence of one region — Central Canada — with common characteristics. It is industrialized, populous, part of the St. Lawrence heartland, the holder of an absolute majority of seats in the House of Commons, and the major beneficiary of national economic, cultural and social policies. The French-English contradiction which appears to separate Quebec from Ontario serves only to force even more federal attention towards this region, almost always at the expense of the West and the Maritimes.[6]

In a similar attempt to define region to suit particular purposes, the government of British Columbia in 1978 issued a series of comprehensive proposals for constitutional reform which in respect to such matters as constitutional amendment and the composition of a reformed second chamber of Parliament gave the former a status as one of Canada's five regions.[7] The British Columbia document advanced arguments from the province's history, economic base, trading patterns, ethnic composition, labour relations and political culture to buttress the argument of regional distinctiveness.

In general, political discourse would be clarified if we ceased to use the term region, and persuasive arguments can be made that neither the Maritime nor the Prairie provinces constitute regions, at least in the political sense. J. Murray Beck, for one, has claimed that neither the Atlantic nor Maritime provinces can in any meaningfull way be considered as a region.

In a 1977 paper Beck wrote of the Maritimes:

> Certainly they do not meet the requirements of the political scientist that the adjacent parts of a region should not only differ from other entities in the political organism but also be capable of being treated as though they were a political actor, nor those of the sociologist who sees a region as part of a national domain sufficiently unified to have a consciousness of its customs and ideals and thus [possessing] a sense of identity distinct from the rest of the country; nor those of the planner who defines a region in terms of a set of problems and then estimates the degree of regionalism by the capacity to respond jointly to them.[8]

In a paper published in 1981, Beck denied that there was an Atlantic political culture and asserted that these areas showed the ''fragmented particularism that is characteristic of non-industrialized societies.'' He wrote:

> The traditionalism and conservatism of the four provinces reinforces their reluctance to establish strong attachments broader than the provincial; so

do the rural values which are highly significant throughout the area. . . . Because distinctive provincial identities and loyalties constitute so important a feature of the political culture. I think it is highly misleading to talk and think in terms of a Maritime or Atlantic political culture. It is much more meaningful to recognize the existence of four provincial political cultures having many values, attitudes and beliefs in common."[9]

Roger Gibbins' *Prairie Politics and Society* published in 1980 was subtitled *Regionalism in Decline*.[10] His basic argument was that "in the early part of the century the Prairie provinces did form a distinctive region in terms of social and economic composition, and a distinctive form of political behavior flowed forth as a consequence. However, social change has sharply eroded the earlier distinctiveness and has left in its wake a relatively enfeebled shell of the earlier regional politics."[11] The grain economy in the period from 1905 to 1939 gave the West "a common set of activities, institutions, grievances and frustrations," and the West was also quite distinct from the rest of Canada in its "ethnic composition, nativity, religious affiliation and rural lifestyle." The relative decline in the importance of the grain economy along with other changes which make the Prairies increasingly less different from the rest of Canada have resulted in the decline of regionalism. However, "the argument that political regionalism is in decline in western Canada does not preclude an emerging provincialism within the prairie region. There are critical differences between regions that are provinces and thus have an institutional, governmental and bureaucratic structure, and pan-provincial regions such as 'the Prairies' that lack the same."[12]

To repeat, Canadians in the peripheries of the country share grievances against various aspects of their domination by Central Canada but have almost no institutional structures of a trans-provincial nature to articulate these grievances. Although there has been little systematic study of this matter, the same appears to be true of sub-provincial areas which differ in attitude and interest from the provinces in which they are located.[13] Significantly, the formula for constitutional amendment which came into effect in 1982 does not recognize regionalism. Thus, the seven provinces containing in total half the provincial population whose consent is required for the most crucial amendments could exclude either three of the Atlantic provinces or three of the western provinces, in each case the most populous of these provinces; although if such an amendment derogated from the rights or powers of the provinces, a province might cause such an amendment not to apply to it.

In recent years there has been a degree of co-operation among the governments of the Maritime and western provinces but none of these jurisdictions has shown any willingness to surrender any of its freedom of action to a trans-provincial organization.[14]

The Prairies and the Canadian Mercantile Order

The Canadian prairies were at the first and to some considerable degree remain an economic colony of the country's central heartland. Chester Morton asserted of the transfer of Rupert's Land and the "North-Western Territory" to Canada in 1870: ''It transformed the original Dominion from a federation of equal provinces each by a fundamental section (109 of the British North America Act) vested with control of its own lands, into a veritable empire in its own right, with a domain of public lands five times the area of the original Dominion under direct federal jurisdiction.[15] Despite the conferring of the jurisdiction over natural resources on the Prairie provinces in 1930, the relations between the central heartland of Canada and its western hinterland have continued to be regulated according to the classic principles of mercantilism:

1. Metropolitan policies have confined the hinterland to the production of staple products exported from the hinterland in a raw or semi-finished state.
2. Metropolitan policies have required the hinterland to buy the manufactured goods of the heartland.
3. Capital development in the hinterland has been carried out by institutions controlled in the heartland.
4. In external economic relations, the interests of the hinterland have usually been sacrificed to those of the heartland.
5. The hinterland and the heartland have been physically linked by transportation facilities controlled by and operated for the benefit of the heartland.
6. Many of the crucial aspects of hinterland-heartland relations have been carried out through the instrumentalities of large business organizations protected by the heartland authorities from both foreign and hinterland competition.

The economic dominance of the prairie region by the commercial-industrial heartland was sustained by political institutions and processes patterned explicitly on those of British imperial rule. Lewis H. Thomas has written this of Ottawa's attitudes and policies in the period immediately after the acquisition of the western territories by the Dominion:

> The imperial-colonial relationship and the process of gradual, unsystematic evolution in that relationship were so familiar, and in many of their aspects so acceptable, as to be one of the assumptions of Canadian political thought. It is not surprising therefore to find the federal government embracing, without any hesitation, the prerogatives of ''imperial'' authority in the North-West.[16]

The Governor of the territory appointed by the Dominion played an important and often decisive role in the area until, after prolonged struggle, responsible government was granted in 1897. Prior to the Prairie provinces being given control over their natural resources in 1931, the Dominion, acting through the Department of the Interior, set the essential patterns of regional settlement and development. When the provinces of Alberta and Saskatchewan were established in 1905, the boundaries were drawn according to the designs of Dominion politicians rather than the needs or desires of residents of the North-West and these provinces began their political lives with premiers chosen by the Laurier government. The federal cabinet used its powers of disallowance more frequently to restrain the western provinces than the others. This pattern of internal colonialism — still prevailing in its essential elements in the Yukon and Northwest Territories — was in marked contrast to the American pattern. One of the last acts of the Continental Congress before its work ended in 1787 was the North-West Ordinance providing for the future government of areas outside the boundaries of the existing states. The Northwest Ordinance specified in some detail the circumstances under which new states equal in constitutional status to the existing ones should be established, and by 1870 some 18 states had been so established.

Recent writings of Doug Owram argue that, in its earlier years at least, the economic and political domination of the Prairies by central Canada was something other than a deliberate plot against the former by the latter.[17] Owram argues that from the beginnings of the expansionist movement in Canada West in 1856 through the end of the century, Canada was perceived largely in agricultural terms, and strong commercial and agricultural sectors required a strong agricultural base. On this basis: "If the agricultural sector was both important and attractive, then it followed that a region centred on agriculture could become as prosperous and as important as a region with a significant commercial or manufacturing component."[18] Neither was it perceived that the Prairies would be subjected to permanent political subordination; according to some of the more enthusiastic supporters of western settlement, it was suggested that in terms of population the new region might in the forseeable future come to be more important than central Canada.

From the challenges posed by Manitoba against the monopoly clauses of the Canadian Pacific Railways (CPR) charter in the 1880s onward, there have been revolts against the Prairies' economic place in Confederation. During the period between 1905 and the collapse of the Progressive party in the mid-1920s the major opposition to central Canadian domination lay in the farmers' movements and Prairie provincial governments closely allied to these movements.[19] In a 1955 essay, Morton suggested that Prairie politics from 1925 to that time had been dominated by "utopian elements," especially as embodied in Social Credit and the Co-operative Commonwealth Federation (CCF).[20] During the interwar period, Prairie protest took many forms and there were several competing and, to an extent, contradictory explanations of the position of the West within Confederation.

In the Progressive movement there was an important element which saw the villain as monopoly — monopolies of banks, railways, elevator companies and so on — whose political power was exercised through the disciplined caucuses of the major parties; the solution was the elimination of monopolies and the establishment of a free-trade order on liberal capitalist lines. Alberta Social Credit believed the solution lay in breaking the power of credit-granting institutions and the establishment of public control over the monetary system. Agrarian socialism, stronger in the most rural province of Saskatchewan, accepted the general outlines of the Fabian solution which had evolved as a response to the conditions of the world's most industrialized nation and proclaimed the desirability of comprehensive economic planning and public or co-operative ownership of the most important elements of the economy. Denis Smith has pointed out that, although the Progressive, Social Credit and CCF movements had their origins and greatest strength on the Prairies, they were not seen by westerners as instruments of regional protest but rather as attempts to force "a realignment of political loyalty throughout the country."[21] Thus: "The professed national aim of each party was to create a national two-party system divided on lines of principle, through which the reforms of each group might be adopted."[22]

From time to time the governments of the Prairie provinces have attempted activities which it was hoped would loosen the region's economic subordination. Just before the First World War, the government of Manitoba established a publicly owned system of grain elevators, an experiment which proved to be a fiasco.[23] In the late 1930s, the Alberta Social Credit government attempted a scheme of provincial control over financial institutions which foundered because of the province's lack of constitutional jurisdiction and the willingness of the lieutenant-governor and the federal cabinet to thwart those measures through the exercise of the powers of reservation and disallowance.[24] After coming to power in 1944, the CCF government of Saskatchewan made some limited and relatively unsuccessful attempts to diversify the provincial economy through small public enterprises and to engage in economic planning.[25] These efforts foundered for various reasons. For the province to obtain access to borrowing at favourable rates in Montreal, New York and Toronto, it had to enter into a tacit agreement "not seriously to exceed contemporary norms for taxation of property income or conduct major transfers of entrepreneurial activity from the private to public sector."[26] Larry Pratt and John Richards write that, "after 1946 senior [Saskatchewan] bureaucrats and ministers displaced their former ambitions to assist public control of economic development into an obsessive concern to perfect the machinery of government."[27]

It was not until the 1970s, however, that the governments of Alberta and Saskatchewan emerged as what Richards and Pratt designated as effective "entrepreneurial actors in staple-led economic development." Prior to that decade, provincial governments in the Prairies had adopted an essentially rentier stance in respect to resource development — most importantly of petroleum, potash and natural gas — and the private corporations which undertook such development did so under relatively light burdens of either taxation/royalties or public regulation. All this changed in the 1970s. In their admirable account of these developments Richards and Pratt show how interventionist provincial governments in Alberta and Saskatchewan were able to alter the terms and benefits of resource development to their advantage in the face of opposition from both Ottawa and private corporations. Perhaps never in the history of Confederation has the economic dominance of the centre been so effectively challenged by the peripheries.

From time to time, Ottawa has gone some distance in meeting Prairie grievances as, for example, the cancellation of the CPR monopoly clause in 1888, the Crow's Nest Pass rail differential, Liberal moves towards lower tariffs in the 1920s, the establishment of the Prairie Farm Rehabilitation Administration in the Great Depression, the National Oil Policy of 1961 and the disposition of the Diefenbaker government to be responsive to Prairie agricultural interests. However, residents of the Prairies have continued to believe that, despite such ameliorative measures, central Canadian interests have successfully sustained the economic subordination of the West.

Prairie resentment of central Canada has never been more profound than in the struggles with Ottawa related to energy development from the mid-1970s to the conclusion of the federal-Alberta energy agreement in September 1981. In his book, *Prairie Politics,* published in 1980, Roger Gibbins wrote that what was commonly called "western alienation" was a thrust towards "greater participation in and recognition by the national government" and that in contrast with the politically alienated elsewhere who have tended to be "the dispossessed, the poor, the economically and socially marginal," those in Alberta who were the "most prominent articulatrors of alienation" tended to be "individuals who have acquired wealth and success in oil, ranching, farming or construction."[28] However, despite Gibbins' claim that western alienation was in the direction of greater participation in national affairs, two other Alberta political scientists wrote in the immediate wake of the proclamation of the National Energy Policy in October 1980 that, "in at least one western province — Alberta — the dominant political and economic elites are in the process of 'contracting out' of the federal system and . . . their support of continuing membership in the federation is increasingly based on utilitarian considerations."[29] As it happened, the short-lived separatist movements were led by right-wing extremists; the core of such movements was restricted to Alberta, and the net effect of such developments seems to have been no more than to increase the determination of mainstream politicians to resist Ottawa.

Prairie resistance to central Canadian economic domination from 1973 to 1981 occurred in a period when there was almost no western representation on the government side of the House of Commons. To add further to western resentment and the conviction that national institutions were hostile to western interests, certain decisions of the Supreme Court of Canada challenged provincial jurisdiction over natural resources.[30] From a Prairie perspective the region's new-found prosperity was based on a favourable conjuncture of circumstances related to resource development — particularly development of petroleum, natural gas and potash — at the very time Ottawa had asserted that such resources should be in large part exploited for national purposes and that the national government should be a significant beneficiary of this process, although in the past the federal authorities had shown little or no disposition to challenge the jurisdiction of other provinces over resources.

It seems now generally agreed that the optimism about natural resource development in the West, which characterized thinking in that region and elsewhere in Canada well on into the 1980s, was ill-founded. On this basis, a further diversification of the economies of the western provinces and a decreasing reliance on resource staples is called for.[31] The degree to which diversification is carried out, as well as the impact of this on the economic subordination of the West to the central heartland remains to be seen.

Cultural, Linguistic and Religious Duality and the Prairies

From Confederation onward, the political elites of Ontario and Quebec have attempted to impose on the Prairies elements of cultural, linguistic and religious dualism which have on the whole been resisted by popular majorities and by governments in these provinces:

1. Section 23 of the Manitoba Act, by which that province was established, provided that the French and English languages should have the same status as in Quebec under Section 133 of the BNA Act of 1867. In 1890, the Manitoba legislature provided that English should be the sole official language of the province, but in 1979 the Supreme Court of Canada decided that this enactment was constitutionally invalid, and Manitoba returned to the official language regime of 1870.[32] The government and Parliament of Canada were deeply involved on the side of the Manitoba francophone minority in struggles about the French language which tore apart the Manitoba community in the early 1980s.[33]

2. Manitoba legislation of 1890 abolishing separate (Catholic) schools whose rights had been guaranteed by the 1870 Manitoba Act led to a major crisis in federal politics. A remedial bill to restore the Catholic privileges was introduced into Parliament by the Conservative government, but before it was enacted the House was dissolved, and in the ensuing general election the Laurier Liberals came to power. Subsequently Prime Minister Laurier negotiated an agreement with the premier of Manitoba providing for instruction in French where there were more than ten French-speaking students and for after-class religious instruction in the public schools.

3. The 1905 federal enactments establishing Saskatchewan and Alberta as provinces provided certain guarantees for separate schools as embodied in Ordinances of the Northwest Territories in 1901 and Section 93 of the BNA Act of 1867. Clifford Sifton, Laurier's most powerful minister from the West, resigned in protest. Anti-French and anti-Catholic sentiments flourished in Saskatchewan in the 1920s, and in 1929 French was eliminated as a language of instruction in the province's publicly-founded schools.[34]

With the important exception of the Manitoba language controversy, the great emphasis given to enhancing the status of French in the Canadian community over the past quarter-century did not bring about important changes in the lives of residents of the Prairies. There was, however, a significant amount of Prairie resentment that, in the context of the 1960s and 1970s, the central Canadian elites were, in effect, asserting that the challenges of the new circumstances of French-English duality were so urgent that they took precedence over other concerns. These elites were also disposed to believe that francophone claims were somehow more worthy than those of westerners which were perceived as being merely economic and, in a period of relative western prosperity, not entirely defensible. However, such views were based on a profound insensitivity to the present circumstances and historical experience of the Prairies. In a paper delivered in 1978, David E. Smith wrote perceptively:

Perhaps the most critical question at this time is the attitude of the west to Canada's fundamental norm of cultural dualism, a norm present for over a hundred years, confirmed in the last decade by the federal government's language legislation and challenged in the west since the beginning of this century. Regional dissent arose originally because the norm did not coincide with the experience of an immigrant, frontier society, and it has achieved new intensity because of federal politics that throw in doubt the legitimacy of that experience. Neither bilingualism/biculturalism nor multiculturalism has roots in the west, each betrays a profound disregard for the region's history.[35]

Interestingly, Smith was highly critical of federal policies of multiculturalism adopted in 1974 and went so far as to say that these policies were an "affront" to the history of residents of the provinces who were neither of British nor French descent. He went on to say: "On the prairies the marriage of bilingualism to multiculturalism will not work harmoniously because the costs of assimilation have already been paid. It is not practicable to suggest that they be recouped through a poorly funded, weak program which has been designed to appeal to the wave of immigrants who settled in Ontario after World War II."[36] A plausible but not, to me, entirely persuasive case can be made that some subordination of Prairie norms of a cultural, religious and linguistic nature to those of central Canada is a necessary price for westerners to pay for the survival of Confederation. This kind of argument was made by W. L. Morton who was, as we have seen, highly critical in 1946 of the Laurentian thesis and the consequent economic domination of the West by the central heartland. In a paper delivered in 1964, Morton attributed the strength of Quebec nationalism in the twentieth century largely to the failure of Ottawa to come to the aid of the French and Catholic minority in Manitoba in the schools crisis of the 1890s.[37] Because the federal authorities had surrendered their rightful role as "the effective and powerful guarantor of minority rights," Quebec had chosen to be "master in its own house" and to turn its back on French-speaking Canadians outside its borders.

To repeat, the cultural, linguistic and religious norms of central Canada are not congruent with the Prairie experience and for more than a century popular majorities and their governments from that area have struggled against the imposition of those norms by the elites of the central heartland. At no time has this struggle been more intense than in the past quarter-century. In an essay published in 1978, David R. Cameron wrote: "Dualism in Canada may generally be classified as the view which holds that the most significant cleavage in Canadian society is the line dividing English from French, and which identifies as the major challenge to domestic statecraft the establishment of harmonious and just relations between the English-speaking and the French-speaking communities of Canada. It is an understanding of the Canadian situation that has its origins in the British defeat of the French forces at Quebec in 1759."[38] This dualistic view became more influential and more clearly defined in elite thinking in Canada during the 1960s and 1970s and was certainly the view articulated so powerfully by Pierre Elliott Trudeau in his shaping of the Canadian political and constitutional agenda during this period. It was a formulation which had little resonance with the history and circumstances of the Prairies.

British Columbia and Confederation

British Columbia has been variously described as the "spoiled child of Confederation"[39] and as "perhaps more international in outlook than any other province."[40] The province began as an area of settlement separate and distinct from the other British North America colonies. R. M. Burns has lucidly summarized the circumstances of its entry into Confederation in 1871:

It is sometimes alleged that British Columbia was a reluctant newcomer to Confederation.... It would be more accurate to say that the marriage was one of necessity, the Colonial office lurking in the background with the shotgun. Canada needed the Pacific colony to tie the national expansion together and to forestall the extension of United States influence in the West. British Columbia needed the financial support of Canada and the offsetting influence it would provide to the growth of active political pressure from below the border.[41]

A contemporary British Columbia politician has nicely stated three major sentiments of his province about Canada: "the aren't we lucky to be living in British Columbia' feeling, a feeling of economic disadvantage by association with Canada, and a feeling of impotence in matters relating to the central government."[42]

As anyone who has had any significant exposure to these two parts of Canada will be aware, the British Columbian attitude to Confederation differs markedly from that of the Prairies. Both these parts of the nation have depended from the early days of settlement on the production of a narrow range of staple products largely developed for exportation outside Canada, and both have had common grievances against national tariff and transportation policies as well as the domination of the federal government by interests of the central heartland. However, the patterns of settlement, the bonds of economic activity on which these two parts of Canada rely along with British Columbia's physical isolation by the Rocky Mountains, have led to significantly different responses and attitudes. The former premier of Saskatchewan Allan Blakeney spoke of the co-operation of the governments of the four western provinces in devising a united front towards Ottawa in preparation for the Western Economic Opportunities Conference of 1972: "Surprisingly perhaps, we found that the conflicts that arose — and that had to be resolved — did not follow political party lines. Such differences as existed tended to be geographically based, particularly between 'the Prairies' on the one hand and British Columbia on the other."[43]

Interestingly, central Canadian interests have never imposed linguistic, cultural and religious duality on British Columbia as has been the case with the Prairies. Neither the French language nor Catholic separate schools had any official recognition in British Columbia either before or after the colony joined Confederation. However, in the latter years of the nineteenth century and the early years of the twentieth, the Dominion authorities nullified provincial laws attempting to restrict Chinese and Japanese immigration into British Columbia and imposing limitations in employment and otherwise on Asiatics in the province. Between 1878 and 1908, no fewer than 20 such laws were disallowed by the federal cabinet.[44] Such actions were not motivated to any significant degree by Dominion concern for the rights of Orientals; they were responses to perceived challenges to federal power over immigration and even more importantly to treaty obligations binding on Canada as a part of the British Empire.

In his 1977 article, Burns wrote: "British Columbia's separatism, to the extent that this exists, is the separatism of the cash register. Its disenchantment with its place in Confederation has a strong foundation in economics."[45] Norman Ruff has summarized the economic demands on Confederation of successive governments of British Columbia in these terms:

Economic Development

• Discrimination in federal fiscal, monetary, international trade and tariff policies against the economic interests of the region.

• Inadequate communications links and excessive transportation costs because of federal policies.

• Inadequate federal capital assistance for a publicly developed economic infrastructure including railways, highways, ferries and port facilities.

Public Finance

• An imbalance between federal expenditures in the province and tax revenues derived from British Columbia.

• The transfer of such revenues to other profligate governments.

• Inadequate recognition of the high operating and capital cost requirements of British Columbia's public services in federal-provincial revenue-sharing arrangements.[46]

In the period between the ascent to power of British Columbia's first Social Credit government in 1952 and the defeat of Social Credit by the NDP in 1972, the province was relatively isolated in federal-provincial relations, although the struggle with Ottawa over the development of the Columbia River Basin in the 1960s was one of the bitterest and most protracted federal-provincial conflicts in Canadian history. Ruff thus describes the 1952–1974 period:

> Under W.A.C. Bennett, British Columbia's sense of geographic and policy isolation from Ottawa took on a concrete reality when he discouraged regular intergovernmental contacts. Conference participation by cabinet ministers and their officials was tightly controlled and at times curtailed. Recruitment to the senior levels of the provincial public service from outside B.C. was rare, and restrictions on travel and long distance telephone calls inhibited participation in the expanding communications network enjoyed by other governments.[47]

The isolation of British Columbia was to a significant extent ended by the coming to power of the New Democratic Party government under Premier David Barrett in 1972, and this greater participation of the province in federal-provincial affairs continued under the regime of Premier William Bennett from 1975 onward. British Columbia participated with the governments of the Prairie provinces and the federal government in the Western Economic Opportunities Conference of 1972 and has continued as a member of the association of western provincial governments. The Barrett administration was less concerned than its predecessors with safeguarding provincial autonomy, and, in Ruff's words, "Jurisdictional questions were secondary to specific policy objectives"[48]; in one bold move, Barrett offered to surrender provincial control over all non-renewable natural resources conditional on the adoption of a national energy policy that provided for the complete public ownership of petroleum and natural gas. The Social Credit governments from 1975 onward have waged the traditional battles of B.C. for jurisdiction without reverting to the isolation of previous years. Meanwhile the province has developed new intergovernmental machinery for participating in the processes of executive federalism through the establishment of a Ministry of Intergovernmental Relations and a small group in the premier's office under an official with the rank of deputy minister charged with such matters.

During the mid-and late 1970s, the government of British Columbia took up the cause of constitutional reform.[49] One demand was that the province be recognized as a region distinct from the Prairies and that it have a veto over constitutional amendments, a demand that was not incorporated into the amending formula put in place in 1982. The centrepiece of B.C.'s constitutional proposals was, however, that the existing Senate be replaced by a body which would be composed of delegates of the provincial governments, an institution modelled explicitly on the lines of the Bundesrat in the Federal Republic of Germany.

British Columbia is a member of Confederation but a somewhat detached member. It has not had the experience of cultural, religious and linguistic duality which in various ways have powerfully shaped the experience of the rest of Canada. Although B.C. has chafed under various national economic policies, its resentment of the central heartland has been more subdued than in the Prairie and Atlantic provinces. Until 1984, it had never had the leader of a major national party and even in this case it was of a man, John Turner, whose roots in the province were somewhat attenuated. British Columbia domestic politics is characterized by a much sharper left-right cleavage than prevails elsewhere in Canada and in this and other ways the province has made its adjustment to its own unique circumstances.

The West and Recent Constitutional Debate

Up until very recently, western Canadians have been constitutional conservatives in the sense that they did not believe that the interests of the part of Canada in which they lived were challenged in any essential way by the twin constitutional inheritances of the Westminster model of parliamentary government and federalism. As we have seen, Prairie Canadians have had several explanations of their economic subordination to the central heartland, and in the interwar period these became embodied in several parties and movements whose major strength was in the West. There has always been a strain of anti-party sentiment in Western Canada, and in the decade immediately after the First World War, particularly, it was common to attribute the domination of the West to the operations of the two major national parties in their disciplined caucus organization and their dependence on central Canadian majorities and on contributions from central Canadian business interests. There was a long struggle for provincial control of natural resources culminating in the turning over of this jurisdiction to the Prairie provinces in 1930. Yet this struggle had as its only objective the accession of these provinces to the same position as the others and did not in any significant way challenge the federal distribution of legislative powers. In brief, westerners challenged the way in which the federal authorities exercised the constitutional jurisdiction that Ottawa possessed rather than the appropriateness of this jurisdiction. There was little or no western perception that the majoritarian dispositions of the Westminster model of parliamentary government jeopardized western interests in any significant way. In Roger Gibbins' terms, western Canadians have up until the last decade failed to develop an "alternative constitutional vision."[50]

From the Confederation of Tomorrow Conference of 1967 to the mid-1970s the constitutional conservatism of the western provincial governments made them ineffective participants in the process of constitutional review and reform. The enhanced recognition of the French language as a response to Quebec nationalism had little significance for the circumstances of the West; neither did influences towards an enhanced scope of provincial autonomy which were pressed by successive Quebec governments. The western governments made a determined struggle to preserve provincial control over natural resources and the revenues accruing from such development. However, although one might plausibly argue that many of Quebec's grievances could be alleviated through an enhanced scope of provincial autonomy, the interests of western Canada could be safeguarded only through changes in the way that Ottawa exercised powers which were almost inherently national — powers over taxation, banking, interprovincial transportation, tariffs, freight rates, and so on.

From the mid-1970s onward, there did develop in the West elements of what one may designate as an alternative constitutional vision. The major thrust of this vision was the demand that the institutions of the government of Canada be restructured so that they would be more representative of and responsive to provincial and regional interests.[51] This kind of proposal has come to be designated as intrastate federalism in contrast to interstate federalism which refers to the constitutional distribution of powers between the federal government and the provinces. Almost all intrastate proposals emphasize the urgency of replacing the existing Senate by a body which would either be popularly elected from each of the provinces or chosen by and acting as delegates of the provincial governments. Other intrastate reforms would change the electoral system by which members of the House of Commons are chosen; loosen party discipline in the House so that MPs could more effectively represent local and provincial interests; provide for provincial participation in the choice of members of the Supreme Court of Canada and in some recommendations of senior officers of federal regulatory agencies and public corporations. In broad terms, intrastate federalism seeks to modify the profoundly majoritarian disposition of the Westminster model of parliamentary government in its Canadian variant and is thus congruent with the interests of western Canada which, in terms of numbers, remains a permanent minority in Confederation.

Although the West made no gains in an intrastate direction in the constitutional settlement which came into effect in 1982, this settlement has several elements clearly tailored to meet the demands of western governments:

1. The formula for constitutional amendment is, in its essentials, a western product. More specifically, the equality of the provinces embodied in this formula and the absence of a Quebec veto over the most important category of amendments came about largely because of the wishes of Alberta and British Columbia.

2. The override provisions of Section 33 of the Charter of Rights and Freedoms, which permit Parliament and the provincial legislatures to enact laws

contravening most provisions of the Charter, were put in place largely to overcome the opposition of the governments of Saskatchewan and Manitoba.
Throughout the constitutional negotiations premiers Blakeney and Lyon had been
persistent supporters of legislative supremacy.

3. The provisions of the Constitution Act, 1982 giving the provinces a limited
jurisdiction over the interprovincial traffic in energy and renewable natural
resources was tailored by Ottawa to win the support of Saskatchewan for the
federal constitutional proposals. As it happened, the province did not respond
positively to such blandishments and joined the "Gang of Eight" in opposition
to the Trudeau government's constitutional initiatives.

Constitutional reform is not now high on the political agenda. There is relative
harmony in federal-provincial relations, and western Canadians have influential
representatives on the government side of the House of Commons. For these
reasons, the thrust towards intrastate federalism is largely in abeyance. However,
it is reasonable to suppose that sometime in the future the intrastate alternative
will resurface as a constitutional vision highly congruent with the durable interests
of western Canada.

The West in the Mulroney Era

The political and economic circumstances of western Canada have changed
dramatically in the period from about 1984 onward. During the late 1970s and
the early years of the next decade, it was reasonable to interpret the West as a
region striving to make its political power commensurate with its burgeoning
economic power. This equation has been radically changed. The plummeting
prices for petroleum, the excess supplies of natural gas, the difficulties of the
British Columbia lumber industry in retaining its American markets and the
generally unfavourable position of western agriculture have contributed to the
adverse economic circumstances of the West. Meanwhile westerners have their
own powerful representatives in the Mulroney government, and this government
has taken several steps perceived to be in harmony with western interests: the
dismantling of the National Energy Policy, the energy accords with producing
provinces, the elimination of restrictions on foreign investment, the commitment
to negotiate a comprehensive free trade arrangement with the United States.

In a perceptive article published in 1985, Gibbins analysed the radically changed
role of Alberta in the federal system in terms which are, in large part, applicable
to the other western provinces. He wrote:

> [T]he 1984 (federal) election has significantly altered Alberta's position
> within the fabric of Canadian political life. In the past, Alberta stood apart
> in Canadian politics through its exclusion from the nation's governing
> coalition, and through the virulent alienation that such exclusion engen-
> dered. Now Alberta no longer stands outside the national mainstream. No
> longer is the province on the outside looking in. At the same time, its
> position within the governing coalition is not one that confers any special
> powers or recognition . . . within the context of the Mulroney government,
> Albertans can be expected to look more to the federal government for

leadership, to take more of their cues from the national Conservative party and the Mulroney government. The 'we-they' distinction that has been so central to Alberta politics has been blurred although not totally erased by the election results.[52]

Gibbins also believes that the situation after the 1984 election has important consequences for provincial politics, and this analysis has implications for other provinces in the West and elsewhere in Canada. On innumerable occasions, provincial governments have run their election campaigns in asking the voters for a strong mandate to deal with Ottawa. As Gibbins points out, such tactics put opposition parties in a difficult position:

> To endorse the provincial government in its battles with Ottawa would be to declare themselves redundant. To accept the provincial government's political agenda, with its emphasis on intergovernmental and regional conflict, was to deny themselves the opportunity to exploit any openings which might arise from discontent with the government's provision of services within the province. To go against the provincial government and side with the national government in federal-provincial disputes was suicidal. To try to outflank the provincial government by being even more strident in Ottawa-bashing was to push opposition parties to the brink of hysteria.[53]

In a more harmonious climate of federal-provincial relations, opposition parties would have better opportunities than before in exploiting purely provincial issues and in holding provincial governments to account in respect to these matters.

The Atlantic Provinces

As is the case with the West, the unity of the Atlantic provinces is more evident to persons outside that part of Canada than to persons who reside there. While there are elements of a regional consciousness and a pervasive sense of regional grievances in Atlantic Canada — taking a form very different in Newfoundland from that in the Maritimes, as British Columbia is detached from the Prairies — the primary allegiances of Atlantic Canadians are provincial and local, and, unlike the Prairie provinces in the period up until the Second World War, there has never been a single staple which shaped a common regional way of life and orientation to the wider Canadian system. With all that being said, Atlantic Canadians do share common grievances and common concerns, and in broad outline these parallel those of the West in respect to the adverse effects of national tariff and transportation policies, a vulnerability to decisions allegedly made in the interests of central Canada and a belief that regional, provincial and local economies are less diversified than they should be because of these decisions. The Atlantic provinces are also the least favoured in terms of the most commonly accepted indices of economic welfare: per capita income, employment rates, labour force participation, and so on. They and their residents are more dependent on federal largesse than the rest of Canada, and in comparison with other parts of Canada, a higher proportion of this is distributed according to the discretion of Ottawa politicians and bureaucrats rather than statutory entitlement. Lastly, the Atlantic provinces are the smallest in population, and even if they were more advantaged financially than they are, it would be impossible for them to provide certain services available elsewhere in Canada except at prohibitively high per capita costs.

Since the Second World War there have been three sets of federal policies which have been designed to or have had the effect of reducing regional economic disparities in Canada, and these policies have been crucial to the Atlantic provinces:

1. *Equalization payments*   The roots of Canada's unconditional equalization payments to the provinces lie in the 1941 tax-rental arrangements by which the provinces were ousted from the personal and corporate income tax and succession duty fields for the duration of the Second World War. From 1967 onward, payments have been based on a revenue-equalization basis which takes into account the hypothetical amount per capita each province would receive from a standard tax levied on provincial revenue sources. These agreements are negotiated for five-year terms and the Atlantic provinces are always "have not" provinces entitled to such compensation. The commitment of the federal government to such equalization was given constitutional recognition in Section 36(2) of the Constitution Act, 1982 in these terms:

> Parliament and the government of Canada are committed to the principle of making equalization payments to ensure that provincial governments have sufficient revenues to provide reasonably comparable levels of services at reasonably comparable levels of taxation.

2. *Federal income support programs*   Keith Banting has pointed out:

> National income security programs redistribute income between regions whenever greater proportions of elderly, unemployed or needy people, or children are found in some regions than in others, or whenever revenues to finance these programs are raised disproportionately from different regions. Both of these conditions are met in Canada and, as a result, the centralization of responsibility for income security in the post-war period has transformed it into a major instrument of inter-regional redistribution, equal in importance to the much more publicized equalization grants.[54]

The Atlantic provinces are major beneficiaries of such equalization and in 1978 received per capita payments as a percentage of the Canadian average on this basis: Newfoundland 145; Prince Edward Island 121; Nova Scotia 110 and New Brunswick 117.[55] [56] These provinces also benefit by federal provisions related to unemployment insurance which extend coverage to self-employed fishermen and by which claimants in areas of high unemployment can receive benefits after fewer weeks of employment and can remain on benefits longer than persons in low-unemployment areas.

3. *Federal efforts to stimulate economic development*   From the late 1950s onward, the federal government has undertaken a number of programs to narrow regional economic disparities through stimulating economic development in the

less prosperous regions of Canada. In the immediate post-war period, Ottawa's management of the national economy mainly through Keynesian-type fiscal measures proceeded with relatively little concern for their differential impact on the various parts of the nation. However, by the time the Diefenbaker government came to power in 1957 high rates of unemployment in various areas caused Ottawa to undertake structural measures to stimulate economic development in parts of the nation which had benefited less than others from post-war prosperity. From this time onward, there has been a changing complex of federal and federal-provincial policies involving public owership, tax incentives and direct grants to private industry, the attempts to create more adequate infrastructures to stimulate economic development, and so on. However, none of these taken alone and together has significantly alleviated the basic economic problems of Atlantic Canada. More than its predecessor, the Mulroney government is committed to encouragement of the private sector as the primary instrument of material development, although there can be legitimate doubts as to the success of this approach in areas of the country in which the private sector is weak.

The dependency of the Atlantic provinces and their residents on the federal government is more pervasive and profound than that prevailing elsewhere in Canada. This dependency conditions the character of Atlantic politics and frustrates indigenous efforts towards effective measures of local, provincial and regional self-help. What Frank MacKinnon has written of Prince Edward Island appears to be generally true of Atlantic Canada:

> The efficiency of government depends substantially on the way it makes use of the ability, money, effort and time that society can reasonably devote to public business. Only a limited proportion of these resources can reasonably be devoted to the mechanics of administration and politics. The major part must necessarily go to the services necessary to society. Herein lies one of the serious problems of Island politics: because the mechanics of politics is so extensive in the Island's large system, the process of "getting" for limited advantage often displaces the process of "doing" for the advantage of all. Every district has something, every denomination that will not tolerate an advantage to another unless it gets a favor, and every organization that puts a price on its citizenship add to the getting process and too often subtract from the necessary doing process.[57]

McKinnon points out that this kind of politics provides for a high degree of popular participation. Despite this, surveys of popular attitudes demonstrate that residents of the Atlantic provinces trust their governments less than other Canadians and feel less efficacious in their capacity to influence these governments.[58] Writing from the perspective of a market economist, T. J. Courchene has argued that past and current federal policies have perpetuated and widened regional economic disparities by removing the incentives for provincial governments and residents of these regions to make rational adjustments to their economic situations.[59] In general terms, the extent of dependency on Ottawa frustrates indigenous elites in the Atlantic provinces from arising and developing effective solutions to the problems of that part of Canada.[60]

Conclusion: The Centre and the Peripheries

The economic relations between central Canada and its peripheries have developed according to the principles and practices of mercantilism, and, in the Prairie provinces particularly, this economic subordination has been compounded by attempts of dominant interests in the heartland to impose cultural, religious and linguistic duality.

It is only in the West, and only in the past decade, that there has grown up among some Canadians in the country's peripheries a recognition that the majoritarian dispositions of the Westminster model of parliamentary government perpetuate the subordination of these peripheries. Thus, belatedly, a connection is being made between the substantive policies of the central government and the constitutional structures within which such policies are formulated and implemented. The Progressive movement in the early interwar period saw the enemy in large part as the disciplined nature of the national political parties and sought to replace this by a structure in which MPs would be delegates of their individual constituencies. As the subsequent history of the Progressives demonstrated, disciplined parties were inherent in the Westminster model, and no effective opposition to the national parties could be mounted by loose groupings of constituency delegates. Proportionate to their respective populations, the majoritarianism of the federal government bears less heavily on the Atlantic provinces than on the West, the former are over-represented in the Senate and the latter under-represented; the circumstance that seats in the House of Commons are redistributed decennially or at longer intervals advantages provinces whose proportion of the national population is stable or declining; other constitutional provisions give New Brunswick and Prince Edward Island more MPs than their proportions of the national population would otherwise warrant, and the conventions of provincial representation in the federal cabinet gives some advantages to Atlantic Canada. Yet until some weakening of the majoritarian elements of the national government is achieved, the peripheral provinces and their residents will to a greater or lesser degree have their interests subordinated to those of central Canada.

Notes

1. David J. Bercuson, ed., *Canada and the Burden of Unity,* (Toronto: Macmillan of Canada, 1977).
2. Ibid., p. 12.
3. Almost all of Creighton's writings eleborate the Laurentian thesis, but see more specifically: *The Empire of the St. Lawrence* (Toronto: Macmillan of Canada, 1970); *The Road to Confederation* (Toronto: Macmillan of Canada, 1964); and *Towards the Discovery of Canada* Toronto, Macmillan of Canada, 1972.
4. W. L. Morton, "Clio in Canada: The Interpretation of Canadian History," in A. B. McKillop, ed., *Contexts of Canada's Past: Selected Essays of W. L. Morton* (Toronto: Macmillan of Canada, 1980), p. 105.
5. Ibid., pp. 108–109. Reprinted by permission of Carleton University Press.
6. Bercuson, *Canada and the Burden of Unity*, p. 2. From *Canada and the Burden of Unity* © 1987, Copp Clark Pitman Ltd. with permission of the publisher.

7. Government of British Columbia, *British Columbia's Constitutional Proposals, Paper No. 2, British Columbia: Canada's Pacific Region* (Victoria: 1978).
8. J. Murray Beck, "The Maritimes: A Region or Three Provinces?" *Transactions of the Royal Society of Canada,* XV, Fourth Series, 1977, p. 302.
9. J. Murray Beck, "An Atlantic region political culture: a chimera," in David J. Bercuson and Philip A. Buckner, eds., *Eastern and Western Perspectives* (Toronto: University of Toronto Press, 1981), p. 165.
10. Roger Gibbins, *Prairie Politics and Society: Regionalism in Decline* (Toronto: Butterworths, 1980), pp. 6 and 8.
11. Ibid., p. 6.
12. Ibid., p. 8.
13. For one of the very few such studies available, see G. R. Weller, "Hinterland Politics: The Case of Northwestern Ontario," *Canadian Journal of Political Science* 10, no. 4 (1977), pp. 727–754.
14. See Morton Westmacott and P. Dore, "Intergovernmental Cooperation in Western Canada: The Western Economic Opportunities Conference" and A. A. Lomas, "The Council of Maritime Premiers: Report and Evaluation after Five Years," in J. Peter Meekison, ed., *Canadian Federalism: Myth or Reality,* 3d ed. (Toronto: Methuen, 1977), pp. 340–352 and pp. 341–353, respectively.
15. Chester Martin, *Dominion Lands Policy,* Carleton Library Edition, edited by Lewis H. Thomas (Toronto: McClelland and Stewart, 1973), p. 9.
16. Lewis H. Thomas, *The Struggle for Responsible Government in the North-West Territories 1870–1897,* 2d ed. (Toronto: University of Toronto Press, 1978), p. 4.
17. Doug Owram, *Promise of Eden: The Canadian Expansionist Movement and the Idea of the West 1856–1900* (Toronto: University of Toronto Press, 1980), particularly Chapters 2, 3 and 4, and also "Reluctant Hinterland," in Larry Pratt and Garth Stevenson, eds., *Western Separatism* (Edmonton: Hurtig Publishers, 1981), p. 47.
18. Owram, *Promise of Eden.*
19. There is a substantial literature on these, but see particularly W. L. Morton, *The Progressive Party in Canada* (Toronto: University of Toronto Press, 1950), and David E. Smith, *Prairie Liberalism: The Liberal Party in Saskatchewan 1905–1971* (Toronto: University of Toronto Press, 1975), particularly Chapters 1–4.
20. W. L. Morton, "The Bias of Prairie Politics", in McKillop, *Contexts of Canada's Past,* p. 156. Morton defined utopianism as "a readiness to adopt untried methods to achieve ideal ends."
21. Denis Smith, "Prairie Revolt, Federalism and the Party System," in Hugh G. Thorburn, ed. *Party Politics in Canada,* 2d ed. (Scarborough: Prentice-Hall Canada, 1967), p. 189.
22. Ibid.
23. Vernon C. Fowke, *The National Policy and the Wheat Economy* reprint (Toronto: University of Toronto Press, 1973), pp. 140–141.
24. J. R. Mallory, *Social Credit and the Federal Power in Canada,* reprint (Toronto: University of Toronto Press, 1976), Chapter IX.
25. John Richards and Larry Pratt, *Prairie Capitalism: Power and Influence in the New West* (Toronto: McClelland and Stewart, 1979), pp. 111–171.
26. Ibid., p. 128.
27. Ibid., p. 142.
28. Gibbins, *Prairie Politics,* p. 168.
29. Larry Pratt and Garth Stevenson, "Introduction" in Pratt and Stevenson, *Western Separatism,* p. 11.
30. Richards and Pratt, *Prairie Capitalism,* Chapter 11.
31. See the 1984 Report of the Economic Council of Canada, *Western Transition* (Ottawa: Minister of Supply and Services Canada, 1984) and the symposium "West Canadian Economic Development: Energy Policy and Alternative Strategies," *Canadian Public Policy* 9, Supplement (July 1985).
32. For an account of the recent situation with respect to official bilingualism in Manitoba, see Bruce G. Pollard "Minority Language Rights in Four Provinces," in Peter M. Leslie, ed., *Canada: The State of the Federation 1985* (Kingston: Queen's University, Institute of Intergovernmental Relations, 1985), pp. 207–216.

33. Ibid.
34. Keith A. McLeod, "Politics, Schools and the French Language," in Norman Ward and Duff Spafford, eds., *Politics in Saskatchewan,* (Don Mills: Longmans, 1968), p. 147.
35. David E. Smith, "Political Culture in the West," in Bercuson and Buckner, *Eastern and Western Perspectives,* p. 170.
36. Ibid., p. 174.
37. W. L. Morton, "The Dualism of Culture and the Federalism of Power," in McKillop, *Contexts of Canada's Past,* pp. 263–264.
38. David R. Cameron, "Dualism and the Concept of National Unity," in John H. Redekop, ed., *Approaches to Canadian Politics* (Scarborough: Prentice-Hall of Canada, 1978), p. 237.
39. From the *Globe,* February 26, 1884, in Robert M. Hamilton and Dorothy Shields, *The Dictionary of Canadian Quotations and Phrases,* revised and enlarged edition (Toronto: McClelland and Stewart, 1979, 1982 reprint), p. 124.
40. Norman Ruff, "B.C. and Canadian Federalism," in J. Terence Morley et al., *The Reins of Power: Governing British Columbia* (Vancouver and Toronto: Douglas and McIntyre, 1983), p. 272.
41. R. M. Burns, "British Columbia: Perspectives of a Split Personality," in Richard Simeon, ed., *Must Canada Fail?* (Montreal and Kingston: McGill-Queen's University Press, 1977, p. 64.
42. Ibid., p. 71.
43. Allan Blakeney, "Western Provincial Co-operation" in Meekison, *Canadian Federalism,* p. 242.
44. G. V. La Forest, *Disallowance and Reservation of Provincial Legislation,* reprint (Ottawa: Department of Justice, 1965), pp. 94–96.
45. Burns, "British Columbia: Perspectives," p. 65.
46. Ruff, "B.C. and Canadian Federalism," p. 290.
47. Ibid., p. 302. For a biography generally sympathetic to the elder Bennett, see David J. Mitchell, *W.A.C. Bennett and the Rise of British Columbia* (Vancouver and Toronto: Douglas and McIntyre, 1983).
48. Ruff, "B.C. and Canadian Federalism," p. 300.
49. *British Columbia's Constitutional Proposals,* 1978.
50. Roger Gibbins, "Constitutional Politics and the West," in Keith Banting and Richard Simeon, eds., *And No One Cheered: Federalism, Democracy and the Constitution Act,* (Toronto: Methuen, 1983), p. 120.
51. For a critical account of this current of constitutional reform, see Donald V. Smiley and Ronald L. Watts, *Intrastate Federalism in Canada,* vol. 39 of the research studies prepared for the Royal Commission on the Economic Union and Development Prospects for Canada (Toronto: University of Toronto Press, 1985).
52. Roger Gibbins, "Alberta: Looking Back: Looking Forward," in Leslie, *Canada: The State of the Federation,* p. 128.
53. Ibid., p. 127.
54. Keith G. Banting, *The Welfare State and Canadian Federalism,* (Montreal: Queen's-McGill University Press, 1982), p. 97. Chapter 6, "Centralization and Redistribution" is a valuable analysis of the impact of federal policies related to income support on provincial economic disparities in Canada.
55. Ibid., p. 100.
56. There is a considerable literature on federal economic policies explicitly related to the reduction of regional economic disparities. See particularly: Anthony D. Careless, *Initiative and Response: The Adaptation of Canadian Federalism to Regional Development* (Montreal and Kingston: McGill-Queen's University Press, 1977); Economic Council of Canada, *Living Together: A Study of Regional Disparities* (Ottawa: 1977); Donald J. Savoie, *Federal-Provincial Collaboration: The Canada-New Brunswick General Development Agreement* (Montreal and Kingston: Queen's-McGill University Press, 1981); and Peter Aucoin, *Regional Responsiveness and the National Administrative State,* vol. 37 of the research studies prepared for the Royal Commission on the Economic Union and Development Prospects for Canada (Toronto: University of Toronto Press, 1986).
57. Frank MacKinnon, "Prince Edward Island: Big Engine, Little Body," in Martin Robin, ed. *Canadian Provincial Politics,* 2d ed., (Scarborough: Prentice-Hall Canada, 1978), p. 230.

58. Richard Simeon and David Elkins, "Provincial Political Cultures in Canada," in David Elkins, et al., *Small Worlds: Provinces and Parties in Canadian Political Life* (Toronto: Methuen, 1980), pp. 37–42.

59. Thomas J. Courchene, "Avenues of Adjustment: The Transfer System and Regional Disparities," in *Canadian Confederation at the Crossroads* (Vancouver: Simon Fraser University, The Fraser Institute, 1978), pp. 145–186.

60. For analysis of the situation of the Atlantic provinces in the light of dependency theories, see Robert J. Bryon and R. James Sacouman, eds., *Underdevelopment and Social Movements in Atlantic Canada* (Toronto: New Hogtown Press, 1979) and Ralph Matthews, *The Creation of Regional Dependency* (Toronto: University of Toronto Press, 1983).

Trudeau to Mulroney

This chapter will relate the persisting circumstances of Canadian federalism to the present and recent past focusing on the relatively abrupt transition from the nationalist and interventionist policies of the Trudeau Liberals (after they were returned to power in early 1980) to the current policies of the Mulroney government.

The Three Axes of Canadian Federalism

In a previous book I designated as the "three axes of Canadian federalism" the relations between (1) French and English, (2) the central Canadian heartland and its eastern and western peripheries and (3) Canada and the United States.[1] The Confederation settlement of 1864–67 and its elaboration in the National Policy of 1878 was a relatively coherent attempt to deal with these three sets of relations: to provide a new kind of French-English accommodation replacing the deadlock between the two communities which had poisoned and paralyzed the politics of the United Province of Canada; to acquire and later develop by the well-understood principles of mercantilism a western hinterland for the central heartland and to establish a new nation separate from the United States on the northern half of the continent. These are the permanent circumstances of Canadian nationhood, and if John A. Macdonald were to reappear among us, he would within a month have a surer grasp of the stakes in our current debates than does the person who is now prime minister. Each of these axes pits territorially defined political communities against one another, and because of this, territoriality profoundly shapes our national life and downplays cleavages which are not spatially demarcated.

Any adequate explanation of the Canadian federal experience would analyse the interrelationships among these three axes over the period since Confederation. I do not have the competence — certainly not the historical knowledge — to attempt such a task, and in this chapter I go no further than to examine the relations between English and French, centre and peripheries, and Canada and the United States in the first half of the 1980s. Perhaps, however, it would be prudent to caution more ambitious scholars that the relations among these axes are very complex and that things are often otherwise than as they seem on the surface. For example:

1. The National Policy of commercial protection, the building of a transcontinental railway wholly on Canadian territory and the settlement of the West are usually regarded as the crucial elements of Canadian nation-building in the first half-century of Confederation, and the subsequent continuance of such policies is often justified on nationalist grounds. However, it can be plausibly argued that the National Policy, whether of Macdonald or Trudeau, has had both continentalist and provincialist consequences. High tariffs have encouraged higher levels of foreign investment in Canada than would otherwise have occurred, particularly in the manufacturing sector, and have resulted in an economy dominated by American capital. A paper by M. W. Westmacott and D. J. Phillips published in 1969 argued that, "since Confederation federal transportation policy has aggravated regional discontent and . . . has been and is a divisive rather than a unifying force within Confederation. The fragility of the Canadian union and the unequal sharing in economic development are symptomatic of the failure of transportation policy in its role as a vehicle for promoting political and economic integration."[2] In the same fashion, tariff policies have led to conflicts between the central heartland and the peripheral regime of Canada. And again, the verdict on whether the policies of economic nationalism undertaken by the Trudeau Liberals after they returned to power is not yet in, but these policies led to both interregional conflict and to American resistance and might be judged in the future to have had both a provincialist and continentalist impact.

2. There is a current of analysis which asserts that provincialism leads to continentalism, that the strengthening of the provinces encourages Canadian-American integration.[3] However, the provincialism-equals-continentalism argument ignores what one might call provincial economic nationalism in terms of which provincial governments have attempted with some success to establish provincial economies, or at least sectors of these economies, with significant autonomy from both national and continental influences. H. V. Nelles has analysed how, in the last years of the nineteenth century and the first decade of the twentieth, Ontario had developed "something akin to a provincial version of the National Policy" by which governmental measures would encourage the processing of raw materials in the province and how such measures were opposed by the federal authorities.[4] Alberta and Newfoundland have in recent years developed economic strategies based on fossil-fuel resources and to varying degrees other provinces have attempted to make their respective economies more autonomous.

The Post-1980 Trudeau Liberals and the Third National Policy

On two occasions prior to the 1980s, federal governments in Canada have adopted comprehensive national policies which gave coherence and direction to the country's development for considerable periods ahead. The first occasion, of course, involved the National Policy of 1878. At the end of the Second World War what may reasonably be regarded as the Second National Policy was adopted — Keynesian-type fiscal management by the central government to ensure full employment and reasonable price stability, the establishment under federal leadership of a developed Canadian welfare state, and the building in co-operation with other nations of a liberal international economy.[5] In their comprehensiveness and coherence the measures undertaken by the Trudeau Liberals after they were restored to power after the short Conservative interregnum of 1979–80 can be seen as Canada's Third National Policy.

The Liberals on their return to office were in a highly confident and purposive mood. The demonstrated ineptitude of the Clark Conservatives in respect to policy matters and in allowing themselves to be defeated in the House of Commons in December 1979 confirmed the Liberals belief in themselves as the normal and legitimate governing party. This confidence was buttressed by the results of the Quebec referendum of May 1980. It is reasonable to suppose that the rejection of the sovereignty/association option was interpreted by the Trudeau Liberals as an indication that not only in Quebec, but in other provinces as well, autonomist sentiments among the public were relatively weak and that in any direct confrontation with the assertion of national power and purpose the provincial governments would not be able to carry the support of their respective residents.

The policies undertaken after the Liberal restoration in 1980 cannot be realistically analysed without reference to Pierre Trudeau. As he again became prime minister, Trudeau remained unpopular with many elements within his own party and the wider public, and the previous election campaign had been one of the most disgraceful in Canadian political history with the major publicity of each of the two largest parties being to emphasize the allegedly undesirable qualities of the leader of the other. Despite this widespread unpopularity, Trudeau was in a very strong position to orient federal policies along the nation-building lines he had come to believe were urgently necessary. In November 1979 he had announced his intention to step down as party leader and when, in the next month, the Liberals had brought down the Clark government, they had no assurance he would withdraw this intention. Had Trudeau not obliged by agreeing to stay on, the Liberals would have faced the unpalatable alternatives of either fighting the election under an interim leader or convening a hurried leadership convention during the campaign.

In a paper "Liberal Priorities 1982: The Limits of Scheming Virtuously," Bruce Doern designated and elaborated the elements of what I have called the Third National Policy as initiatives in respect to the Constitution, the National Energy Program (NEP), a new approach to economic development, the establishment of a Western Development Fund (along with other efforts to improve relations with western Canada) and the renegotiation of program funding and equalization payments with the provinces.[6] The first two of these initiatives — those relating to the Constitution and the NEP — were more critical than the others. Another federal thrust which Doern does not designate but which was of considerable importance was Ottawa's attempt to remove provincial barriers to the mobility of people, goods and capital within Canada.[7]

The nature of federal initiatives on the Constitution which began soon after the Quebec referendum of 1980 and ended with the agreement between Ottawa and the governments of nine of the provinces in November 1981 has been examined in earlier chapters. There was, of course, a nationalistic thrust here in the desire to eliminate the anomalous situation in which the most important elements of the Constitution could be amended only by the action of the parliament of the United Kingdom. Further, as I have argued, it was hoped and expected that the Chapter of Rights and Freedoms would undercut the allegiances of Canadians to their respective provinces by guaranteeing rights on a uniform nation-wide basis.

The major goals of the NEP, announced in the same month that the constitutional resolution was introduced into Parliament, were: to provide national security of supply in energy and the ultimate independence of Canada from the world energy market; to Canadianize the energy industry (especially with respect to petroleum), and to share the benefits of expansion in the energy industry among Canadians by increasing the federal share of oil and gas revenues and by establishing a uniform nation-wide price for petroleum and natural gas.[8]

Security of supply was to be attained by reducing the demand for oil (through various types of conservation and substitution measures) and by increasing supply (through emphasis on exploration and development on the northern frontiers outside provincial boundaries as well as by the building of a natural gas pipeline through Quebec to Atlantic Canada). Various measures were taken to Canadianize the oil industry by requiring foreign operators to take on Canadian partners before production licences on Canada lands would be issued and by the expansion of Petro-Canada through the takeover of foreign firms. The goal of redistributing the benefits of expansion in the energy industry was pursued by a common domestic price and by increasing Ottawa's share of revenues attendant on energy development.

In the early 1980s also, the federal government showed more disposition than before to formulate and implement a relatively coherent strategy for national economic development. This development was to be centred on the development of natural resources and on a group of mega-projects, the latter mainly related directly to resources. A Board of Economic Development, later to become a cabinet committee, was established under its own minister, and, more than before, all departments and agencies of government were required to concern themselves with the impact of their activities on development. These interventionist measures were aimed at enhancing federal visibility by procedures in which federal authorities would deal directly with individuals, businesses and other social groups rather than by channelling federal support through the provincial governments.

With the Quebec referendum over, the Liberals in 1980–81 turned their full attention to attempting to woo western voters with the establishment of a Western Development Fund of $5 billion of which $2 billion was to be spent in 1981–82. Although many believed that these moneys would be widely distributed among western communities deemed "winnable" by Liberal party strategists, the government decided that most of the fund would be used to rationalize and improve railway transportation in the West and to deal with matters attendant on the phasing of the Crow's Nest Pass subsidies.

The Third National Policy was a coherent attempt to deal with the three axes of Canadian federalism:

1. In relation to the French-English dimension, the objective was that members of the two linguistic communities should as individuals have equal rights, including the crucial rights to education and to deal with the public authorities in whichever of the official languages they chose, wherever in Canada this was at all practical. Thus, French Canada was not to be confined to Quebec, and Ottawa as well as Quebec City had the right to speak for francophone Canadians.

2. The federal government was to play an important and visible role in the western and eastern peripheral regions of Canada, particularly in the economic development of those regions.

3. The federal authorities were to take active steps towards the Canadianization of those elements of the economy deemed central to national autonomy and towards domestic control over the most important aspects of national economic development.

The common impulse behind the various elements of the Third National Policy was that of countering the provincializing influences in the Canadian polity and economy by making the federal government more pervasive and visible in the lives of individual citizens and thus to reinforce the allegiance of citizens to the national political community. In the constitutional discussions and in the federal propaganda in support of Ottawa's position on these matters, the Trudeau government exploited widespread public support for an entrenched Charter of Rights and Freedoms — now redesignated by the federal authorities as "The People's Package" in contrast to the "Power and Institutions Package" related to the powers of governments — and it was expected that the Charter, by conferring rights on all Canadians wherever in the country they lived, would be a nationalizing instrument to be authoritatively interpreted in the last instance by a national institution, the Supreme Court of Canada. More tangibly, the NEP would benefit consumers by keeping the domestic price of petroleum below world prices. The Liberals had been gratified by widespread public opposition to the hesitant moves of the Clark government towards privatizing Petro-Canada, and on this basis, the Liberals no doubt believed that there was a good deal of latent popular support for economic nationalism. As we have seen, there was a pervasive thrust in federal policy towards enhancing the public visibility of Ottawa's activities and giving the national government political credit for them. In short, there was a comprehensive and coherent attempt to reorient the Canadian community in a more nationalistic direction.

It would be an exaggeration to say that the Third National Policy had proved to be a complete failure by the time that Trudeau left office in mid-1984. Both a domestic amending formula and a Charter of Rights and Freedoms had become parts of the Constitution. The Quebec independence movement was in disarray. Writing in late 1984, Bruce Doern and Glen Toner argued that certain elements of the NEP were likely to persist for the foreseeable future.[9] With the support of the two opposition parties in the House of Commons, Parliament had enacted legislation imposing financial penalties on provinces whose medical and hospital insurance plans permitted user fees for health services. Changes had been effected in regional development policies to enhance Ottawa's control and visibility.

Notwithstanding the important achievements mentioned above, the Third National Policy had not been a notable success. To obtain the support of nine of the provinces for the constitutional settlement of November 1981, Ottawa had had to compromise some of its basic objectives in accepting an amending formula which the federal government did not like, in agreeing to the "notwithstanding" provisions of the Charter, in putting aside a procedure by which disagreements about constitutional matters between the federal and provincial governments would be resolved by referendums and so on. Furthermore, the Quebec government had refused to accept the legitimacy of the settlement, and Ontario had successfully resisted pressures to make that province officially bilingual. The underpinnings of the NEP and the mega-projects strategy for economic development inextricably related to the NEP had been withdrawn because of declining world prices of petroleum, an eventuality which federal planners had apparently not taken into account. In the face of domestic opposition and intense pressure from the government of the United States, Ottawa showed a declining will either to restrict foreign investment or to use the Canada Development Corporation as an instrument of national economic development. The federal government had not put in place measures to extend its powers in relation to post-secondary education. Although the Charter of Rights and Freedoms had guaranteed the rights of individuals to "move to and take up residence in any province" and to "pursue the gaining of a livelihood in any province," this did nothing to remove provincial barriers to the free movement of goods and capital, and any province which had rates of employment below the national average might establish programs restricting individual mobility; further, in an attempt to secure Saskatchewan's support for its constitutional initiatives, Ottawa had accepted as part to the Constitution provisions which would give the provinces certain powers in respect to the extra-provincial movement of natural resources.

In the article cited above, Bruce Doern wrote:

> We conclude that the Trudeau Liberals deserve considerable credit for the constitutional and energy initiatives of 1981 but that they face potentially unmanageable problems in 1982 and beyond. These problems emerge from the fact that it is virtually impossible for any federal government — let alone one without a strong base in all regions — to politically manage what is effectively the non-military equivalent of a five-front war. Motivated to an excessive degree by the consuming desire for federal visibility and identity, the Liberal initiatives on the Constitution, the NEP, economic development, Western Canada, and social programs are constructed on too fragile a political and philosophical base.[10]

We must await future historians for an account of how the restored Liberals committed their party to a much more activist and interventionist set of policies than those which had been adopted by successive Trudeau governments prior to the 1979 election. The development of the new initiatives appears to have involved only a very small group of persons with little prior discussion in the party or at the senior and decisive levels of the federal bureaucracy. Certainly there was little notice given to the Canadian public in the 1980 elections of such impending changes.

The Trudeau Liberals were ill-equipped to fight "a five-front war." They had, it seems, seriously underestimated the strength of the opposition to their nationalistic measures. In the complex constitutional situation as it developed in 1980–81, a very large number of actors emerged, all of them in one way or another frustrating Ottawa's plans: the governments of eight provinces, the official Opposition in Parliament, the appeal courts in three of the provinces and the Supreme Court of Canada, representatives of the native peoples and women, and certain elements in the Parliament of the United Kingdom. The western strategy had done nothing to bring residents of that region to the support of Ottawa, and the NEP along with other nationalistic policies had further exacerbated relations between the West and the federal government. Further, the Trudeau Liberals had not anticipated the vigorous opposition of the American authorities to their policies. In an essay published in early 1982, W. Irwin Gillespie and Allan M. Maslove wrote: "The strategy that lies behind the recent federal initiatives might well be characterized as the 'new nationalism'. It is offered not as a counter to internationalism or continentalism but rather in opposition to provincialism or regionalism."[11] In his book-length account of Canadian-American relations in the early 1980s, Stephen Clarkson wrote:

> The new centralism implied that the [federal] government would play a larger role in directing the economy. Although greater government intervention in the economy would necessarily have a great impact on an industry overwhelmingly owned and controlled by American companies, there was no thought among the architects of the new Liberal strategy that their plans would lead them to a direct confrontation with Washington.[12]

Not only had the Trudeau government underestimated the strength of the opposition to its nationalistic policies, but it had also failed to develop an effective strategy for mobilizing elite and mass opinion behind these policies. Clarkson points out that in the early 1980s there was an emergent corporate elite of nationalist disposition from companies "that had direct connections with either the energy industry or markets dependent on government procurement."[13] Over the long run it is possible that the careful cultivation of such corporate nationalists with a direct stake in the success of the Third National Policy might have provided an effective counterweight to the predominant impulse of the Canadian business community towards continentalism and hostile to government interventionism. More significantly perhaps, the Trudeau government showed neither taste nor talent for mobilizing popular opinion in support of its policies. During the period between the early 1960s and the coming into effect of the new constitutional arrangements in 1982, the federal and provincial governments and the articulate Canadian elites had been engaged in an intensive process of defining the essential nature of the Canadian political community. David Elkins and Richard Simeon have designated the three alternative definitions emerging from these debates as nation-centred, Quebec nation-centred and province-centred.[14] However, it appears that most Canadians forthrightly refused to be mobilized behind any of these conflicting options and to believe that one could at the same time have allegiances to both province and nation and, in Quebec, to be something of a Quebec nationalist and yet support the continuing membership of that province in Confederation. The response of the Canadian public to the United States was similarly ambivalent, and, although Ottawa made some not very successful attempts to mobilize popular opinion against the provinces, the federal authorities showed no corresponding disposition to appeal to the public in face of the intense pressures of the Reagan administration against Canadian economic policies.

Canadian Federalism in the Mulroney Era

The Liberal interregnum under Prime Minister John Turner in mid-1984 was too short to see any decisive developments in the Canadian federal system emerge. Turner had been in private life when the Third National Policy was put in place, and his personal ideological dispositions were cool or hostile to such interventionist and nationalistic directions. Whatever might have happened had the Liberals been returned to office in the general election of September 1984, the changes in the Canadian federal system between the last years of the Trudeau period and the early Mulroney era were profound.

Under Mulroney's government, the intensive redefinition of the Canadian political community which had gone on since the early 1960s ended. Constitutional discussion and reform inevitably involved such redefinition, and the Progressive Conservatives, both before and after the 1984 election, made it known that their priority was the economy, with the unstated corollary that the new patterns of relationships between governments and the private sector and the other economic reforms which the PCs wanted to bring about did not necessitate constitutional change. As we saw in Chapter III, there were two pieces of unfinished constitutional business left over from the 1982 settlement: the adherence of Quebec to this settlement and the definition of the rights of the aboriginal peoples. In response to the action of the Liberal majority in the Senate in holding up a government financial measure, the government sponsored a constitutional amendment curtailing the powers of that body, but after the immediate controversy died down, the Conservatives showed little disposition to press ahead in securing the required provincial consent for this change. In general, constitutional matters had been put on Ottawa's back burner.

In respect to the first axis of Canadian federalism, French-English relations, the Mulroney government began in a peculiarly favourable position. Unlike any previous anglophone prime minister, Mulroney understood the intricacies of Quebec politics and was perceived as an authentic *québécois* by even the most nationalistic persons in that province. As Leader of the Opposition, he had gained political credit with francophones throughout Canada by rallying his party in support of the rights of francophones in Manitoba against the Progressive Conservative opposition in that province. In 1980, while president of Iron Ore of Canada, he had vigorously supported the No option in the Quebec referendum but subsequently had taken the position that the referendum results had settled the independence issue once and for all and included in his cabinet and among his advisors persons who had supported the sovereignty/association option. Unlike other prime ministers in the recent past, Mulroney could adopt a stance of impartiality towards Quebec provincial politics because, soon after the PCs came to power, the PQ dropped its commitment to Quebec independence.

Notwithstanding all the assets mentioned above, the PC position in Quebec remains vulnerable. The Quebec electorate is very volatile, and one cannot make any confident judgements about its disposition to support the PCs in future Quebec elections. Apart from Mulroney himself, Quebec has been very weakly represented in the federal cabinet, particularly (in contrast to the Trudeau Liberals) in important economic portfolios. Further, the ideological disposition of the PCs towards non-intervention in the economy and their concern with the federal deficit impose some restrictions on the courting of Quebec voters with the free-spending policies of former federal governments.

The Mulroney government has had considerable success in creating more harmonious relations between Ottawa and the Atlantic and western provinces. This has come about largely because of the elements of the NEP, the signing of accords with several of these provinces related to energy matters and the loosening of restrictions on foreign investment in Canada. However, as in Quebec, the anti-interventionist ideology of the PCs may constitute an obstacle to their fortunes in Atlantic Canada; in an area where the private sector is weak, market-driven economic activity is unlikely to be effective.

In general then, relations between English and French and between the central heartland and the peripheries of Canada are now characterized by less conflict than in the Trudeau era. There are, of course, continuing strains in federal-provincial relations, particularly in respect to federal measures limiting increases in financial assistance to the provinces. Unlike the preceding period, however, these conflicts are being waged apart from contradictory ideological definitions of the nature of the Canadian community.

The third axis of nationhood, relations with the United States, is now higher on the Canadian political agenda than the other two. There is now virtual unanimity among those who speak for the Canadian business community that moves towards a comprehensive free trade agreement with the United States are urgently necessary, and this view is endorsed by the Macdonald Commission and accepted by the Mulroney government.

Serious students of such matters agree that the major stake in the current proposal is not the elimination of explicit tariffs between Canada and the United States and that these are not now the major barriers to trade and to enhanced economic integration between the two countries. The vital issues relate to the modification or abolition of what have come to be called non-tariff barriers (NTBs), that is, actions of governments which advantage or disadvantage particular firms or industries in competition with firms or industries located outside the boundaries of these jurisdictions. On this basis, almost any significant public policies which differ among jurisdictions, national or sub-national, within Canada and the United States might plausibly be regarded as a NTB whether such policies involved differential rates of corporate taxation, measures to narrow regional economic disparities, social or cultural policies or government attempts to protect the natural environment.

The free trade proposal has inevitably become a federal-provincial matter, although as the debate emerges, it is unlikely that the lines of cleavage will follow provincial or regional lines exactly. In the past, the provinces have successfully asserted their right to be consulted in respect to matters of international trade, specifically in respect to GATT negotiations. More significantly perhaps, a comprehensive free trade agreement with the United States would require the provinces to abolish, or at least to modify radically, the barriers they have imposed on the free movement of the factors of production within Canada. There has been a considerable amount of recent analysis as to the nature or the effect of such restrictions.[15] Contrary to some of the more alarmist estimates of such barriers the (Macdonald) Royal Commission on the Economic Union and Development Prospects for Canada concluded: "The direct costs of existing interprovincial trade barriers appears to be small. There are many barriers to interprovincial trade and factor mobility, but their quantitative effect on the level of economic activity is not sufficient to justify a call for major reform."[16] However, in respect to particular kinds of activity, barriers are significant and the Commission recommended an amendment to Section 121 of the Constitution to prohibit barriers in services as well as goods and the agreement of the federal and provincial governments on a code of economic conduct to reduce barriers to factor mobility, to be policed by a federal-provincial council of ministers of economic development, advised and assisted in this task by a commission of independent experts. At any rate, the provinces are inevitably involved, to a greater or lesser extent, in any free trade negotiations with the United States, both because of Ottawa's acquiescence to their demand to be consulted on all trade matters and because provincially-erected NTBs will be a subject of discussion in such negotiations.

The thrust of the free trade proposals is towards the harmonization within Canada and the United States of policies involving benefits for or burdens on private economic activity. In the current context this will mean a much more extensive reliance than at present on unregulated market forces, particularly in Canada where, in the broadest of terms, governments have shown more disposition than in the United States to control private economic enterprise for a myriad of purposes. However, a free trade agreement would not be self-enforcing and would require a supranational agency able to police effectively the actions of national and sub-national governments in their inevitable tendencies to erect NTBs, sometimes in collaboration with powerful private interests within their respective boundaries.

The free trade proposal challenges the fundamentals of Canadian nationhood. Contrary arguments are of course made. Some suggest that our nationhood is so well established as to be able to withstand further economic integration with the United States; others suggest that trading relations have little, if anything, to do with national independence. It is also said that the increases in material wellbeing allegedly to be realized through free trade will strengthen nationhood and ameliorate some of the conflicts among provinces and regions resulting from protectionist and interventionist policies. Such arguments are utterly misleading.

Canada is pre-eminently a political nation, and what its citizens share is a common set of governmental institutions operating within the framework of the law and conventions of the Canadian Constitution. National and sub-national governments in Canada have used their powers in pursuit of a wide variety of purposes. Such powers are, in fact though not in law, limited by the circumstances of interdependence and, in particular, by the domination of foreign multinational corporations over many sectors of the economy and on occasion by direct pressures from the government of the United States. Despite these constraints, Canadian governments have, in respect to many matters, established policies differing from those of the United States, even, in some cases, against powerful opposition from American business and governmental interests. It is this range of freedom of action which supporters of a free trade arrangement with the United States would have Canadians surrender.

The Mulroney government has brought about a pattern of relations with the private business sector, the provinces and the executive branch of the government of the United States relatively free of the intense conflict which prevailed under the Trudeau Liberals after they were restored to power in 1980. The price of such change, however, has been a profound absence of national direction. Without such direction and without any coherent national vision articulated by the leadership of the federal parties Canadian politics becomes little more than a "scuffle of private interests."

Notes

1. Donald V. Smiley, *Canada in Question: Federalism in the Eighties,* 3d ed. (Toronto: McGraw-Hill Ryerson, 1980), Chapter 8.
2. M. W. Westmacott and D. J. Phillips, "Transportation Policy and National Unity," in R. B. Byers and Robert W. Reford, eds., *Canada Challenged: The Viability of Confederation* (Toronto: Canadian Institute of International Affairs, 1979), p. 294.
3. For expressions of this view, see Kari Levitt, *Silent Surrender: The Multinational Corporation in Canada,* student edition (Toronto: Macmillan of Canada, 1970), pp. 142–153, and Donald Creighton, "Canadian Nationalism and its Opponents" in Donald Creighton, *Towards the Discovery of Canada* (Toronto: Macmillan of Canada, 1972), pp. 271–185.
4. H. V. Nelles, *The Politics of Development: Forests, Mines and Hydro-electric Power in Ontario, 1849–1941* (Toronto: Macmillan of Canada, 1973).
5. On the Second National Policy see Donald V. Smiley, *Constitutional Adaptation and Canadian Federalism since 1945,* documents of the Royal Commission on Bilingualism and Biculturalism (Ottawa: Queen's Printer, 1970), chapter II.
6. G. Bruce Doern, "Liberal Priorities 1982: The Limits of Scheming Virtuously," in G. Bruce Doern, ed., *How Ottawa Spends Your Tax Dollars: National Policy and Economic Development 1982* (Toronto: James Lorimer, 1982), pp. 1–36.
7. See the federal document introduced into the constitutional discussions by the Minister of Justice Jean Chretien in July 1980, "Powers over the Economy: Securing the Canadian Economic Union," C.I.C.S. Document 830-81/036.
8. For a comprehensive account of NEP, see G. Bruce Doern and Glen Toner, *The Politics of Energy: The Development and Implementation of the NEP* (Toronto: Methuen, 1985).
9. Ibid., pp. 491–492.
10. Ibid., p. 2.
11. W. Irwin Gillespie and Allan M. Maslove, "Volatility and Visibility: The Federal Revenue and Expenditure Plan," in Doern, *How Ottawa Spends Your Tax Dollars,* p. 43.
12. Stephen Clarkson, *Canada and the Reagan Challenge* (Toronto: James Lorimer, 1982), p. 21.
13. Ibid., p. 19.
14. David Elkins and Richard Simeon, *Small Worlds: Provinces and Parties in Canadian Political Life* (Toronto: Methuen, 1980), pp. 285–312.

15. See John A. Hayes, *Economic Mobility in Canada: A Comparative Study* (Ottawa, Minister of Supply and Services Canada, 1982) and M. J. Trebilcock, J. R. S. Prichard, T. J. Courchene and J. Whalley, eds., *Federalism and the Canadian Economic Union* (Toronto: University of Toronto Press, 1983).

16. *Report of the Royal Commission on the Economic Union and Development Prospects for Canada,* vol. 3 (Ottawa: Minister of Supply and Services Canada, 1985), pp. 133–134.

IX

Retrospect and Prospect: Provincialist and Non-Provincialist Influences in the Canadian Governmental System

Governmental System

The Canadian federal system is in process of continuing transition. The changes of the past 25 years have been dramatic indeed. The 1960s and 1970s were characterized by the emergence of competent and aggressive provincial governments willing and able to challenge Ottawa on a wide variety of fronts and in so doing to make appeals to the allegiances of their respective residents. With the Trudeau Liberal restoration to power in 1980, there was a reassertion of federal power and purpose and in 1980–81 a period of federal-provincial conflict of a virulence unprecedented in Canadian history. The early years of the Mulroney government have seen a radical dampening of this conflict and the relegation of federal-provincial relations to a lower place on the national political agenda than in the preceding quarter-century.[1]

This concluding chapter will analyse the federal system in terms of the interplay between the provinces and other institutions and processes which either divide or unite Canadians along axes other than those demarcated by provincial boundaries.

The Strength of the Provinces

The provincial governments in Canada are perhaps more powerful than the constituent units of any other contemporary federation. In contrast to the United

States, these jurisdictions are small in number, and the two largest of them contain about two-thirds of the national population. The provinces have legislative jurisdiction over a large number of important matters — including some related to international affairs — and, again in contrast to the United States, the Supreme Court of Canada plays an active role in delineating the jurisdictions of the two orders of government and, in the process, protecting provincial powers. The workings of the Westminster model of parliamentary government permit provincial leaders to rank and co-ordinate provincial objections. Unlike the Australian states, the provinces have important sources of revenue independent of the national government. The confederalization of the party system which has been analysed in Chapter V means that provincial political leaders are supported by party apparatuses almost entirely focused on provincial electoral success and independent of the respective federal wings. Finally, the provinces have a considerable hold on the allegiance of their residents, an allegiance buttressed in the case of Quebec by sentiments of national identity.

The strength of the provinces is subject to challenge from two sorts of influences: (1) those of a spatially demarcated nature not delineated by provincial boundaries; (2) those of a pan-Canadian nature which either unite Canadians or divide them along axes other than spatially delineated ones. Each of these will be discussed in turn.

Spatially-Delineated Forces other than Provincial

There are three spatially-delineated elements of the Canadian political system other than provincial:

1. *The local governments*   Despite their importance to the welfare of Canadians and the relative Canadian success in making cities liveable, Canadian local governments have little autonomy. In contrast to the United States, mayors of the larger cities are not important national figures; municipal political groupings are only weakly integrated, if at all, with national and provincial parties, and there are almost no direct fiscal and administrative linkages between Ottawa and local authorities. Broadly speaking, the tradition of local government autonomy in Canada is weak, and these jurisdictions, in fact as well as in law, are creatures of the provinces.

2. *The local constituency organizations of the political parties*   A spatially-delineated element of the Canadian political system which is unduly neglected by observers is the local constituency organization of the national and provincial political parties. These organizations are less important in the distribution of patronage than in earlier periods of Canadian history and in election campaigns increasingly work under the direction of the professionalized elements of the national and provincial parties. However, as David E. Smith points out, the initial recruitment of elective politicians is usually through the local party organization, and in such recruitment "it attracts interest and support, it educates, and it provides aspirants with an introduction to the skills of leadership and elections."[2] Except in rare instances, candidate selection is a local matter, and "Candidates are normally local residents who are conscripted or co-opted by

local party leaders to run for nomination; parachuting of candidates by central headquarters is almost non-exitent."[3] Furthermore, the majority of delegates to national and provincial leadership conventions are selected by local party organizations.

3. *Spatially-delineated groupings of rights-holders*   Although, as we shall see, the general thrust of the Charter of Rights and Freedoms is to define the rights of Canadians as such wherever in the country they reside, there are countervailing elements in the Charter which have at least the potentiality of protecting the rights of territorially-defined groupings. French and English language rights in respect both to the provision of federal services and to education are to be defined by the courts in terms of the concentration in particular areas of significant official-language minorities. Also, the extent to which the Charter gives an impetus to aboriginal self-government and to the enhanced recognition of native land claims, the beneficiaries will be spatially-demarcated groupings of native peoples.

In broad terms, none of the territorially-delineated influences which have been outlined above is very important in the total structure of political power in Canada. Neither are there effective institutions, governmental or otherwise, for articulating the interests of sub-provincial groupings (Labrador, Northern Ontario, the interior of British Columbia, for example) or trans-provincial groupings like the Prairies or the Maritimes. Thus, provincialism can be effectively tempered only by what one might reasonably call pan-Canadian institutions and processes which either unite Canadians or divide them along axes other than territorial ones.

Pan-Canadian Institutions and Processes

It might be thought that the very existence of a central government in Canada would be an instrument of national integration or at least would divide citizens along axes other than those demarcated by the boundaries of the provinces. Like the provinces, the federal government has resources of jurisdiction, revenues, a party apparatus, a competent bureaucracy and a hold on the allegiances of Canadians. Yet it is not inevitable that these resources will be used in a pan-Canadian way as this term has been defined above, and it is at least conceptually possible to see the central government primarily as an aggregator of interests and values specific to the provinces. Supporters of what has come to be called "intrastate federalism" argue that the main institutional deficiency of the Canadian governmental system is that the central government is insufficiently representative of and responsive to the interests of the provinces and regions, and a number of reforms have been recommended to remedy this alleged deficiency: the replacement of the existing Senate by a body composed either of members popularly elected in the provinces or of delegates of the provincial governments; changes in the electoral system of the House of Commons to bring about a closer correspondence between the proportion of the popular vote that the parties get in the provinces and the proportion of seats they obtain; a loosening of party discipline to allow MPs to be more effective representatives of their provinces and ridings; provincial participation in the choice of members of the Supreme Court of Canada and various federal executive agencies and so on.[4] Many of the intrastate reformers argue that only through such reforms can Ottawa mount an effective challenge to what are perceived as the excessive powers of the provinces based on the claims of the latter to be the exclusive representatives of provincially-bounded interests. Thus, according to the intrastate norm, the government of Canada should be primarily an outlet for provincially and regionally demarcated interests.

There are three institutions and processes in the Canadian governmental system which work against intrastate federalism and towards pan-Canadianism:

1. *The organization of the federal government*   The ways in which most departments and agencies of the federal government are organized give an important pan-Canadian dimension to the political system. The late Donald Gow argued that the foremost concern of most federal departments and sub-departmental groupings was either with particular industrial sectors such as agriculture, forestry, transportation and so on, or with particular social categories such as veterans, Indians and old people.[5] He wrote:

> Unless a minister was very clever, the problems which got identified and had their issues stated were those within the department's frame of reference. Since the frames of reference are drawn on the basis of industries or social categories, those problems which come up within a regional or cultural context are ignored, or not seen clearly. With an eye to the integrity of their "little society" almost any bureaucracy will resist answers to cultural and regional problems which may involve loss of function.[6]

In 1982, the federal government undertook a series of reforms aimed at making the executive apparatus more sensitive to regional and provincial values and concerns.[7] However, despite these reforms and the circumstance that, from Confederation onward, the federal cabinet has been chosen according to traditions of provincial representation, the structure of the government of Canada retains a pervasively pan-Canadian disposition.

2. *The national party leadership convention*   The national party leadership convention is the most pan-Canadian of our national political institutions.[8] The rule that votes for the leadership are cast by secret ballot denies candidates the opportunity of attempting to piece together coalitions of provincial or regional power-brokers and encourages at least the serious candidates to seek the support of individual delegates throughout the country.[9]

3. *The Charter of Rights and Freedoms*   The Charter of Rights and Freedoms is, at least potentially, a powerful pan-Canadian influence and was conceived by Prime Minister Trudeau and the more perceptive of his colleagues and supporters as a device to counter provincialism. Tom Axworthy, Mr. Trudeau's senior policy adviser in the constitutional debates of 1980-81, wrote in a paper delivered in 1985:

> What can be stated with confidence now is that the debate leading up to (the accord of November 1981) was revealed in pristine clarity two compelling visions of Canada. One was a dream of nation-building. Individualism formed the core of this belief. Individual Canadians, possessed of inalien-

able rights, including linguistic rights, make up the national community in which the people are ultimately sovereign. The other was a paen to province-building: parliamentary sovereignty is the central concept, diversity and particularism are the emotive forces, and sovereignty rests on a provincial compact.[10]

Section 33 of the Constitution Act, 1982 which permits both Parliament and the provinces to enact specific laws notwithstanding certain provisions of the Charter was a major concession to the provincialist view. However, in broad terms, the Charter is a pan-Canadian instrument. Whether and to what extent it contributes to national unity remains to be seen. Alan Cairns has suggested that the Charter may become a unifying device by which "the citizens of a fragmented society may achieve an integrating collective sense of themselves from their common possession of rights and the availability of a common language of political discourse."[11] A contrary view was expressed by the legal philosopher Ronald Dworkin in a 1970 essay analysing the current domination of American political debate by the language of rights: "The concept of rights, and particularly the concept of rights against the government, has its most natural use when a political society is divided, and appeals to co-operation or a common goal or purpose are pointless."[12] Whether the Charter develops as an influence towards unifying Canadians or dividing them, it will almost inevitably be a counterweight to the pervasive provincialism which characterized the governmental system in the 1960s and 1970s. A common national institution, the Supreme Court of Canada, is in process of giving final and authoritative definition of common nation-wide rights and even if this gives rise to new sources of political conflict, the resultant cleavages and mobilizations will, in all likelihood, divide Canadians along axes other than those delineated by provincial boundaries.

Beyond the pan-Canadian influences that have been discussed above, successive federal governments since that of John Diefenbaker have, as we saw in Chapter V, developed a marked disposition to elevate to importance issues which do not divide Canadians along provincial or regional lines and, in respect to such issues, to seek the support of citizens wherever in the country they live. It is likely that, to a greater or lesser extent, this will continue, if only because pan-Canadian strategies are useful for federal politicians in countering the power of the provincial governments.

Pan-Canadianism, Provincialism and Class

Canadian politics is based less on class polarization than that of other western nations, whether class is defined in the Marxian sense or as categories related to income, occupation and social status. Federalism itself frustrates such polarization on a Canada-wide basis; persons are divided for important purposes and to varying degrees define themselves as *québécois*, British Columbians, Nova Scotians, and so on, rather than as workers and employers, Canadians who are disadvantaged and those who are not, and so on. The regional character of Canadian economic development results in the dominance of various fractions of the bourgeoisie in particular provinces and, sometimes, in the influence of these fractions on the provincial governments to defend their interests against other fractions of the dominant class. On the other side, many of the critical interests of workers are matters lying within provincial rather than federal legislative jurisdiction, and this contributes to the fragmentation of the trade union movement and the power of provincial labour congresses against national federations of unions.

If we move away from structural factors, it may plausibly be argued that the relative absence of class conflict in Canadian politics is a resultant of the widespread definition of such politics as being about something other than class. This is the thesis of Janine Brodie and Jane Jenson in their perceptive book on party and class in Canada. One of the basic functions of political parties is to provide voters with "a definition of politics."[13] Thus: "They [the parties] define for the electorate the content of politics and the meaning of political activity. In other words, at the level of ideology, political parties shape the interpretation of what aspects of social relations should be considered political, how politics should be conducted, what the boundaries of political discussion properly may be and what kinds of conflicts can be resolved through the political process."[14] Brodie and Jenson describe how the dominant Canadian parties have been relatively successful in defining the political as having to do with matters other than class conflict, and they show how radical parties have, on the whole, failed to mount effective challenges to such definitions as sustain the power of the bourgeoisie.

While the Brodie-Jenson analysis is valuable in turning our attention to the role of parties in defining politics and consequently the nature of political conflict, they tend to overlook the role of other institutions in this process, particularly the media and the universities. For example, this book defines the persisting circumstances of Canadian nationhood in other than class terms; it speaks in terms of the relations between English and French, between the central provinces and the peripheries, and between Canada and the United States.

It seems unlikely that, in the forseeable future, Canadian politics will come to be based largely on class, even more unlikely if class is defined in the Marxian sense. It is more probable that cleavages will emerge dividing Canadians along lines other than those of their residence in particular provinces.The Charter of Rights and Freedoms and the women's movement have potentialities for such pan-Canadian mobilization. Relations with the United States are now higher on the Canadian political agenda than they have been in recent decades and, although cleavages about such issues may in part follow provincial lines, it is more likely that nationalist and continentalist influences will be distributed, albeit unevenly, throughout Canada.

Perhaps we are on the verge of new kinds of pan-Canadian mobilization. In their introduction to the OTHER *Macdonald Report,* Daniel Drache and Duncan Cameron identify a "popular sector" consensus which they believe has emerged to counter the "business agenda" allegedly articulated by the Royal Commission on the Economic Union and Development Prospects for Canada.[15] The "popular sector" consists of "churches, trade unions, women's groups, social agencies and organizations representing Native Peoples, farmers and the disadvantaged." While somewhat different views are represented in what Drache and Cameron see as this emergent coalition, the popular sector proposes "a radically different economic order in which democratic control of the economy and the state is strengthened by creating new forms of participation."[16] The OTHER *Macdonald Report* is a collection of briefs from organizations in the popular sector which portray "Canada as seen from the factory, office and farm, as seen from the unemployment line and the welfare office."[17]

With their characteristic opportunism and pragmatism, it is likely that most Canadian political parties, federal and provincial, will avoid a straightforward choice between the two agendas rather starkly delineated by Drache and Cameron, although the NDP has opted for the popular agenda and Social Credit in British Columbia has accepted the business agenda in a fairly undiluted form. What is more likely is the mobilization of persons and organizations representing the two competing visions in relation to particular issues such as free trade with the United States, women's issues, the preservation of universal access to health care and the rights of labour unions. In such mobilization, it is improbable that the primary lines of cleavage will be cultural or provincial.

Notes

1. As a harbinger of these new developments, see two recent books on Canada written by journalists, Richard Gwyn *The 49th Paradox: Canada in North America* (Toronto: McClelland and Stewart, 1985) and Andrew Malcolm *The Canadians* (Toronto: Paper Jacks, 1986). The emphasis in both books is Canada's place in North America, and there is relatively little attention given to the French-English and federal-provincial dimensions which so preoccupied the country in preceding decades.
2. David E. Smith, "Party Government, Representation and National Integration in Canada," in Peter Aucoin, research coordinator, *Party Government and Regional Representation in Canada,* vol. 36 of the research studies prepared for the Royal Commission on the Economic Union and Development Prospects for Canada (Toronto: University of Toronto Press, 1985), pp. 10–12.
3. Ibid., p. 11.
4. For a comprehensive analysis, see Donald V. Smiley and Ronald L. Watts *Intrastate Federalism in Canada,* vol. 39 of the research studies prepared for the Royal Commission on the Economic Union and Development Prospects for Canada (Toronto: University of Toronto Press, 1985).
5. Donald Gow, *Canadian Federal Administration and Political Institutions,* unpublished Ph. D. dissertation, (Kingston, Queen's University, 1967).
6. Ibid., p. 96.
7. Peter Aucoin, *Regional Responsiveness and the National Administrative State,* vol. 37 of the research studies prepared for the Royal Commission on the Economic Union and Development Prospects for Canada (Toronto: University of Toronto Press, 1985).
8. John Courtney, *The Selection of National Party Leaders in Canada* (Toronto: Macmillan of Canada, 1973) and Donald V. Smiley "The National Party Leadership Convention, A Preliminary Analysis," *Canadian Journal of Political Science* 1, no. 4, pp. 373–397.
9. At the Progressive Conservative leadership convention of 1983, Joe Clark's support on the final ballot ranged from 23 per cent of the delegates from P.E.I. to 62 per cent in Manitoba; Mulroney's from 64 per cent in New Brunswick to 35 per cent in Manitoba. Patrick Martin, Allen Gregg and George Perlin, *Contenders: The Tory Quest for Power* (Scarborough: Prentice-Hall Canada, 1983), p. 257.

10. Thomas S. Axworthy, "Colliding Visions: The Debate over the Charter of Rights and Freedoms 1980–81," Paper Presented to the Conference on the Canadian Charter of Human Rights and Freedoms, University of British Columbia, March 1985, mimeo, p. 2.

11. Alan C. Cairns, "The Canadian Constitutional Experiment: Constitution, Community and Identity," Killam Lecture, Dalhousie University, November 24, 1983, pp. 51–52. Quoted in Peter Russell, "The First Three Years in Charterland," *Canadian Public Administration* 28, no. 3 (Fall 1985): p. 396.

12. Ronald Dworkin, *Taking Rights Seriously,* (Cambridge, Mass: Harvard University Press, 1980), p. 184.

13. M. Janine Brodie and Jane Jenson, *Crisis, Challenge and Change: Party and Class in Canada* (Toronto: Methuen, 1980), p. 8.

14. Ibid.

15. Daniel Drache and Duncan Cameron, eds., "The OTHER *Macdonald Report* (Toronto: James Lorimer, 1985).

16. Ibid., p. ix.

17. Ibid., p. x.

INDEX